AMERICAN ORIGINS
TO 1789

SIX-VOLUME SET

AMERICAN ORIGINS TO 1789

DUMAS MALONE
COLUMBIA UNIVERSITY
and UNIVERSITY OF VIRGINIA

•

BASIL RAUCH
BARNARD COLLEGE
COLUMBIA UNIVERSITY

APPLETON-CENTURY-CROFTS

DIVISION OF MEREDITH PUBLISHING COMPANY

New York

COVER ILLUSTRATIONS

FRONT: *Top,* Captain John Smith's Map of New England, 1614
  William L. Clements Library, University of Michigan

  Right, Detail from Portrait of George Washington, by John Trumbull
  Yale University Art Gallery

  Left, Detail from Portrait of Benjamin Franklin, by Duplessis
  Metropolitan Museum of Art

  Bottom, A New Jersey Dining Room, Cumberland County, 1725
  H. F. du Pont Winterthur Museum

BACK: *Top,* A Virginia Mansion, Carter's Grove
  Virginia Chamber of Commerce

  Left & Right, Details from Painting of the Declaration of Independence, by John Trumbull
  Yale University Art Gallery

  Bottom, Fort Michilimackinac, Michigan, 1695
  Michigan Tourist Council

To

the students we have been privileged to teach —at COLUMBIA, BARNARD, YALE, the UNIVERSITY OF VIRGINIA, the UNITED STATES NAVAL ACADEMY, and elsewhere—*we gratefully dedicate this book.*

PREFACE

THIS IS ONE OF SIX PORTIONS OF OUR WORK OF HISTORY WHICH WAS FIRST published in two volumes under the title, *Empire For Liberty: The Genesis and Growth of the United States of America.* Extended to include the Kennedy-Johnson administration, and also brought up to date in other respects, the work is now presented in six paperbound books for the convenience of students and the public.

Each of these books represents a chronological segment of American history and is a self-contained unit—with bibliography, appendices, and index. To each book we have given a descriptive title because, besides being usable in any combination with the others, it stands alone.

In preparing a new edition we have corrected such errors as were reported to us by those who have used the work and have availed ourselves of various helpful suggestions. The treatment of recent events, of course, is fresh, and minor changes have been made in the text elsewhere as a result of further study. There have been numerous additions to and some omissions from the original bibliographies.

Remaining mindful of the continuity as well as the variety of the American story, we repeat here parts of the original preface in which we tried to sum things up.

We believe that if history is to come alive in the minds of readers it must be presented primarily as a story. Therefore, this work is predominantly narrative in form. Within the inexorable limits of space, we have tried to do justice to all the important aspects of American history— political, economic, constitutional, diplomatic, social, religious, artistic, and intellectual.

In the process of selection, we have laid emphasis on two themes of special interest today. The course of world affairs in our century has magnified the importance of American foreign policy, and in this work we have emphasized international relations. In response to the crucial importance of ideology and movements of thought in our time, we have also given special attention to these. But we do not forget that the American story is one of human beings rather than impersonal forces. We have paid special attention to the people and their leaders in all fields at each stage.

We are wedded to no single thesis, knowing of none by which the whole of our history can be adequately explained. But we do see, as a thread running through the entire fabric, the idea of the free individual. And we

vii

repeat, as designating a major historic goal of our growing society, the Jeffersonian quotation from the original titlepage: "Such an Empire for Liberty as She has never surveyed since the Creation." (To Madison, April 27, 1809).

As used here, the word "empire" connotes no exploitation of subject regions on this continent or anywhere else. Its meaning has been newly illustrated by the admission of Alaska and Hawaii as full-bodied members of the Union of self-governing states. The vision of a better life for every human being, with faith that it would result from maximum liberty compatible with public order, inspired all the most fruitful public and private actions of Americans from the beginnings of English settlement. If this vision was temporarily blurred after the Civil War, it has gained renewed life because of events in the twentieth century, especially the rise of totalitarianism in the world.

The threat to the free individual that is implicit in the consolidating tendencies of our generation, both at home and abroad, intensifies the need to grasp the meaning of the American experience. Americans and all others who believe that man fulfills himself in conditions of political, social, economic, and cultural freedom should understand that American history is less important as a success story in material terms than as a struggle to fulfill human potentiality. The authors will be grateful to readers who accept this work as an effort to contribute to such understanding.

In the preface to the first edition, after expressing our gratitude to all those who had helped us through the years to understand our country better, we named a number of individuals who had rendered us special services. The list of helpful friends has now become so long that we must content ourselves with a general expression of thanks, without reference to particular persons. We should be remiss, however, if we did not say that we are more grateful than ever for the good counsel of our publishers.

Since the labor and judgment of both authors have gone into all parts of this history, no precise apportionment of responsibility between them is possible. In the full meaning of the term this is a joint product. In restudying and resurveying the whole of our country's past we have enjoyed a very great experience. We hope that this book will serve as an invitation to others to explore that past and share that experience.

D. M.

B. R.

CONTENTS

MAPS and CHARTS

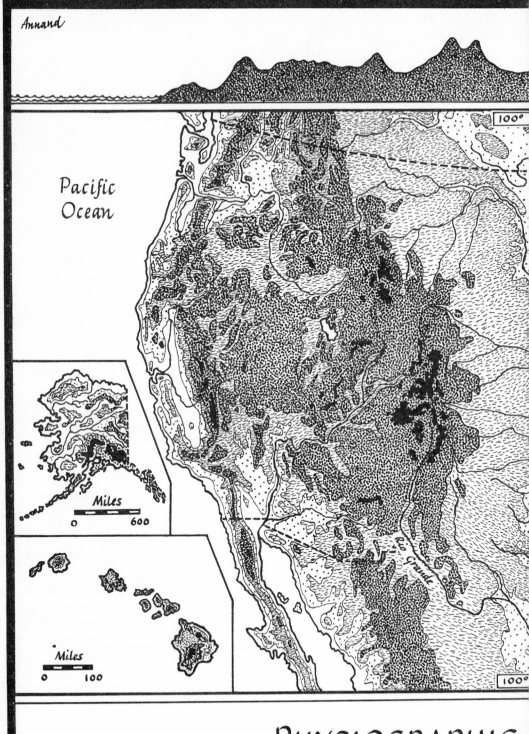

Annand

Pacific
Ocean

Miles

0   600

Miles

0   100

Rio Grande

100°

100°

PHYSIOGRAPHIC

Profile

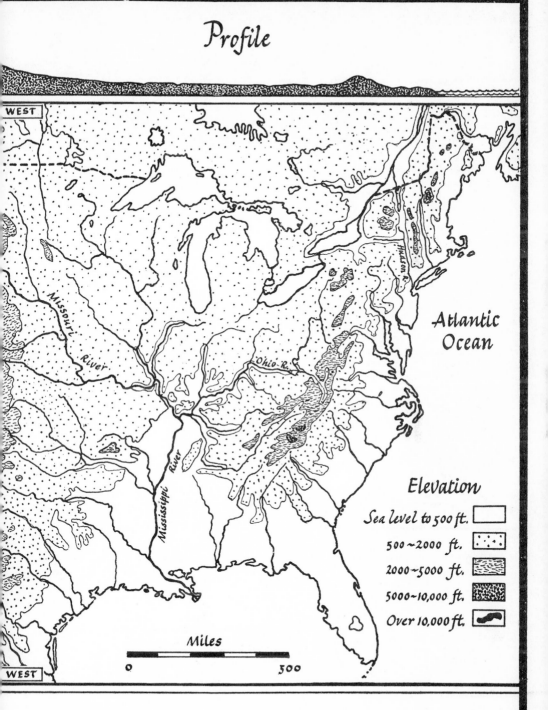

WEST

WEST

Missouri River

Mississippi River

Ohio R.

Hudson R.

Atlantic Ocean

Elevation

Sea level to 500 ft.

500~2000 ft.

2000~5000 ft.

5000~10,000 ft.

Over 10,000 ft.

Miles

0   500

UNITED STATES

Part I

COLONIAL FOUNDATIONS
TO 1763

CHAPTER 1

European Backgrounds

THE MIGRATION OF EUROPEANS TO AMERICA WAS ONE of the greatest folk movements of human history. In the vast and rich new land mankind was given a fresh chance to create on this planet a civilization more nearly like its dreams. Men of all sorts and conditions sought to seize upon unparalleled opportunities for more abundant life, and their continuing efforts comprise the essence of the American story. The desire to create a new and better society has been a leading motivating force in American history from the beginning. It is necessary, however, to inquire why Europeans left their homes and began to come to the New World at a particular period of time. At least one "discovery of America" was made long before the birth of Columbus, but this did not result in permanent trans-Atlantic settlements.

Iceland, a steppingstone to America on the northerly sailing route, has been occupied by Europeans since the seventh century, A.D. Irish immigrants lived there first in small numbers. The boldness of the Irish in going as far as Iceland can be related to the burst of creative energy in many aspects of life that characterized the Ireland of this period, when the rest of western Europe slept in the Dark Age between the breakup of the Roman Empire and the rebirth of civilization in the later Middle Ages. But the Irish did not now venture farther westward.

Scandinavians, thrust out to sea by the inhospitable nature of their rugged peninsula, became the greatest voyagers of the Dark Age. In the ninth century they pushed the Irish out of Iceland and made that island their base for voyages to Greenland. Eric the Red founded Brattahlid on the west coast of Greenland in the tenth century. In the year 1000, which some Europeans feared would witness the end of the world, Leif Ericsson or Leif the Lucky, son of Eric the Red, touched the coast of the North American continent, though scholars cannot agree just where. He was pleased with what he saw, and called the country Wineland the Good.

About a dozen years later, Thorfinn Karlsefni tried to found a colony on the coast where wild grapes grew. He and his little band lived for more than a year at a spot which may have been on the banks of the Saint Lawrence River. Indians, whom the Norsemen called Skrellings, were unfriendly, and the colonists left. But the experiences of Ericsson and Karlsefni were not forgotten. Their stories were repeated among their descendants from generation to generation and written down in the fourteenth century. Scandinavians from time to time voyaged to the remembered coast. It is possible that English fishermen, who sailed to the Grand Banks off Newfoundland years before the first English colony was established in America and who sometimes went ashore, had learned the way from the Scandinavians. Yet nothing permanent resulted from the Scandinavian voyages, for the settlement at Greenland disappeared.

The "rediscovery" of America by Columbus on October 12, 1492, might have been just as indecisive as the adventure of Leif the Lucky, had not Europe undergone revolutionary changes which made the settlement of a new hemisphere a practical, almost a necessary, enterprise.

THE COMMERCIAL REVOLUTION

When Leif stepped ashore at Wineland the Good, and for several centuries thereafter, European society was organized to suit the requirements of an inefficient agricultural economy. Farming methods were primitive and did not produce enough food to support any considerable increase in population, or to free more than a tiny privileged minority from subsistence labor. There was little trade, since local agricultural groups did not depend on it for the necessities of life, and almost all effective political authority was in the hands of local landowners or feudal lords. Religious activity was international in scale and directed from Rome for all Christendom, but efforts to create a parallel political organization in such experiments as the Holy Roman Empire were, on the whole, a failure. The Church itself supported agriculture as a way of life more conducive than trade to Christian virtue.

Successful military chiefs in the Middle Ages made themselves and their heirs lords of the lands they conquered. These lords with bands of fighting men provided armed protection to those who worked the land as serfs. The serf, unlike a slave, enjoyed rights, chiefly security under the lord in his tenure of his strips of land; but it was the lord who interpreted the rights and duties of all within his domain, and he was often undisposed to heed the injunctions of any higher religious or political authority.

Every manor and castle with the serfs' huts around it tended to be an independent community. Artisans produced rudimentary manufactured articles, and little contact with the outside world was necessary. A priest in charge of spiritual life was likely to be the only person who could read and write. Monasteries and cathedral towns were often centers of learning and art, but they were organized much like the manors, with serfs to till the land and an abbot or bishop as both the secular and spiritual head of the community.

The most striking feature of medieval society was its immobility. It was virtually impossible for anyone to escape the social status and occupation of his parents unless he entered the ranks of the clergy. Freedom of opportunity to better one's condition, or, in the phrase of the sociologist, vertical mobility, an outstanding characteristic of modern American society, was practically nonexistent. Medieval society—hierarchical, authoritarian, and hereditary—seemed frozen in a rigid mold. Yet no sooner was medieval order victorious over the chaos created by the destruction of the Roman Empire by barbaric invasions than the system began to yield, little by little, to forces of change. Barely perceptible in the eleventh century, these forces steadily accelerated the dissolution of medieval society and substituted the forms of life that we call modern. By the sixteenth century, change had progressed far enough to release the extraordinary energies which transplanted European civilization to America.

One of these great changes was the Commercial Revolution. It did not put an end to agriculture as the occupation of the great majority of Europeans. That was left for the later Industrial Revolution to accomplish. But trade and banking became dominant forms of economic activity in addition to agriculture.

Trade had not entirely died out in Europe after the dissolution of the Roman Empire. The use of money for exchange gave way to simple barter of one local product for another. Market days and fairs were customary occasions when surrounding farmers brought their small surpluses of products to a village to exchange them with their neighbors. Towns grew up around such markets, and their year-round population slowly increased. Artisans, whose craft skills created demand for their wooden, metal, leather, or glass wares, set up shops. Officials, notaries, and innkeepers thrived by serving the needs of the market. Merchants bought the surplus of one town and its surrounding countryside and carried it to another for sale at a profit. Prosperous merchants accumulated their profits in the form of gold and loaned it out at interest to lesser merchants, to lords and kings, and even to the Popes of Rome. The Church rule that interest was usury and a sin, because money cannot "breed" money, was relaxed when churchmen realized that trade redounded to the common advantage and that lenders must be compensated for their risk.

The merchants and artisans of the medieval towns fought hard to free their communities from the control of their lords with their incessant demands for soldiers and taxes. Town leaders demanded the right to govern their communities independently in ways conducive to commercial prosperity. They asserted the right to make a serf who escaped from the land and sought refuge and a better livelihood inside the town walls a *freeman* of the town.

The growth of trade and the towns introduced a new factor of vertical mobility into medieval society. Craft artisans banded together in guilds to protect the price and quality of their products. The merchants' guild effectively governed the town. Trade with other towns and distant lands loosed the bonds of superstition and ignorance among townsmen sooner than among country people. The beginnings of technological improvements of manufacturing processes were conducive to scientific advance. The medieval towns, step by step, won their fight for freedom against the lords of the land and became centers of wealth, power, and culture.

In some parts of Europe, especially in the areas of modern Italy and Germany, towns became so powerful that they dominated the surrounding countryside. They developed into city-states, and partly for this reason, Italy and Germany did not become national states until the nineteenth century was well advanced. In other parts of Europe, however, especially in England and France, kings found willing allies in the towns in their struggles to suppress the local princes and nobles and unify their kingdoms under strong central governments.

During the Crusades of the twelfth and thirteenth centuries, generations of warriors from the castles of Europe found in the Near East spicy foods, silken garments, gorgeous tapestries, art and architecture which made their own lives seem tasteless and rude, almost barbaric. When they returned, they were dissatisfied with the productions of Europe. Merchants eagerly invaded Eastern markets to buy the products which the wealthy of Europe demanded.

The self-sufficiency of the manor gave way to dependence on towns and merchants. In England many of the serfs were freed to starve or find work in the towns as best they could while their lands were enclosed for sheep pastures and the wool was sold abroad. Elsewhere serfs were encouraged to raise crops that could be sold, as the lords demanded gold with which to buy luxuries. Serfs were, therefore, transformed into tenants, and diversified farming was increasingly replaced by the production of staples.

Trade by barter gave way to the use of money. Merchants organized trade routes and merchant-bankers financed manufacturers to swell their stocks. They invented basic devices of modern business, such as the chartered company and the letter of credit. They ruled cities, became the paymasters of armies, raised up kings, and patronized artists and scholars. Rightly they were called *merchant-princes*.

By the end of the fifteenth century the Commercial Revolution had progressed far enough to permit daring new ventures beyond the boundaries of Europe and the Near East. Merchant-adventurers and ambitious governments sent ships into the seven seas to discover new supplies of goods Europe wanted and new markets for European productions. The search for gold and silver was especially keen because Europe produced almost none, and its trade with the Orient drained accumulated stores of the precious metals to the East. European merchants became impatient with the cumbersome method of trading with the Orient through middle-men, each of whom made his own profit. They resented the trade monopoly of the Italian city-states. Besides that, an old route through Constantinople was less profitable after 1453 when the city was con-quered by the Turks. The hope of breaking the monopoly of the Italian cities led to a search for a new route to the Orient and the "rediscovery" of America.

The event was an incident in the world-wide quest for trade and gold. The Commercial Revolution had introduced a dynamic factor into European society, and the transplanting of European civilization to Amer-ica, though not wholly attributable to it, was one of its results.

THE RISE OF NATIONAL MONARCHIES

A second great change which helps to explain the settlement of America occurred in the political organization of the western European peoples. The fifteenth century witnessed in Spain, France, and England the rise of national governments controlled by absolute monarchs. Mon-archical government in which the king personally wields ultimate power has in our century passed from the European scene. But nationalism has steadily increased in force until today it is perhaps the most important single determinant of society. It deserves particular attention by Ameri-cans because, although they have rejected monarchy, they have adopted nationalism with little modification.

After the breakup of the Roman Empire, Europeans dreamed of some day restoring such a universal government with its many advantages of peace, law, and unity for the known portion of humanity. The Church of Rome adapted to religious purposes the universal organization of the Empire, and to some extent it succeeded in encouraging a single law for Christendom, but Europeans were unable to achieve political unity or peace.

In the later Middle Ages a new principle of political organization emerged. It was in a sense a compromise between the localism under which men suffered and the universalism of which they dreamed. This was the principle of nationalism. It meant the political organization under one central government of people speaking the same language, occupy-ing a particular geographic area, sharing a common historical tradition and a common destiny. Individuals were ready to serve this new order, co-operating to create a coherent economic system, and tending towards religious unity or, in the nineteenth and twentieth centuries, agreeing upon tolerance of religious differences. Nationalism was slow in growth, often involving civil war before a country accepted it, and it has assumed protean forms, but we may detect its earliest beginnings in the very system of feudalism it destroyed.

Increasingly during the Middle Ages, feudal lords allied themselves to each other in bonds of fealty under which the one gave service, military and financial, and the other gave protection against enemies. Intermarriage among the nobility of Europe, and ownership by one family of widely scattered lands and castles, strengthened these ties. It often happened that one lord was linked to dozens of others, to some of whom he gave service, while from others he received protection. These alliances by no means united contiguous geographic areas, but the convenience of such contiguity created a steady tendency towards the amassing of holdings in one region. Furthermore, feudal lords who claimed kingship struggled to bind all the lords of their kingdom, and even other kings, in personal fealty to themselves. At the same time, the Commercial Revolution encouraged larger political units.

In the climactic wars of the Middle Ages two tendencies were visible. First, the attempts of kings to subject distant kingdoms to their rule failed. Thus the Hundred Years' War of the English kings to make good their claim to rule France resulted in defeat and the political independence of both countries. Second, the attempts of kings to subject the lords of their own kingdom to their rule succeeded, notably in Spain, France, and England.

In Spain, the struggle took the form of centuries-long wars of Spaniards to expel the Moors, and this resulted in a high degree of political and religious unity among all Spaniards. Feudal lords consented to the leadership of their local monarchs, and the famous marriage of Ferdinand of Aragon and Isabella of Castile united under one dynasty the last two separate Spanish kingdoms. Success against the Moors followed. They were finally defeated in 1492, the very year of Columbus's first voyage. In that year also, Ferdinand and Isabella expelled the Jews from Spain. A powerful kingdom emerged, intolerant of racial or religious differences from the Spanish Catholic norm, experienced in war and arrogant with power, ready for new adventures to spread Spanish Catholic civilization to new lands, and eager to gather riches from them to pay for the wars and bring luxury to the rather barren Spanish Peninsula.

In France, free of alien intruders like the Moors, national unity was achieved less dramatically and less quickly but nonetheless surely. The French feudal aristocracy was particularly factious and only the most skillful king could hold the lords in check. Francis I was such a king. Early in the sixteenth century he achieved so much authority that France seemed about to rival Spain in capacity for national enterprise beyond her borders. But a succession of weak kings after Francis allowed the country to be distracted by civil wars in which old feudal rivalries and new antagonism between Catholics and Huguenot Protestants intermingled. Only in the seventeenth century did France become effectively unified under a single king who was more absolute than those of Spain or England. Then France created a colonial empire to serve the wealth and power of *Le Roi Soleil,* Louis XIV.

In England, the Wars of the Roses between factions of feudal lords supporting rival contenders for the throne ended in 1485 with the triumph of the Tudor Henry VII. He and his descendants, especially Henry VIII and Elizabeth, ruled England cautiously to build up her unity and power against foreign enemies, ultimately Spain. They recognized the value of trade in achieving their goals, encouraged merchants, and made allies of them to offset the feudal aristocracy at home and to advance their ambitions abroad.

Portugal and The Netherlands in lesser fashion exemplified the rule that nationalism first succeeded in countries fronting the Atlantic Ocean. Elsewhere in Europe the principle of nationalism did not overcome feudalism and produce successful central governments until the eighteenth and nineteenth centuries. The rise to power of the Atlantic nations shifted the political and economic center of gravity from the Mediterranean, where it had been focused for more than four thousand years, to western Europe and the vast ocean westward to America. The age-old rivalries of Mediterranean cities and empires for wealth and power in that theater gave way to a new era of rivalries among Atlantic states in a world setting that included the American hemisphere.

The great advantage of national monarchy as a political form in this new era was that it enabled a single authority to control large combinations of economic and military power and achieve success in large-scale enterprises of peace and war. Highly trained professional armies, using the new gunpowder and firearms, succeeded militias of knights and footmen. Only a king receiving taxes from a large population could afford to support such an army. Similarly, only a wealthy king could build huge navies of big sailing warships carrying several decks of guns, which displaced the Mediterranean rowing galleys. Presently the naval battles of European monarchs were being fought in American waters and even in the Pacific and Indian oceans.

Wielding such awesome weapons, able to enforce their wills around the world, the new national monarchs acquired prestige approaching worship among their subjects. Little wonder that they were acclaimed as rulers by *Divine Right.* The poorest subject of such a king could identify himself with his glorious deeds and, by faithful obedience, bask in reflected glory. In the new nation-states, the fealty of the serf to the local landowner gave way to the loyalty of the free subject to his king. True, this was still loyalty to a person, not patriotism towards a nation, but the king acted for the nation. In the course of time it became possible for the individual to regard the interests of the nation as supreme even over those of the monarchy, and unpopular monarchies could be overthrown by patriots in favor of rulers more responsive to the popular will. Such a development occurred in England and The Netherlands in the seventeenth century, and it signified the ultimate triumph of nationalism as the dominant force of modern politics.

Today, as inheritors of this ultimate nationalism, we are inclined to criticize the national monarchies of the early modern period as inferior to our own republican government. But to the people of western Europe in the fifteenth and sixteenth centuries, those governments represented release from the evils of feudalism. Merchants in particular enjoyed a sense of freedom and opportunity under the new system and made the most of it. Their business within the kingdom was immensely facilitated by the slow substitution of one national system of taxation for the multitude of inhibiting levies that feudal lords had imposed on trade at the boundaries of their petty domains. Beyond the frontiers of the kingdom, the merchant-adventurer was encouraged by the king to seek new markets and sources of goods wanted at home. He was protected by the diplomacy, the army, and the navy of his government in his competition with the merchants of rival kingdoms and in his exploitation of weak peoples and "backward" lands.

Kings regarded the private profits and public taxes which foreign and domestic commerce might yield as secondary considerations compared with economic benefits which increased the power of the kingdom. In the economic theory of the time, the precious metals were looked upon as the true wealth of nations. To stop the drain of gold and silver out of the kingdom and insure the accumulation of a goodly supply of them inside its boundaries became the prime economic object of every national monarchy. There were two ways in which this could be done: by conquest and despoilment of lands possessing supplies of the precious metals; or by managing foreign trade in such a way that goods of greater value were exported than imported and the favorable balance was paid in specie. Both methods were aggressively pursued by the monarchs of western Europe. The system of governmental regulations which was designed to insure success is called mercantilism. It was the characteristic economic policy of European governments until it was to some extent supplanted in the nineteenth century by the policy of free trade.

The mercantilist system was only gradually worked out by the national monarchies, and they adjusted it in detail according to their varying problems. Spain was most successful in finding and appropriating new sources of gold and silver in America. France imposed the most rigid mercantilist regulations upon her foreign trade, but was only partially successful in conquering and colonizing lands suited to mercantilist exploitation. The Dutch organized a rich trade in spices with the East Indies, and established their rule over many of those islands, but their larger ambitions were frustrated by the weakness of their position in Europe. Portugal opened up new trade routes from which stronger countries chiefly profited. England, the last comer in the race for power through trade, and the least rigid in her mercantile regulations, was nevertheless the most successful of all. Why this should have been true will become clear later in our study.

At this point we can safely say that the political and economic energies of the new national monarchies in western Europe, which emerged from feudalism during the fifteenth century, help to explain why the isolation of the Western Hemisphere since the dawn of time was suddenly and irrevocably destroyed in 1492.

THE RELIGIOUS REVOLUTION

We should commit a serious historical error if we were to read our own preoccupations with politics and economics into the minds of our ancestors and minimize that aspect of life which they regarded as most significant of all: the effort to know and obey God's will. For Europeans of the fifteenth century this all-important effort was unthinkable without the aid of the One, Holy, Roman, Catholic, and Apostolic Church. The Church provided not only certitude of knowledge of God and his Divine Plan for mankind, but also rules of conduct and sacramental means guaranteed to provide the obedient soul with eternal happiness. The Pope of Rome was Vicar of Christ on earth, administering the temporal power and the spiritual treasury of grace which Jesus had entrusted to Peter for the comfort and salvation of humanity. The authority of the Pope, and therefore of God, reached down along the descending levels of the Church hierarchy of cardinals, archbishops, bishops, and abbots into every hamlet of Europe in the person of the local priest. It was an impressive structure, this international organization and hierarchy, wealthy and powerful in temporal things beyond lords and kings, yet still more wealthy and powerful in the realm of the spirit, because it held the keys to Heaven and Hell for all humanity. It controlled minds as well as souls, bodies as well as minds. Its power, the reflection on earth of the Divine Will, was all-pervasive: in art and science as well as theological and philosophical speculations; in the processes of governments as well as the conduct of serfs; in daily life as well as Sunday religious service and the myriad festivals of the saints in Heaven.

The Church used its vast power and wealth in many beneficent ways. It fostered art, architecture, and learning, so that the high medieval culture emerged from the semibarbarism that followed the fall of the Roman Empire. It ministered to the sick and the poor, so that the monasteries and houses of charity of medieval Europe performed some of the functions which private charity and governmental assistance perform in modern society. It tempered the barbarism of the early invading hordes and the cruelties of the powerful with the Christian law of love. It mitigated the pride and bitterness of caste by preaching that, in the eyes of God and the Church, lord and serf were equally destined for eternal glory. It even reduced the scourge of war occasionally by invoking the "Truce of God." Most important of all, the Catholic Church held before men's eyes a spiritual vision of Divine Order and noble destiny for man which redeemed the sorrows and futilities of this world. Through Christ, the Church conquered death itself.

The Church claimed that its civilizing and spiritualizing mission justified the obedience and material support it demanded from the mighty and the humble. Europeans for the most part responded willingly to its demands. Here and there a recalcitrant king or a doubting reader of the Bible challenged the authority of the Church and pointed to abuses of its power. But the Church resisted the argument that abuses by its ministers justified rejection of its authority, regarding it as heresy and a threat to its mission. It did not claim that its officials were never sinners, but it denied that their sins justified overthrow of their authority. Pious churchmen called for reform *within* the Church.

Corruption grew among the clergy during the later Middle Ages in some proportion to the ever-increasing wealth of the Church; and, more and more, men questioned the divinity of an institution that seemed so obviously temporal in its interests. Laymen, gaining in instruction, became ambitious for equality with the clergy. The lowest serf compared his own hunger and rags with the luxurious life of the fat prelate wrapped in furs and supping on rare food and wine. Ambitious kings looked enviously at vast lands engrossed by the Church and at its chests of gold and jewelry which yielded no increment to the wealth and power of their kingdoms. Particularly they resented the huge quantities of precious metals which the Church drew to Rome from every domain in Europe that imported them. Also, the Pope was a rival temporal king among kings, as well as spiritual Vicar of Christ, and the loyalty he claimed from all Christians he sometimes used to further the interests of his temporal kingdom, so that other kings found their subjects divided in their loyalty. The popes seemed to chaffer in the marketplace for gold; to play chess in the power politics of Europe with kings as pawns and the unfair advantage of hidden armies of loyal subjects inside every kingdom; to relish the vices and luxuries of the ancient Roman emperors; and their claim to be the surrogates of Jesus Christ fell into disrespect.

Prior to the sixteenth century, the Church put down religious rebellions by force, and for centuries more it continued to use force against them. But on October 31, 1517, a German monk named Martin Luther raised a banner of revolt which the Church could not suppress. On that day, Luther nailed to the church door in Wittenberg his famous Ninety-five Theses opposing doctrines and practices of the Church. Millions rallied to the standards of Luther and other reformers until North Europe, after more than a century of ferocious religious wars, established its religious freedom from Rome.

Luther protested against the sale of indulgences, which are remissions of temporal punishment after death for sins. He proposed a doctrine which deprived the Church of most of its function as intermediary between God and man. The essence of this was that men could achieve salvation by faith without works. By "works" he meant chiefly the sacraments which the Catholic Church claimed were essential to salvation and which could be administered by its priests alone. Luther reduced the number of sacraments from seven to two, baptism and communion, and reduced the importance even of these. He abolished monastic orders and the celibacy of the clergy. For a time he attempted to win the approval of Church authorities for his doctrines, but when they refused, he denied the authority of the Pope. A large part of Germany and all of Scandinavia quickly adopted Lutheranism. Princes and kings were particularly enthusiastic. They found in the new doctrines justification for depriving the Church of Rome of its possessions and power in their domains. They established new churches which took on the character of national institutions.

Lutheranism was conservative in comparison with new revolts which followed—especially the Peasants' Revolt of 1525 in Germany. This was directed against the land-owning aristocracy and both Catholicism and Lutheranism; and it coupled economic and political radicalism with extreme religious individualism. Martin Luther supported the violent suppression of the Peasants' Revolt, and the "radical sects" were persecuted by both Lutherans and Catholics. In the seventeenth century, some of the German sectarians found refuge in America, particularly in William Penn's tolerant colony of Pennsylvania where they still maintain their beliefs and unique social customs. Lutheranism itself as a state church never found a habitation in the New World, but in later generations it appeared there, in one form or another, among immigrants from Germany and Scandinavia.

In Switzerland a revolt broke out which had great significance for America. Ulrich Zwingli in 1527 repeated Luther's action and went farther. He abolished all ritual and attributed only symbolic meaning to the sacraments. Religious war broke out in Switzerland and Zwingli was killed in 1533, but a Frenchman, John Calvin, carried on the work in Geneva, which became the capital from which revolt spread far and wide. In 1536 Calvin published *The Institutes of the Christian Religion,* the manual on which all subsequent varieties of Calvinism were based.

The chief doctrine of Calvin was predestination, according to which God had determined from the beginning of time which human souls were destined for Heaven and which for Hell. This denied free will to human beings. But even though his doctrine meant that nothing could be done to change one's ultimate fate, Calvin taught that a devout and virtuous life was a visible sign that God had "elected" an individual for Heaven. Calvinism therefore led its adherents to engage in continuous self-examination and rigorous self-improvement, in the hope that one might discover that he belonged to the elect rather than the damned.

The question of the individual's election was important not only to himself but also to his co-believers because of the system of church organization that Calvin established. The local congregation with its minister was the sole structure. It was controlled, not by the whole congregation, but only by those who were thought to be elect in co-operation with the minister who was the final judge. Later in New England, participation in government was also restricted to church members, that is, the elect led by the clergy.

Calvinism was a harsh but powerful creed. It spread rapidly into France, where its adherents were called Huguenots, into The Netherlands (Dutch Reformed Church), into Scotland (Presbyterians), into England and the English colonies in America (Puritans—Congregationalists), and elsewhere. Worldly pleasure, even of sorts that others regarded as innocent, Calvinists rigorously forbade to themselves and their neighbors because they regarded it as a visible sign of an unregenerate heart. Outwardly and inwardly, the Calvinist was severe and somber—in keeping with his vision of God as an unpropitiable and inflexible Master. Some historians believe that the Protestant religions in general and Calvinism in particular reflected the new economic system of merchant-capitalism. They point out that the individual responsibility of the Protestant for his religious life parallels the individual enterprise of the capitalist, and that codes of religious ethics which imposed thrift and sobriety were better suited to a rising capitalism than the tolerance of human weakness characteristic of Roman Catholicism.

However that may be, it seems clear that the Protestant Revolution contributed to the growth of nationalism and to the expansion of European powers overseas. This can be seen not only in countries where Protestantism was successful, but also in France and Spain, where the Catholic Counter-Reformation defeated Protestantism. With the spread of revolt, the Catholic Church organized a defensive campaign against it. Many of the abuses of which reformers complained were stopped. The Society of Jesus, or Jesuit Order, made up of devoted "Soldiers of Christ," was founded by Ignatius Loyola of Spain in 1540 to combat heresy by militantly propagating the Catholic faith. It sought new converts for the Church everywhere in the world, to compensate, as it were, for losses in Europe. The colonial enterprises of France and Spain were partially designed to further such missionary work. The Counter-Reformation also inspired international and civil wars against Protestantism.

These wars, which ended only with the Peace of Westphalia in 1648, while they were mainly religious, also strengthened nationalism in Europe. Kings exploited the religious fervor of their subjects in order to advance their personal and national interests against rival monarchs, so that sometimes Catholic governments fought Catholic governments. At the same time, monarchs strove to put down religious dissent within their territories, in order to add religious unity as an element of national strength to political unity. At the end of the Thirty Years' War, which involved practically all of Europe, the peacemakers in 1648 turned to a principle other than religion as a basis for peace. This principle was nationalism, which dictated boundaries roughly corresponding to those of Europe today. Each ruler was permitted to determine for himself the religion which should be supported by his government and imposed on his subjects. Thus nationalism triumphed while the religious issue was compromised. Thenceforth religion, when it played a political role at all, was subordinated to the power of the nation-state.

The case of England was special in many respects, but there, too, nationalism triumphed over the Universal Church. The refusal of the Pope to annul the first marriage of King Henry VIII and the favors shown by the popes to rival kings led Henry to put through Parliament in 1534 the Act of Supremacy, which denied the authority of the Pope and made the King head of the English Church. This permitted Henry to appropriate to his own uses the vast lands and wealth of the monasteries. He distributed much of the land to faithful supporters of the Tudor dynasty, especially merchants, thereby creating a new aristocracy loyal to the Crown and the nation and further undermining divisive feudalism. At the outset the Anglican Church did not differ doctrinally from Roman Catholicism. Bishops became the effective leaders of the hierarchy, and for this reason the Church came to be called Episcopalian in the United States after the achievement of independence.

Lutheranism and Calvinism as well as radical sectarianism won many adherents in England in the sixteenth century, and they sought to reform or overthrow the Anglican Church as they did the Roman Catholic Church elsewhere. Queen Elizabeth, the last Tudor, temporarily settled the issue in favor of national peace by according, in 1558, a degree of tolerance to doctrinal differences within the Church of England. After her death in 1603, the Stuarts of Scotland came to the English throne, and critics and opponents of the Established Church were persecuted. James I and his son, Charles I, believed in their Divine Right to rule and the duty of the people and Parliament to obey in secular as well as religious matters. Many of the English settlers in America, especially the Puritans of the Great Migration to New England during the decade beginning in 1630, were motivated by a desire to escape the Stuart tyranny.

In 1642, civil war broke out in England between the Royalists, or Cavaliers, and the Parliamentary Party, or Roundheads. The landowning noblemen and "High Church" Anglicans supported the King. Parliament drew its strength from the rural gentry, merchants, and artisans of the towns, who were Puritan or Congregationalist Calvinists; from the Presbyterian Calvinists who were strong in Scotland; and from many more radical varieties of dissenters. Oliver Cromwell organized the "Ironsides," an army fired with religious zeal, and easily overcame the King's forces. In 1649, Charles I was convicted of treason and executed. Oliver Cromwell became Lord Protector—in effect, dictator. When he died the English people and Parliament were ready to accept promises by the exiled son of Charles I that he would rule with due respect for Parliament. He was invited to the throne as Charles II in the Restoration of 1660, and for twenty-five years ruled England on the Tudor model.

His brother and successor, James II, threatened to restore Catholicism and reassert the old Stuart claims to rule by Divine Right. Parliament deposed him and made his daughter, Mary, with her husband, William of Orange, joint sovereigns. Parliament passed in 1689, and the monarchs of England thereafter adhered to, the several acts that constituted the "Glorious Revolution." These acts included a Bill of Rights, an Act of Toleration applying to all Protestants, and in general allowed the growth of the authority of Parliament to rule England. This settlement was the foundation of an era of religious and civil peace within England which persists to our day and is unrivaled in modern history.

Most of the English colonies in America were founded during the troubled seventeenth century. Unlike the Spanish and French colonies, the English settlements as a group were heterogeneous in the religious composition of their populations, and they enjoyed in varying degree the privileges of self-government. These circumstances were peculiarly favorable to the growth of free institutions in English America. The Religious Revolution which Luther launched led Spain and France to build in America new strongholds of the old Catholic faith, but in one or another of the English colonies an adherent of any Christian religion might find a haven.

THE INTELLECTUAL AWAKENING

The Intellectual Awakening of the fifteenth and sixteenth centuries also helps to explain the European expansion. In general, the mind of man was freed from control by religious and political authority and men set out to discover the truth about humanity, society, nature, and the universe, guided solely by observation and individual reasoning power. The Renaissance, that is, the revival of ancient Greek and Roman learning and arts, began in Italy in the thirteenth century and spread throughout Europe. It created the intellectual climate in which modern science and culture were born.

At first the scholars and artists of the Renaissance did not challenge the authority of Church or State. Indeed, the great thirteenth-century theologian Saint Thomas Aquinas reconciled pagan philosophy, especially that of Aristotle, and Catholic faith. Some of the popes and many feudal lords and kings were patrons of the new learning and art. But the thrill of rediscovering ancient culture led bold thinkers to add new discoveries of their own by questioning accepted notions and following the dictates of observed fact and reason, and these discoveries sometimes required the defiance of religious and political authority.

Such a discovery was made by Nikolaus Copernicus (1473-1543), a Pole or German who lived in Italy. He conceived that the earth was a planet revolving around the sun. His proofs of this heliocentric theory were inadequate, and he hesitated to publish them, but his hypothesis upset the accepted view, derived from the Greek philosopher Ptolemy, that the earth was the center of the universe. The implication of the Ptolemaic view that man, the highest form of life on earth, was the most important entity in the universe, fitted well the Christian view that man was God's climactic creation and the special object of his Divine Plan. The heliocentric view seemed to undermine these foundations of Christian faith. The Copernican hypothesis was partially proved by the Italian mathematician and astronomer Galileo Galilei (1564-1642), but the Roman Catholic Inquisition required him to deny its truth.

In Protestant England scientific advance was not restricted. Issac Newton in his *Principia* of 1687 established the laws of physics which were accepted by scientists until further discoveries partially modified them in the twentieth century. The English also excelled in the invention of practical applications of scientific principles in devices and machinery which helped them to lead the world in efficiency of industrial production. The English colonies were the heirs of English science. In Benjamin Franklin they produced an experimental scientist capable of advancing human knowledge, especially in the field of electricity, and Americans eventually equalled the British in practical inventions.

The same pattern may be observed in the history of the social sciences. The application of reason to the laws of human society was encouraged by the rediscovery of ancient writers and reached a culmination in the work of the Englishman, John Locke (1632-1704). Rationalist social scientists believed that government, economics, and all social institutions were, or should be, subject to natural law in the same manner as the physical universe. Locke declared that natural law and human reason justified the

Glorious Revolution of 1688. His theories were applied even more rigorously by the authors of the American Declaration of Independence in the next century.

As Europeans came to make empirical science the sole criterion of truth and to subject all aspects of reality to human reason, they turned to the exploration of the surface of the earth in order that it, too, might yield its secrets. The great explorers provided experimental proof of the hypothesis that the earth was round. The fifteenth and later centuries saw a long procession of such "experimenters" set sail from Europe to seas and shores unknown. The thirst of these explorers for knowledge, far surpassing that of the Scandinavians of earlier centuries, would not be satisfied until every foot of the globe was studied and charted. Thus it was that the "rediscovery" of America became an incident of the Intellectual Awakening.

The revolutionary ferment of Europe, which began in the thirteenth century and touched all phases of economic, political, religious, and intellectual life, is the essential explanation of the settlement of America.

CHAPTER 2

Continental Powers
and the New World

THE AGE OF DISCOVERY WHICH BEGAN IN THE FIFTEENTH century has gone on until brave men have reached the poles and scaled the earth's highest mountains in the twentieth. Furthermore, the discoveries and explorations of the fifteenth and sixteen centuries ushered in a new and unparalleled era of trade and settlement which is best summed up by the phrase, the expansion of Europe. The process of expansion whereby a small and relatively impotent continent achieved undisputed world leadership continued for upwards of four centuries, until the great powers fell to fighting among themselves in 1914. Australia and New Zealand were eventually colonized by the British, while Asia was penetrated by Europeans and parts of Africa were settled by them; but the conquest and colonization of the Americas comprise the most significant phase of European expansion. For long generations the star of empire was brightest in the West, and the struggle for position there was a major element in the conflicts among European nations, at least until the winning of independence by the United States. Even after the republics of North and South America were established, they carried on European languages and civilization, modified though these were by New-World conditions. Viewed in the world setting these countries were outposts of Europe, and their colonial history is a part of European history.

We must lay chief emphasis on England, but other nations of the Old World played an even more conspicuous part in the early saga of discovery, exploration, and conquest. In a brief survey of their accomplishments it is impossible to do justice to the bold mariners who braved the perils of vast and unknown waters, to the explorers who treaded the trackless forests and overcame the mountains, to the conquerors who invaded and took over the fastnesses of ancient Indian potentates, to the traders who plied the seas. These audacious men were seeking treasure, to be sure, but they faced incalculable dangers in the name of national patriotism and their holy religions; and, despite the many stains of cruelty on their records, they were heralds and pioneers of European civilization.

PORTUGAL

Prince Henry of Portugal (1394-1460), called "The Navigator," was the precursor of the Age of Discovery. His chief accomplishment was a series of voyages, led by himself or navigators he had trained, along the uncharted western coast of Africa. In his career may be observed the transition of Europe from medieval to modern interests. He began as a religious crusader conquering the infidels of Africa; he ended as a political and economic imperialist expanding the power and wealth of the Portuguese monarchy. He advanced the science of navigation and European knowledge of geography as means to religious and secular triumphs.

Portugal was in a strategic position for such adventures in the fifteenth century when Spain was still partially occupied by the Moors. Prince Henry was zealous to win new territory for Christendom, and the popes issued Bulls calling upon the kings of Christendom to help Portugal in holy war against the African Muslims. But rising nationalism was fast destroying the ardor of kings for international religious crusades, and Henry received no help. His capture of Ceuta in North Africa was a national victory for Portugal. He conquered the Atlantic islands—Madeira, Cape Verde, and the Azores—and became more and more interested in a plan of empire for his country. The gold and slaves of Africa tempted him to send his navigators down along the coast of the unexplored continent.

After Henry's death, Portuguese navigators continued to lead Europe in explorations. In 1488, Bartholomew Diaz sailed around the Cape of Good Hope. India lay ahead, and Vasco da Gama in 1498 reached that fabled land. But by this time Spain, newly unified and triumphant over the Moors, had superseded Portugal as the leading promoter of explorations. The Portuguese navigator Magellan was in the employ of Spain when he set out to circumnavigate the globe in 1521. Portugal during her brief era of glory had won footholds overseas which she retained as trading posts, and the Pope awarded her a monopoly over the southern sea route to India and title to Brazil, but she was unable to compete with the more powerful Atlantic monarchies for the chief prizes.

SPAIN

Columbus

Jealousy of Portuguese achievements incited Ferdinand and Isabella of Spain to surpass them. The Genoese trader and navigator Christopher Columbus gave them their opportunity. Almost every aspect of Columbus's early career is in dispute, but this much may be fairly stated: he was learned in the geographical knowledge of his time and his determination to extend it was of heroic proportions. He knew the earth was round, he was familiar with Atlantic wind currents, and he was an expert navigator. He may have known of the voyages of the Scandinavians beyond Iceland and he was certainly well acquainted with the explorations of the Portuguese. He made an inspired guess on the basis of fragmentary knowledge that new lands existed westward beyond the Azores. Whether he expected to find "unknown" lands or Cypangu (Japan) and Cathay (China) is in doubt. But it cannot be doubted that he possessed the mentality and character of a "modern" man—persistence in the study of available facts, boldness in projecting startling hypotheses, and determination to subject his dreams to the test of evidence.

Besides this, Columbus was persuasive in argument and skilled in leadership. He offered his enterprise to one sovereign after another, promising them glory, gold, and converts. Finally the Spanish monarchs financed the speculation. They made him commander of a fleet comprising the *Niña, Pinta,* and *Santa Maria,* vessels about 75 feet long, well equipped and manned. They sailed from the Spanish port of Palos on August 3, 1492. It was an easy voyage, marred only by a mutiny on October 10 which Columbus quelled by promising to turn back after three days more. At two o'clock on the morning of October 12 the *Pinta* sighted San Salvador, now called Watling Island, one of the Bahamas. After exploring several islands and erecting a fort on Hispaniola (now Haiti and Santo Domingo or Dominican Republic) and leaving a small garrison there, Columbus returned to Spain, where he and his men were greeted with excitement and joy.

Another Genoese, John Cabot, was employed by King Henry VII of England and made two voyages to America in 1497 and 1498, but nothing came of them except an English "legal" title to North America. England was not yet ready for overseas expansion. But Spain was ready. The voyage of Columbus was a national enterprise and it was made to serve the national interest.

The Spanish monarchs provided Columbus with seventeen vessels for a second voyage to establish Spanish rule firmly in the West Indian islands. The garrison at Hispaniola had been wiped out by Indians. Co-

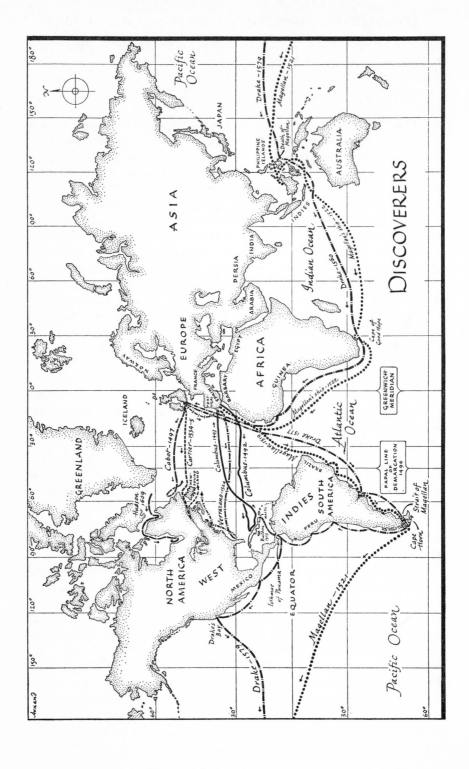

DISCOVERERS

lumbus selected another site on the island and founded a colony that became the center from which the Spanish Empire in America expanded within a generation. Conversion of the natives to Catholicism was an important activity of the Spaniards, and it was not thought incompatible with brutal exploitation. First the Spaniards traded with the natives for gold, then took it by force, and finally drove them to labor in mines until within a few years the Indians of all the islands were exterminated by cruelty, overwork, and European diseases. Then slave-hunting expeditions sought new supplies of labor for the islands on the mainland of South America, and African Negro slaves were bought from the Portuguese.

Spanish colonists were largely unemployed veterans of the Moorish wars who regarded work in the mines and on the land as beneath their dignity. A system of *encomiendas,* comparable to European feudal estates, with Indians as serfs and Spaniards as lords of the land, was gradually developed. Columbus died in obscurity in Spain after a fourth voyage to America, but his work was carried on by *adelantados* and *conquistadores.* His family relinquished to the Crown his claims to hereditary authority over America. Everywhere in the New World governors appointed by Spain followed the explorers and conquerors. As viceroys and captains-general they exercised the absolute authority of the Crown.

Conquest and Colonization

Puerto Rico, Jamaica, Cuba, and other islands were quickly conquered and colonized. Cattle ranches and sugar and cotton plantations flourished. But the Indians' stories of untold wealth in gold, of natural marvels and great cities, led one expedition after another to the mainland. Juan Ponce de Leon discovered and named Florida in 1513 while searching for a legendary spring that would restore youth to the aged. Vasco Núñez de Balboa with several hundred Indians and Spaniards searched for the fabulous Inca Empire of Peru. He crossed the Isthmus of Panama and, "silent, upon a peak in Darien,"[1] in 1513 gazed upon the great body of water afterwards named the Pacific Ocean.

Hernando Cortés with 550 Spaniards found in Mexico the advanced civilization of the Aztecs and vast quantities of gold. Some of the Indians greeted him as their legendary "Fair God" and helped make him in 1521 master of an empire. By 1535, Francisco Pizarro had conquered the equally rich empire of the Incas in Peru. Tales of more rich cities and civilizations led intrepid explorers into the territory from present South Carolina to California, but they found nothing to match Mexico and Peru. The Spaniards never established more than weak frontier outposts along the North American Gulf Coast and westward into New Mexico and California. They

---

[1] From Keats's sonnet "On First Looking into Chapman's Homer." Keats made an error in this poem by naming Cortés as the discoverer of the Pacific.

concentrated their efforts in Central and South America, where, by the middle of the sixteenth century, Spanish civilization and Christianity flourished over the ruins of the Indian states. The Portuguese had won a foothold in Brazil, and in 1580 Philip II succeeded to the thrones of both Spain and Portugal, so for a brief era Spanish glory was unrivaled. The Philippines had been conquered by the Spaniards after Magellan's discovery. The wealth of the Orient as well as of the New World made Spain perhaps the richest empire yet known on earth.

The Spaniards were the first of the modern empire builders and their methods provide a norm with which other imperial systems may be compared. From such comparisons explanations may be drawn in answer to the significant question, why the Spanish Empire, at first so brilliantly successful, lost first place in less than two centuries to the British Empire, that seemingly haphazard creation of latecomers.

The foundations of the Spanish imperial system were Bulls issued in 1493 by the Spanish Pope Alexander VI. In them the authority of the Papacy gave sanction to a division of the whole world into Spanish and Portuguese spheres of influence. Portugal was dissatisfied with its share and Spain consented in the Treaty of Tordesillas in 1494 to a Line of Demarkation running north and south 370 leagues west of the Azores, so that Portugal could enter Brazil. But the Papal Bulls of 1493 had established several great principles. These were: (1) that discovery of non-Christian lands gave legal title to those lands to the Christian sovereign whose agents or subjects discovered them; (2) that the subjects of other sovereigns were forbidden to enter territory legally held by a Christian prince; and (3) that the trade of a colony was an absolute monopoly of its mother country. The other maritime governments paid no attention to Papal Bulls which would have excluded them forever from colonial power. Francis I of France, when he sent Jacques Cartier to the Saint Lawrence, told Spain he wanted to see "Adam's will to learn how he had partitioned the world."

England flouted the Bulls even before Henry VIII displaced the Pope as head of the English Church, and after that event competition with Spain was stimulated by religious rivalry. But Spain proceeded to build her empire on the principle of absolute monopoly. To its political and economic control was added the absolute authority of the Crown of Spain over the religious institutions of the colonies when the Pope conveyed to it the *patronato real*. Under this power of royal patronage the King of Spain controlled all ecclesiastical appointments and benefices in the empire and enjoyed the power of taxation over Church properties. He could even prevent papal orders from being promulgated in the empire by the clergy. In return for these extraordinary privileges, the Spanish Crown had responsibility for the conversion of the natives to Catholicism and the general welfare of religion.

Thus no limit was placed on the authority of the Spanish monarchs in their overseas domain. The Council of the Indies was established in Spain in 1524 to rule the colonies in the name of the king. It made laws, appointed governors and officials, heard cases as the court of final appeal, and supervised the economic life of the colonies. This latter function was the special province of the *Casa de Contratación,* an agency in Spain subordinate to the Council of the Indies. The Casa managed the trade of the empire as a monopoly of the Crown, with the particular purpose of making it yield maximum profits in gold and silver. No Spanish merchant could do business with the colonies except through the Casa and under its rules. No colonial merchant could deal with any other Spanish colony or with any foreign colony or nation—only with Spain, and in Spain only with the Casa. Virtually all colonial activities, personal as well as economic, political, and religious, were heavily taxed for the benefit of the Crown. No share in government was allowed the Spanish settlers in the colonies, and much less did the bulk of the population, Indian serfs or Negro slaves, enjoy power. In the course of time, corruption and inefficiency mitigated the rigors of Spanish rule, but they only substituted other evils.

The great purpose of the Spanish colonial system was to provide the Crown with the wealth in the literal form of gold and silver which spelled luxury and power. Spain might have used this wealth as capital to establish industries at home and supply the colonies with the manufactures they needed. Instead, such manufactures were purchased in northern Europe, where industries consequently thrived on the Spanish market. The Spanish government also wasted the wealth of America on wars intended to make it supreme in Europe—an ambition which was rudely shattered by the destruction of the Armada in 1588. The English even dared to rob Spain of her American profits by attacks on fleets carrying gold in the Spanish Main.

Strength and Weakness of the Spanish System

Spain was a modern power insofar as the country was united under a powerful centralized government, and the life-blood of her empire was trade, regulated according to mercantilist principles. But in most other respects Spain and her empire were medieval. Social organization was even more rigidly defined by hereditary class and caste distinctions in the colonies than at home. The Reformation was countered in the colonies as at home by the Inquisition, which forcefully stamped out heresy, and by the Jesuits, so that Catholicism was at least outwardly strengthened in the process. Although two universities were founded at Mexico City and Lima, Peru, at an early time, the intellectual life of the colonists was subject to censorship in order to prevent infiltration of modern thought. In all that pertained to political and economic freedom, the colonies were equally excluded from participation in modern developments. The wealth of the Indies slipped through Spanish fingers, leaving hardly a trace beyond the transitory luxuries of the few. Within a century after the voyages of Columbus, the Spanish Empire had passed its apogee.

For three more centuries Spain gave ground slowly before the incursions of rival empires and revolts of its subjects, until in 1898 in the Spanish-American War Cuban rebels and the United States delivered the *coup de grâce.* If one chief reason for the failure of the Spanish colonial system can be detected, it is that it stifled rather than encouraged the participation of the colonial peoples in the development of modern social, economic, political, and religious institutions. Nevertheless, the positive gifts of Spain to the Empire, especially in the fields of religion, literature, language, and art, brought millions out of barbarism and remain today as a precious heritage of their descendants in Latin America.

FRANCE

The exciting news of gold in the world that Columbus had discovered acted like a magnet in drawing adventurers of all the Atlantic states across the ocean. Fishermen frequently sailed from France and England to the Grand Banks of Newfoundland, where nets were rarely pulled in empty. French sea dogs raided Spanish settlements and waylaid gold fleets during the years after the conquests of Mexico and Peru. Papal Bulls, the Ten Commandments, and Spanish power were all inadequate to protect the Spanish monopoly of the New World.

Early Explorers

France soon sent the explorers de Gonneville and Verrazano to search out a suitable place for permanent French settlement. Francis I decided that the St. Lawrence River might be a Northwest Passage to the Orient, and in any case was the route to a fabled interior kingdom rich in diamonds and gold. He sent Jacques Cartier on three voyages in 1534, 1535, and 1541. On the third trip, Cartier built a fort on the site of modern Quebec, established a colony, and set out to find the mythical kingdom. Within a year the whole venture was abandoned and the French returned home. The enormous debts Francis I bequeathed to his successors and the civil wars in the kingdom postponed the building of a French empire.

But the claim by discovery and exploration was not forgotten. In better times, during the truce between Huguenots and Catholics under the Edict of Nantes, King Henry of Navarre granted in 1603 to a Huguenot nobleman, Sieur de Monts, feudal and trading rights to a vast strip of North

America lying between the 40th and 46th parallels. This overlapped territory that England claimed and began to settle a few years later. The Anglo-French rivalry for empire in North America was one of the causes of a series of great wars during the next two centuries.

Samuel de Champlain (1567-1635) was an outstanding empire builder of his time. He was a tireless explorer who penetrated the interior of North America and, when too old to go himself, sent young men into the forests and along the lakes and rivers until Frenchmen had traversed the whole area from the Saint Lawrence River to present-day Minnesota and Missouri. Champlain was a diplomat who organized alliances between the King of France and the Algonquin-Huron Confederation of Indian tribes. He helped these tribes expel the Iroquois from the Saint Lawrence Valley and thereby secured a monopoly of the rich fur trade for France. The King of France gave monopoly rights over the fur trade to other favorites, but Champlain and de Monts ignored the royal decree and re-established a colony at Quebec which became the headquarters of the trade in treasured beaver skins. Champlain ruled over savage Indians and hardy Frenchmen until he died in 1635.

The fur trade gave France a source of American wealth less spectacular but more enduring than the gold of the Spanish Empire. The wearing of fur was a sign of wealth and dignity in all Europe. Kings, nobles, and merchant princes paid well for furs trapped by Indians and sold in Quebec for knives and trinkets. The fur trade largely determined the character of the French Empire in America. Because the Indians performed the main task of providing the pelts, French rule over them was benevolent and hardly disturbed the Indians' way of life. The French carried on agriculture only in a limited strip of land on the banks of the Saint Lawrence. There *habitants* tilled the soil as virtual serfs of feudal landholders and created a reproduction of the rural life of old France which has persisted to this day.

In 1632, the first Jesuit missionaries reached Quebec. They were fearless and tireless in the work of exploring the continent and converting the Indians. Thus the Counter-Reformation won new adherents for Catholicism in North America to make up for Protestant inroads in Europe. France might have built a Catholic-Indian empire in the vast region of the Mississippi Valley and the Great Lakes but for the failure of her Indian allies to withstand the Iroquois. The Five Tribes of the Iroquois Confederation—the Mohawks, Oneidas, Onondagas, Cayugas, and Senecas—living then in the present area of New York State, formed ties with Dutch traders at Albany, and later with the English, which made them more than a match for the Algonquin-Huron Confederation. The Iroquois wars, beginning in 1642, disrupted the fur trade and led King Louis XIV to strengthen French rule in America.

Building an Empire

Coming to the throne in 1661, Louis XIV consolidated his absolute rule at home and at the same time made himself personal master over New France. In this work he was influenced by the mercantilist ideas of his principal minister, Colbert. Canada was converted into a royal colony ruled by an *intendant* who exercised the authority of the king in America. The first intendant, Jean Talon, invaded the Iroquois country and defeated the Five Tribes in 1666. Then he reorganized French relations with the Algonquin-Huron tribes whom the Iroquois had scattered as far west as Minnesota, and regularized the fur trade to provide maximum profits for France. In 1673, the Jesuit priest Jacques Marquette and Louis Joliet discovered the upper Mississippi River. Talon's successor, Louis Count de Frontenac, and the explorer Sieur de La Salle, boldly planned to build a string of forts along an interior route that would tie the Saint Lawrence to the Mississippi. La Salle built forts along the route as far as the Illinois River, then he went to France and organized an expedition to invade the Spanish Empire to the south and establish a fort at the mouth of the Mississippi River. He was killed in 1684 by his own followers when they failed to find the difficult entrance to the "Father of Waters." But France was deeply committed now to the struggle for empire in North America.

In 1689, Louis XIV refused to recognize William of Orange as King of England. This was the starting point of four wars between England and France which had for their greatest prize supremacy in the whole of North America. As the fortunes of war favored now one, now the other of the two great contenders, there hung in the balance not merely the question of which Old World monarchy should rule the new continent, but whether it should be held in fief for the Indians and the fur trade, or should be settled by farmers seeking homes in the wilderness.

THE DUTCH

In the sixteenth century, the kings of Spain ruled The Netherlands by virtue of dynastic marriages. But Calvinism won over a large part of the Dutch people, they were jealous of their ancient rights of self-government, and Spanish religious and military rule were severe. Revolt followed revolt, until the Dutch finally won their independence in 1648 and established a republic ruled by the States General (parliament), and the eldest male of the House of Orange as hereditary *statthalter*. England had helped the Dutch against Spain, and after the defeat of the Spanish Armada the Dutch exploited their excellent geographic position to build an overseas trading empire. The Dutch Calvinist merchants and sailors made up in vigor and persistence what their country lacked in power to compete with the Spanish and the Portuguese. The Dutch East India Company, founded in 1602, was granted extensive political, military, and trade rights. It expelled the Portuguese from much of their East Indian empire and became the chief purveyor of spices to Europe. The Dutch West India Company, founded in 1621, was granted similar powers over American and African trade. Within a few years the Dutch gained a foothold on the coast of Brazil, several West Indian islands, including St. Eustatius and Curaçao, and founded New Amsterdam on the island of Manhattan. Thus the Dutch Republic boldly challenged Portugal, Spain, and England for trade and empire.

New Netherland

Henry Hudson was looking for a shorter route to Asia when, in 1609, he sailed up the majestic American river that bears his name. The Dutch West India Company founded New Amsterdam as a trading post in 1624 and this became the governmental seat of the colony of New Netherland. From this center, Dutch settlements spread eastward into Connecticut and Long Island, northward along the Hudson River, westward into New Jersey, and along the lower Delaware River. But the Dutch had now committed themselves to imperial enterprises so farflung that they could not conduct all of them effectively. They were chiefly interested in Oriental trade and neglected American ventures in favor of the East Indies. Nevertheless, the settlements they made in the present area of the United States were destined to leave a permanent impress upon the country. Dutch architecture provided excellent models for American builders. Dutch tolerance quickly fixed the cosmopolitan character of life on Manhattan Island, where languages, peoples, and religions mingled in carefree confusion. The neat husbandry and solid business methods of the Dutch, their love of plain comfort and domesticity, entered into the American heritage.

In spite of the advanced self-governing character of the Dutch at home, no popular representation was allowed in the government of the New Netherland colony. A governor and council appointed by the Dutch West India Company had sole authority. The governors, such as Wouter van Twiller, Willem Kieft, and Peter Stuyvesant, were regarded as petty tyrants. They mishandled relations with the Indians. The company imposed a feudal land system on the rich Hudson Valley which remained as a relic of medievalism until long after the American Revolution. Anyone who would settle fifty families of tenants at his own expense was granted a large tract of land with rights as *patroon* over the tenants. The patroons exercised political, judicial, and economic authority in their domains. Vast quantities of the best land were kept out of cultivation because the patroons could not attract many farmers to work under this archaic system.

Peter Stuyvesant, the last Governor (1647-1664), injured the commercial prosperity of New Amsterdam by ending the free-trade policy which had promised to make the settlement the headquarters of American commerce. He antagonized the burghers of the town by violating the company's grant to them of self-governing privileges. He imprisoned many who objected to his tyranny. A small Swedish settlement on the Delaware River was taken over by the Dutch, but in the east the English settlers came in such numbers that the Dutch were pushed back. The authorities in Massachusetts in 1659 encouraged migration to the Hudson Valley and sanctioned an English post near Poughkeepsie to attract the Iroquois trade. The Dutch West India Company went bankrupt when its invasion of Brazil failed and it could not support New Amsterdam against the English.

Yielding To The English

After the Spanish danger receded, the English and the Dutch had fallen out. Through the seventeenth century they fought several wars. These ended in 1674. The Statthalter William III of Orange married the daughter of James II of England in 1677, thus paving the way for his accession to the English throne in 1689. The Netherlands retained much of her eastern Empire, but the English in 1664 pushed her out of New Netherland and renamed the colony New York. Weakened by neglect and misrule, it was surrendered by Peter Stuyvesant to an English expedition without a blow.

The English used their victory wisely. The Dutch colonists transferred their loyalty to England and remained an important, even dominant element in the population long after they were outnumbered by English newcomers. The patroons emerged as a provincial aristocracy whose daughters' hands were eagerly sought in marriage by the English merchants of New York City. The Dutch origins of names famous in later American history—such as Schuyler, Van Buren, Vanderbilt, and Roosevelt—attest the enduring importance of the Dutch contribution to American civilization.

❖   ❖   ❖

Trade, religion, and national power were the chief incentives leading Portugal, Spain, France, and The Netherlands to explore and colonize the New World. Portugal, Spain, and France successfully established colonies organized on absolutist and monopolistic principles. Native populations and Negro slaves performed the hard labor of winning wealth for European settlers, who were exploited in turn for the benefit of their mother countries. It hardly entered the minds of Portuguese, Spaniards, and Frenchmen that the destiny of America might be to give Europeans, much less other peoples, a chance to build societies on any other model than one determined for them by the kings of Europe. The opportunity they perceived in America was for kings and their governments to realize their dreams of wealth and power. Consequently, absolutism and monopoly were imposed on the colonies even more harshly than at home.

The official motives of the English government in its colonial policy were not greatly different from those of the continental governments. England attempted to establish an economic monopoly over her American colonies according to the Spanish norm. But the English Crown lacked money to finance colonial enterprises, and had to make concessions to the private groups who did finance them. More important, the traditions and institutions of the English people favored a degree of personal liberty and self-government unknown in Portugal, Spain, and France. In practice, the English government permitted its American colonists wide latitude in economic, political, and religious matters. Thus it became possible for the English colonies to serve not the interests of the king so much as the interests of the colonists themselves. Finally, these colonists carried to America visions of an ideal society far different from the societies the other powers created there.

CHAPTER 3

Early English Settlements: Virginia and Maryland

THE ENGLISH RESPONSE TO THE DISCOVERY OF AMERICA was suggested by Sir Thomas More in his famous book *Utopia*, published in the sixteenth century. Utopia was an ideal society on an island in the New World and it has given its name to all such visionary schemes. But some of the most important features of social organization in Utopia that seemed impossible dreams then are commonplaces of American life now. Such were the nine-hour working day, inventions to save labor, city planning, free and compulsory education, intellectual and religious freedom, and, most significant of all, government by representatives chosen by the citizens.

Englishmen were not content to dream about a better and happier society. They founded one colony after another in America to carry into practice one scheme or another for attaining it. The states of the Union and the federal government itself are practical applications of the utopian dream of freedom and self-government, and Americans to this day consider it their birthright to criticize public evils and devise improvements which will bring the ideal society a little closer to realization. The peculiar English and American combination of social vision and common-sense practicality underlies the whole course of American history.

SIXTEENTH-CENTURY ENGLAND

At the beginning of the century, England was poor and weak. Henry VIII built up the Royal Navy to protect the homeland from invasion and the colonies from imperial rivals. To encourage the merchant class which supported it against unruly nobles, the Crown, in the middle of the century, chartered the Muscovy Company to trade with Russia. This was a joint-stock company of a type that was destined to play a large role in English colonization. Membership in such a company could be obtained by contributing a sum of money for the purchase of stock, and the members organized themselves as a self-governing body. The company exercised authority outside the kingdom, chiefly economic but also political, which was bestowed by the king in a "charter of privileges." Profits from the business activities were distributed among the members in proportion to their ownership of stock. It can be readily seen that such an organization was an ancestor of the modern business corporation, but its importance goes far beyond the business field. The practice of self-government and the exercise of political authority by companies chartered to colonize America provided experience which led directly to the organization of governments on the same principles.

Rivalry with Spain

England prospered during the sixteenth century in part because the gold of Mexico and Peru was used by Spain to buy English woolens and other products. Also, the religious quarrels between Catholic Spain and the Protestant England of Queen Elizabeth gave English seadogs an excuse to capture treasure ships before they arrived in Spain. When Francis Drake dropped anchor at London with a cargo of Spanish gold, Good Queen Bess paid him the signal honor of visiting him aboard his ship, where she knighted him—and shared his treasure.

Englishmen took over the external trade of their kingdom which had formerly been in the hands of foreigners. Daring English traders even invaded the commerce of foreign empires, as John Hawkins did when he carried African slaves to Spanish America in defiance of the Papal Bull and the laws of Spain and Portugal. The ideal of economic self-sufficiency appealed greatly to Englishmen. Colonies able to provide not only gold but also the commodities that England had to import, such as tar and timber for shipbuilding and all kinds of semitropical products, and capable of buying English manufactures in exchange, were essential to the developing English scheme of self-sufficiency. Besides this, Protestantism could be strengthened by extending it to colonies and thereby limiting the expansion of Catholicism. Thus dreams of national power, national wealth, and national religious security all entered into the creation of an English empire in America.

Spain had no intention of allowing the bold English heretics to destroy her monopoly in the New World. Spurred on by the semipiratical raids of the seadogs, Spain organized the Invincible Armada for the invasion and conquest of England. When the 132 Spanish ships, carrying 3165 cannon and thousands of soldiers, stood in the English Channel in 1588, the future of America hung in the balance. But the seamen of England rallied to the national defense, the Royal Navy was expanded by numerous ships faster and more skillfully managed than the clumsy Spanish galleons, and, under the leadership of Drake, Hawkins, and Howard, the Spaniards were defeated and their proud vessels scattered. A storm off the Hebrides completed the destruction of the Armada, and England was delivered. The joy and patriotic fervor of Englishmen knew no bounds. Their new-found greatness manifested itself exuberantly in literature, notably in the immortal works of William Shakespeare. It also expressed itself in colonial enterprises.

England Turns to America

Up to the time of the Armada, English explorers, beginning with John Cabot, had been chiefly concerned with finding a passage through or around America to the Orient. In 1576, Sir Martin Frobisher thought his expedition to find a Northwest Passage was successful when he entered the region of Hudson Bay. Sir Humphrey Gilbert in 1583 laid claim to Newfoundland in the name of the Queen. In 1600, the East India Company was chartered, and it eventually controlled most of the trade of India, paving the way for that country's addition to the British Empire. Richard Hakluyt and others compiled accounts of English voyages which were exceedingly popular reading matter in Elizabethan England. But attempts at English settlement in America in the sixteenth century were not successful. Sir Walter Raleigh, under a patent from the Queen, claimed all North America north of Florida, named it Virginia in honor of his sovereign, and in 1585 planted two colonies on the sands of Roanoke Island, in what is now North Carolina. The first group of colonists went back to England after a year, and the second had mysteriously disappeared without a trace when ships returned to America in 1590.

In 1603, Elizabeth died. Her successor, the Stuart James I, made peace with Spain, thus releasing English soldiers and sailors for American adventures. The business of capturing Spanish treasure ships now declined, and merchants sought other outlets for their venture capital. Thousands of English farmers had been thrown off the land by the enclosures which joined tillage tracts into sheep meadows to provide wool for the textile industry. The Elizabethan Poor Law of 1601 had made such unemployed "sturdy beggars" the charges of the local parishes, which were anxious to get them off their hands. England, suddenly at peace, found herself suddenly overpopulated. Poor families begged for employment for their hands and rich men sought employment for their capital. At the same time, Puritans and Dissenters feared the High-Church Anglicanism of the Stuarts, which seemed but a disguise of Roman Catholic leanings and, worst of all, friendliness to the great enemy of the English patriots—Spain. Furthermore, the Stuarts—James I and his son Charles I

—seemed bent on destroying the ancient rights and privileges of Englishmen, particularly the powers and privileges of Parliament. When the House of Commons adopted the Great Protestation of 1621, including the assertion, "That the liberties, franchises, privileges, and jurisdictions of Parliament are the ancient and undoubted birthright and and inheritance of the subjects of England," the King tore the page from the journal, dissolved Parliament, and imprisoned its leaders.

With the King riding roughshod over his subjects, it seemed to many Englishmen that escape to the New World was the only chance to secure their freedom from Stuart tryanny. Yet it must be realized that the very willingness of the Crown to allow rebellious subjects to go to America was in sharp contrast to the Spanish requirement that none should go to America except Spaniards of proved loyalty and religious orthodoxy. The English settlements in America were unique in that they were largely populated by the poor and the rebellious who were determined to create a society designed for their own well-being rather than the mere aggrandizement of their monarch. The first permanent settlement, however, at Jamestown in 1607, was made under the auspices of a company of merchants and other adventurers whose motives were patriotic as well as commercial.

THE FOUNDING OF VIRGINIA

The King, on April 10, 1606, issued a patent authorizing two companies to set up colonies in what was known as Virgina—the region between the 34th and 45th parallels of latitude, that is, between the Cape Fear River and the present site of Bangor, Maine. The London Company was to begin settlement in the southern part of the territory, the Plymouth within the northern. The specific lands granted were to center in the first seat of settlement in each instance, extending 50 miles north and south along the coast and 100 miles inland. The charter provided that the companies should elect resident councils to govern each colony. A Royal Council in England, appointed by the king, was placed over the resident councils to supervise them in the national interest. This contained persons identified with the companies. Also, the rights of the colonists as Englishmen were guaranteed. Colonists of Spain and France were considered to be outside the law and subject to the arbitrary rule of their kings. But in the charter of the Virginia companies, all "liberties, franchises, and immunities" enjoyed by Englishmen at home were guaranteed to English settlers and their children in America. Among such rights were trial by jury, habeas corpus, and the ownership and inheritance of land. At the same time, the colonies were placed outside the kingdom for purposes of customs duties and in the matter of representation in Parliament.

Jamestown

Members of the companies subscribed money to finance the settlements. The charters enjoined the duty of converting the natives to Christianity, and it was hoped that gold might be found. In spirit the companies were intensely patriotic, but their major immediate purpose was to establish a profitable trade in fish and furs. Only the London Company concerns us here. On December 20, 1606, it sent three ships, the *Susan Constant*, the *Goodspeed*, and the *Discovery*, with 144 men under the command of Captain Christopher Newport, on the southerly route to America. After sailing among the West Indies, the ships entered Chesapeake Bay on April 26, 1607. They were instructed to settle on the river which seemed most likely to afford a Northwest Passage, and away from the coast for security against the Spaniards. Therefore the ships entered the river that was named the James, and on May 24 the site of Jamestown was chosen. Thirty-nine men had died on the long voyage. The survivors built a fortified enclosure for a church and houses and set about exploring the low and heavily wooded country.

These first Englishmen to establish a permanent settlement in America had more liking for adventure than for labor and hardships. They hoped for quick riches by barter with the Indians or the discovery of gold, and they became unruly when threatened by starvation and disease in this rich but untamed land. One mutiny was put down only by executing its leader, Captain George Kendall, and all but thirty-eight men died before the year had ended. Supply ships from England, a new group of immigrants that included more craftsmen and laborers, and the firm rule of Captain John Smith, who became president of the Resident Council in September 1608, saved the colony. The redoubtable Captain put all hands to work and threatened to send shirkers into the forest to starve.

The zeal and intelligence of the leaders of the company in England ensured the endurance of the little settlement. They studied the weaknesses of the venture and worked hard to correct them. They decided that the secret of success was not quick riches, but a stable life for families tilling the soil. Sir Edwin Sandys, an able member of the Royal Council, obtained in 1609 a new charter from the King which enlarged the bounds of the colony to include Chesapeake Bay and gave the officers of the company greater control over the government of the colony. Sir Thomas Smith, an outstanding businessman who was highly experienced in commerce and government, became treasurer and head of the company and he supervised its affairs with skill. A great public campaign was opened to obtain subscribers and settlers. One circular declared that the objects of the company were to spread the Gospel, "to plant an English nation" in America, and to establish a trade which would secure Englishmen from being "eaten out of all profits" by foreigners. Enthusiasm ran high. Guilds and clergymen joined in supporting a heroic new effort. Purchasers of stock were promised their pro-rata share of "Golde, Silver and other mettals or treasure, Pearles, Precious Stones or any kind of wares or Merchandizes, commodities or profits whatsoever." Enough money was raised to outfit nine ships and about a thousand immigrants. In money and in human life the cost of this patriotic enterprise was high.

The company had decided to make Lord De la Warre "Lord Governor and Captain General of Virginia" as a virtual dictator. Sir Thomas Gates went out in May 1609 with the first expedition as De la Warre's deputy. A hurricane forced Gates's ship to Bermuda but the others reached Jamestown, and Captain John Smith gave way reluctantly to Captain George Percy as head of the Resident Council. Disease and Indian attacks quickly played havoc with the newcomers. There followed the grim "Starving Time," which every colony in America seemed fated to endure until the skills and organization necessary to establish a colony were at length attained. By the end of the next winter less than half of the colonists were alive, and these were famished and beseiged by Indians. Gates arrived from Bermuda in May 1610, but when food for only sixteen days remained, the settlers boarded ship for Newfoundland where they hoped for help from fishermen.

Jamestown was abandoned in June 1610, and the fleeing ships were some miles down the river when they met a fleet under the command of Lord De la Warre, with reinforcements and supplies from England. Gates and his men turned about and the whole company reoccupied Jamestown. The Starving Time was past. De la Warre returned to England in March 1611, but Sir Thomas Dale, Sir Thomas Gates, and Captain Samuel Argall successively ruled the colony and placed it on a permanent footing. Settlements on more healthful sites than the one at Jamestown were founded, peace was established with the Indians, and artisans and farmers were more numerous among new immigrants. The rulers of the colony were harsh, but they had to gain some security before they could allow much freedom.

In 1612, Sir Thomas Smith and his associates obtained another revision of the charter, which proved to be the final one. This now gave title to Bermuda. Soon transferred to a subsidiary company, Bermuda was permanently occupied by the English from this time on. Also, the company gained full control of the Royal Council. The affairs of Virginia were completely under the company hereafter until 1624, when the royal period began.

Virginia under the Company

Sir Thomas Dale in 1613 introduced a new land system of great significance for the future of English colonization. Up to this time, the company had retained title to the land, agricultural products were placed in the common storehouse, and supplies were distributed among the colonists according to need with little regard to the labor individuals performed. Dale allotted to every man three acres which he might cultivate for himself in return for a fixed annual payment of produce as rent to the company. Thus an incentive was provided for the individual colonist to work hard. John Rolfe in 1612 began experiments to raise tobacco for export which met with great success. Encouraged by the opportunity to make private profits, the colonists turned eagerly to tobacco production. In 1617, £20,000 worth was sent to England. The economic foundations of Virginia were being firmly laid in smoke.

Sir Edwin Sandys realized that the colony could be rapidly populated only if immigrants were granted an opportunity to own land outright. Beginning in 1618, the company offered fifty acres to anyone who bought a share of stock in the company. Land was also granted to the Church of England for the support of parish churches and clergymen, and to a college which the company hoped to found. Finally, the famous "headright" system was adopted, whereby the company granted fifty acres of land for every person transported to America. An individual could collect a headright for himself and also one for every member of his family or servant he brought with him. Thus an Englishman of small means could transform himself into a landowner in America, and a person of means might establish a large plantation.

Sandys and his associates showed far-sighted statesmanship. They gave up the search for immediate profits for the company in order to create a prosperous colony based on private ownership and private profits which, in time, would redound to the benefit of England and its merchant class as a whole. Moreover, the headright system, which persisted and was afterwards extended to other colonies, facilitated the development of a society composed of self-reliant freemen in sharp contrast to the feudal system of Spanish America. By 1618, however, the Company was heavily in debt. In an effort to recover their losses, members of the company now joined with outsiders to form subsidiary associations and engage in particular enterprises which might be profitable. A number of great plantations, modeled on the English village and its outlying lands, were established or projected by associations of adventurers and planters who received patents from the company. The Pilgrims who ended up at Plymouth had set out to establish one of these Virginia plantations. Other associations were formed to engage in manufactures, but the cultivation of tobacco superseded all other activities.

The anxiety of Sandys to make Virginia attractive to the best type of settler was responsible for the first institution of popular self-government in America. Colonists complained of the tyrannical practices of their rulers, particularly Captain Samuel Argall, and the company in reply bestowed a Charter of Grants and Liberties in 1618. This declared that Virginia should be constituted a "free popular state," and that no government should be imposed on the colonists without their consent. A new governor, Sir George Yeardley, was sent out with the charter in 1619 and instructed to call a general assembly of the planters every year. Each "corporation" in Virginia, that is, each settlement, hundred, and plantation, was permitted to elect two burgesses as delegates to the assembly, for the purpose of doing "those things as might best tend to their good."

Yeardley called the first meeting of the famous Virginia House of Burgesses in July 1619. He proclaimed the annulment of "cruell lawes" established by his predecessors, and declared that henceforth Virginia would be ruled by the "free lawes" that prevailed in England. Elections for the House of Burgesses were extraordinarily democratic, even servants and youths of seventeen years taking part. When the twenty-two burgesses met in the church of Jamestown, no other colony in the Western Hemisphere could match Virginia's progress towards that ideal society of which Sir Thomas More had dreamed. The experience of Englishmen in their ancient Parliament in London and, more directly, the experience of the colonists with the corporation form of business organization, had provided excellent training. The burgesses immediately organized themselves on the pattern of the House of Commons and proceeded to enact laws for the government of the colony and draw up petitions to the company for the enlargement of their sphere of power. One of these petitions resulted in an important concession by the company in 1621 that none of its orders should be carried out unless it was approved by the House of Burgesses.

The company had now divested itself of a large share of its political as well as economic reason for existence, and several difficulties hastened its dissolution. The first of these involved the new staple crop of tobacco. The craze for smoking the "sotweed" created a great market in England and Europe. Many moralists, led by King James I, spoke out violently against the habit of "drinking" smoke, but their efforts seemed only to popularize it. The English government imposed a heavy import duty on Virginia tobacco and forbade the colonists to export it to any other country, in return for which cultivation of the plant was forbidden in England. Also, the right to import tobacco was granted by the King to his favorites as a monopoly privilege. The situation was made worse when Sandys obtained for the company a monopoly contract to import tobacco into England, because this contract promised a large share of the profits to the King and various officials. The leaders of the company fell to wrangling, Sandys was defeated, and the tobacco contract was dissolved. Henceforth, tobacco could be imported by anyone into England upon payment of a duty. The English market was protected and the situation was favorable to the Virginia colonists, but the greatest potential source of profit to the company had been lost.

Meetings of the company in London became contests between embittered factions. Meanwhile, in 1622, a large number of the Virginia colonists were massacred by the Indians, and many of the company's properties, including experimental factories, were destroyed. King James became convinced that the company had mismanaged its affairs, and it was true that defenses had been neglected in favor of the universal cultivation of tobacco. The King moved through his Privy Council to take control of Virginia. Leaders of the company attempted to raise the issue in Parliament but James denied Parliament's authority and was upheld by the courts. The company was dissolved by court order and Virginia became a royal colony in 1624. The new King, Charles I, appointed a governor and council to rule under royal instructions. The colonists preferred this to the company's rule, and were gratified to find that their legislature and local courts of law were not disturbed under the new regime.

Life in the First Colony

Thus Virginia evolved into the first royal colony in America while enjoying a high degree of self-government. Immigration proceeded apace, yet it never caught up with the demand for labor on the tobacco plantations. Indentured servants provided the bulk of the labor supply until the last quarter of the seventeenth century, when Negro slaves were imported in increasing number from Africa. During the middle of the century, as many as 1500 indentured servants came to Virginia every year. They usually had volunteered to serve a master from two to seven years in return for transportation and an "outfit" of clothing and equipment. Then, at the end of their term, they became free citizens, and, obtaining land of their own on easy terms, they often rose rapidly in the social and economic scale.

This transformation of poor Englishmen into landowners enjoying political privileges set a pattern which was to give special character to life in the English colonies. The number of immigrants who belonged to the families of the English nobility was negligible. The first "ruling class" in Virginia as elsewhere in the English colonies was chiefly composed of members of the merchant and yeoman farmer classes who had enough money to bring servants with them and obtain large tracts of land. They formed the "plantation aristocracy" of the new colony, and some Cavaliers joined them later, but their ranks were continually swelled by "new men" rising in the social scale.

Not all of the immigrants came to Virginia and the other colonies voluntarily. English judges sentenced criminals to transportation to

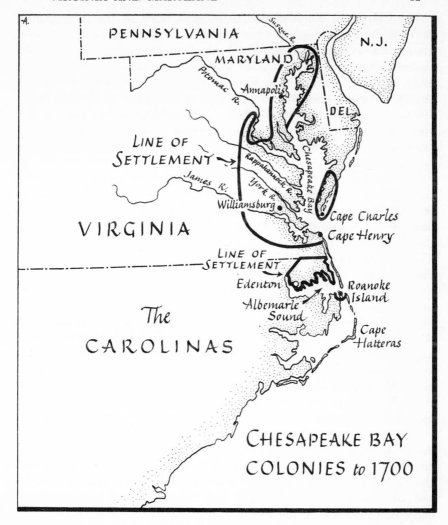

CHESAPEAKE BAY
COLONIES to 1700

America and overseers of the poor got rid of their charges in the same way. Parliament sometimes banished political offenders to the colonies. Poor children were sent over, as were women to provide wives for the settlers. Prisoners of war, especially Irish, were sometimes transported. Illegal methods of populating the colonies were also used: kidnappers "crimped" the unwary and shipped them off in virtual slavery. The vast majority of involuntary immigrants were unfortunate rather than vicious, and they generally turned into excellent citizens in the New World. As the English poet and divine, John Donne, said, colonization was "not only a spleen to drain ill humours of the body, but a liver to breed good blood."

The Church of England was early established as the state church of Virginia. Provisions were made for its support by means of land grants and tax funds. As settlement advanced along the rivers and into the interior, parishes were defined and placed in charge of clergymen in much the same manner as in England itself. But conformity was never strictly enforced, even after the House of Burgesses in 1642 passed a law to expel dissenters from the colony. The need for settlers and laborers was too compelling for landowners to support any effective campaign against members of dissenting sects or even against clergymen who ministered to them.

The worst hazard of life in the low-lying Tidewater areas was malaria, but when quinine was discovered it helped to mitigate the scourge. The Indian menace declined after several bloody outbreaks. The company had tried to establish friendly relations with the natives and to pay them for their lands, although their legal title was never admitted. The general rule in English as in Spanish America was that any Christian king whose subjects seized territory belonging to infidels acquired title thereby. For some years trouble was avoided in Virginia by the marriage to John Rolfe of Pocahontas, daughter of the Indian Chief Powhatan. She warned the colonists of impending attacks by her tribe. After her father died, his brother Opechancanough led the fearful massacre of 1622. This caused the company to import antiquated weapons, armor, and artillery from the Tower of London, and these medieval arms were employed with great effect in the American wilderness, so that thereafter, except for one uprising in 1644, Virginia was very little troubled by the natives.

The Spanish claimed as their own the lands on which the first English colony in America was established, and they went so far as to send reconnoitering expeditions to Jamestown. But they were convinced that the colony would fail for lack of gold or silver mines, and they would not risk another war with England over territory that seemed so useless. They remained a potential threat, however, and actually the boundary between Spanish and English territory in North America remained in dispute for two centuries, being inherited and finally settled by the United States. France claimed territory indefinitely southward from the Saint Lawrence region, and for a time there were French settlements at Mt. Desert in the present state of Maine. But Sir Samuel Argall wiped these out, and after 1616 Virginia felt secure for some years against the French.

By establishing and maintaining this first colony, the English became successful contenders in the contest of European powers for imperial position in America. According to Spanish standards, Virginia was a useless possession, requiring backbreaking labor of white men and yielding little wealth to the mother country. The population was a "foul brood of heretics," undisciplined and ambitious for personal rather than imperial gain. Even in imperial terms, however, the English had follov·ed wise policy. Time was to show that the institutions of self-government and private ownership of readily available land were more productive of wealth and human happiness than was the system of absolutism and feudalism that Spain brought to the Western World.

MARYLAND

The colony of Maryland began, not under the auspices of a trading company, but of a proprietor. Its political, economic, and social system proved to be much the same as in Virginia. Maryland was originally the feudal domain of a noble Catholic family. George Calvert, Lord Baltimore, obtained in 1632 from King Charles I a grant of nearly ten million acres lying between the Potomac River and the 40th parallel of north latitude. He and his heirs were created "Absolute Lords and Proprietaries" with power to make, with the consent of the freemen, any laws that were consonant with the laws of England. They were empowered to make grants for subordinate feudal manors, to fix rents and levy duties and taxes. In return, the King received two Indian arrows annually in token of feudal service. The Calverts were poor and hoped to make their fortune in America and also to establish a haven for Catholics. The proprietors encouraged Protestants as well to settle in their domain, realizing that Catholics wishing to migrate were not numerous enough to build up the colony.

On the death of George Calvert in 1632, the year of the grant to him, his son Cecil became Lord Baltimore, and the latter appointed his brother, Leonard, Governor of Maryland. Several hundred colonists of various faiths voyaged to the Chesapeake in 1634 aboard the *Ark* and the *Dove*. Catholics chiefly settled around Saint Mary's, Protestants in and around Providence, later called Annapolis. Immigration proceeded, and soon the Tidewater region was dotted with tobacco plantations. The Marylanders learned the technique of successful colonization from the Virginians and suffered relatively few hardships. All the settlers were tenants of the Calverts. Some, mostly Catholics, were granted manorial privileges and great tracts of land. These men farmed their lands with tenants of their own and servants, and paid quitrents to Lord Baltimore. Yeoman farmers leased land from the proprietor, used their own labor supplemented sometimes by that of a few servants, and also paid quitrents.

The Lords Baltimore drew up the laws for their colony and sent them to a representative assembly of the freemen for approval. From the beginning the Assembly asserted its right to introduce laws. The officeholders, unlike the population, were in majority Catholics, but they were jealous of the proprietors' pretensions to absolute power. The Assembly enacted a law of religious toleration in 1649, which gave assurance to Protestant immigrants that they would not be persecuted, and many Puritans answered the invitation. Englishmen in Maryland, especially the Protestant majority, continued to challenge the absolute authority of their feudal Catholic rulers, and sporadic civil conflicts marked the history of the colony. The Puritans of Maryland won power for a time during the rule of Oliver Cromwell in England. They did not hesitate to persecute Roman Catholics and to repeal the Act of Toleration in 1654. With the Restoration in 1660, the Calverts regained control and established an uneasy peace. More important than religious disputes in causing unrest in Maryland was the unwillingness of yeoman farmers to pay their quitrents—small money payments representing a commutation of feudal dues and services which were payable to the proprietor by freeholders. Like other frontiersmen in America, they believed they had a God-given right to absolute ownership of the land they cleared and farmed. Despite its proprietary form, Maryland became another nursery of individual freedom, and another school of self-government.

Negro Slavery in the Tobacco Colonies

The supply of indentured servants from England proved insufficient to meet the demand for labor on the expanding Tidewater tobacco plantations of Virginia and Maryland. The theory that England was overpopulated, which had impelled the first colonial settlements, gave way in the 1660's to the opposite view that the mother country was suffering from a shortage of labor. Epidemics of the plague wiped out a sizeable fraction of the poorest classes in England, the shortage of labor sent wages skyrocketing, and loud complaints were made against the draining of artisans and farmers to America. One of the acts of King Charles II after he came to the throne was to charter the Royal African Company to invade and monopolize the slave trade of Portugal. Subsequently, by the *Assiento* (1713), Spain granted Englishmen the privilege of selling African slaves into the Spanish Empire. The trade in slaves to the English colonies was even more lucrative, and it solved their labor problem at the cost of fastening on English America its most inhuman institution.

The usual justification for slavery at the time was that it permitted the conversion of the Africans to Christianity and their general advancement in civilization. But the slave trade, conducted by means of warfare and the corruption of African tribal life, frustrated the development of native civilization in Africa. Also, it killed off many more Negroes than those who were submissive and healthy enough to survive the infamous "middle passage" to America, and the cruel "breaking-in" process which made them amenable to disciplined labor.

Chattel slavery as a legal institution was established in the English colonies almost by accident. Such a form of servitude was unknown in English law. The first Negro slaves in the mid-seventeenth century were regarded as servants who would normally obtain their freedom after a term of labor. But they had no indentures to present to a court to prove their right to freedom, and the temptation to hold them and their children in bondage was too strong for the labor-hungry planters to resist. Late in the seventeenth century large numbers of slaves were brought into the colonies and their status was fixed in codes of laws passed by provincial legislatures. The standard slave codes in English colonies were more severe than among the Spanish and Portuguese, insofar as they left the slaves with no rights against their masters which could be enforced at law. The typical slaveowning planter of Tidewater Virginia and Maryland was kind and patriarchal towards his human chattels, particularly towards those who served him personally, but he was greatly interested in "getting a crop," and he generally left the field hands to the mercies of overseers, who were notoriously brutal as a class.

The introduction of Negro slaves had the effect of expanding the large plantation system. The best Tidewater tobacco lands in Maryland and Virginia came under the ownership of great planters who used gangs of slaves to work them. Small farmers who could not afford to buy slaves found it hard to compete for good land or to sell tobacco as cheaply as the large planters. Many of them eventually turned westward to the Piedmont region, the foothills of the Blue Ridge Mountains, though even there the lands were often opened up first by planters. Lesser men tended to engage in diversified agriculture on family farms similar to those in the northern colonies. In Tidewater a plantation aristocracy grew up. The culture and way of life of the English country gentry were taken as models by this new colonial class. Replicas of English country homes were built along the rivers, sons were educated in England, ships brought the latest English books and fashions to the planters' own wharves and took away the tobacco crop, and hospitality was dispensed lavishly.

For the owner of thousands of acres and dozens or hundreds of slaves, whose father in many cases had left England a poor man, America had indeed proved to be the land of promise. Along with relative ease and luxury, however, went a high sense of social and political responsibility, which was well exemplified in the next century by George Washington, Thomas Jefferson, and other leaders. Public life was considered the proper career for the masters of great plantations, and they schooled themselves in the law. The planters dominated the Virginia and Maryland legislatures and they strengthened their position as a privileged class by statute. Laws of primogeniture and entail were intended to secure family position in future generations, but they were of much less importance in the New World than, the Old because of the abundance of land. The apportionment of seats in the legislatures gave disproportionate representation to the older counties, and this became an increasing grievance as population grew to the westward. On the foundation of Negro slave labor, a society was erected in the tobacco colonies which seemed to be divided into castes, and certainly was divided between slave and free. But the large area of unoccupied land offered real opportunity to poor settlers and servants whose indentures had run out, and society remained fluid to a degree that was not matched in Europe.

CHAPTER 4

The New England Colonies

THE COLONY OF VIRGINIA WAS IN MOST RESPECTS A reproduction of English society and institutions—more flexible in offering greater opportunity to the poor and more rigid in that it was based on a staple agricultural economy and eventually on Negro slavery. New England, on the other hand, became in the seventeenth century the seat of a series of experiments in the establishment of colonial societies on original patterns—according to specifications which were found by religious enthusiasts in the Bible. These zealots were in varying degrees rebels against the Church of England, and nothing distinguished English colonial policy from that of the other European powers more than the toleration, even the encouragement, of the rebellious utopian experiments that were carried on by the Pilgrims of Plymouth, the Puritans of Massachusetts Bay and Connecticut, and the Baptists of Rhode Island. At the beginning religious and social idealism were virtually unalloyed by commercialism in these colonies.

THE PILGRIMS

In the same year, 1607, that the first settlers sent by the London Company arrived at Jamestown, the Plymouth Company sent out two vessels with 120 men to establish a colony in the northern section of the vast region then called Virginia. These men reached the coast of Maine in August, entered the Sagadahoc (Kennebec) River and built a fort on its banks. Gardens were planted and trade was opened with the Indians for furs. But all the difficulties that beset Jamestown, except fevers, were encountered by the settlers in Maine, and no strong leadership or aid from England carried the colony through the first severe winter. The factious settlers returned home before the year was out. The timber and furs and fish of the district attracted numerous expeditions during the following years. Fishermen sometimes stayed ashore through the winters, and trading posts were maintained on the rivers. New England was not an unknown territory when the Pilgrims arrived at Plymouth in 1620.

The Pilgrims were Separatists, believing that salvation could be attained only outside the Church of England, and followers of the Brownist principle of church organization. The Brownists abolished all officialdom and authority in religion except what was set up by a voluntary association of individuals who "covenanted" together. A clergyman held office only by consent of the members of the covenanting body, and Brownists would not recognize any office or organization above that of minister. This extremely democratic religious policy made Brownists anathema to conservatives of all faiths. One such congregation of Scrooby, Nottinghamshire, fearing persecution after an investigation by Anglican authorities, fled in 1609 from England to Holland, where religious eccentricity was tolerated. Led by their minister, John Robinson, a graduate of Cambridge University, they settled in Leyden and for a decade were quite content.

They were simple folk, intent on pursuing godliness, modest in behavior, mild and kindly even to adherents of other faiths. Personal holiness and virtue were the extent of their ambition in this world. But as time passed they saw that their children were losing their English speech and, what was worse, were failing in piety and turning to dissolute ways. They feared that Spain would resume her rule of Holland and that they would be thrown into the torture rooms of the Inquisition. Meanwhile, they found in this placid and tolerant society no real opportunity to advance their vision of the Kingdom of Christ on earth. The community in its little meeting-house in Bell Alley carefully debated the best course. They felt that God called them to the New World, but they lacked money, powerful friends, experienced leaders—everything that seemed necessary for the dangerous adventure.

Leaders of the Virginia Company of London, who were casting about for groups to swell the population of their colony, decided that the Leyden Separatists were likely material. Their religious radicalism could be overlooked in favor of their willingness to work. Thomas Weston organized a stock company subordinate to the Virginia Company to use a land patent the parent company gave to him and associated capitalists. A generous offer was made to the Leyden group. They should go to Virginia not as employees of the company, but as stockholders, partners, and freemen. Those who could not afford to pay for stock would receive one share in consideration of their labor. For seven years all the products and property of the colony would be owned in common, then a general distribution among stockholders in America and in England would take place. A group of workmen from London, some of them artisans and the others servants of the company, would be added to the Leyden farmers and craftsmen.

The Leyden flock divided on the question of accepting the offer. Many were fearful that persecution would meet them in the Anglican colony of Virginia. A minority dwelt hopefully on the possibility that they might maintain their identity in America as an independent civil and religious community. After prolonged negotiations and debate, thirty-five "saints" from the Leyden minority joined sixty-six "strangers" from London to make the memorable voyage in the *Mayflower* from Plymouth, England, in September 1620.

Immediately the passengers elected one of the Leyden men, John Carver, as their Governor. The ship was overcrowded and scurvy broke out because of poor diet. Yet only one passenger died on the way, and two children were born, who were given the names Oceanus and Peregrine. On November 9, Cape Cod was sighted. This was recognized as being outside the boundaries of the parent Virginia Company, but the passengers were sick, winter was at hand, and the possibility of estab-an independent Separatist community far from Jamestown was inviting. On November 11, anchor was dropped in the harbor of present-day Provincetown inside the tip of the Cape. A better site was found across Massachusetts Bay on the mainland where Indians, recently ravaged by an epidemic, had abandoned their cultivated land. The strangers were threatening to strike out for themselves on the argument that the site was outside the jurisdiction of the company. Therefore the saints, before going ashore, drew up a compact of agreement that laws consented to by the majority would be accepted as binding by all, and Carver was confirmed as Governor to rule the community ashore. This *Mayflower* Compact is ever memorable as a primitive American constitution of self-government. It was no sudden invention: the Brownist practice of church government by covenant and the stock-company practice of self-government by shareholders were both familiar to the saints and strangers of the Plymouth colony. But these religious and economic precedents were now extended to cover political government by compact, and this was a new thing in the world.

On Christmas Day, 1620, the little band began to build their first house, and they labored through the winter despite scanty food, sickness, and the death of half the company including Governor Carver. William Bradford was elected in his place. The survivors refused to give up, for, as Bradford later wrote in his history of the colony, "they knew they were pilgrimes, and looked not much on those things, but lift up their eyes to the heavens, their dearest cuntrie." In the spring, the Indian Squanto showed them how to plant maize, the New World corn which, by the abundance of its yield, saved many an American colony and frontier settlement from starvation. Each man built his own house along a street running up the hill from the harbor and planted his own garden behind his house, while a stockade surrounded the whole. On the hill a meeting-house was built with a flat roof where six cannon were mounted. This building, where religious services and town meetings were held, was at the same time a fort to defend the Pilgrims' experiment in freedom against all enemies—a fitting symbol of Plymouth Colony.

In the fall of 1621, the ship *Fortune* with supplies and new immigrants arrived. A good harvest was gathered, turkeys and deer were shot, and a feast of Thanksgiving was celebrated for three days, with the Indian chief Massasoit and ninety aborigines as guests. The remarkable industry of the settlers produced a valuable cargo of oak timbers and beaver furs to be sent home in the *Fortune*. The colony survived, although it grew slowly and contained only 300 settlers after ten years.

In 1627, to prevent distribution of the property of the colony among the shareholders, including those in England, Governor Bradford and seven Pilgrims bought out the London shareholders and distributed the land and cattle among the residents of Plymouth. Thus in this colony, as at Jamestown, individual ownership succeeded the joint-stock system. Gradually offshoots of the Plymouth settlement were established in the surrounding country, but Plymouth never became large enough to rival the later Puritan settlement at Boston.

Charles M. Andrews, the New England historian, has declared: "The Pilgrim Fathers stand rather as an emblem of virtue than a moulding force in the life of the nation." Their simplicity in faith, heroism in labor, and innovation in political self-government have made them spiritual ancestors of the American people. Their form of government was democratic, although they retained one of the minor social distinctions of England, that between "master" and "mistress," and "goodman" and "good-wife." Education was not particularly valued by them. They found in the Bible all their learning, and they read the Bible not for insight into problems of theology, which did not interest them, but for encouragement of plain virtue. While they were mildly disposed towards other faiths, they did not believe in religious freedom within their own community. When a clergyman of the Church of England, the Reverend John Lyford, came to Plymouth to administer the sacraments to those desiring them, he was tried and driven out of the colony.

In practice the government was under the control of Governor Bradford, who was annually re-elected twenty-nine times, and his council of assistants, who were also elected by the freemen. After ten new towns had been settled, the meeting of all the freemen gave way in 1643 to a representative assembly with two delegates from each town elected by its freemen. Bradford and his successors tried to obtain a charter from the Crown legalizing their government as a separate colony, but they failed. In 1691, Plymouth was annexed to Massachusetts. Thereafter the Pilgrims suffered some loss of religious independence. They were forced to pay for the support of Puritan clergymen, although they continued for many years to maintain their own clergy as well. Eventually they lost their identity as a distinct element in Massachusetts. Nevertheless, the Pilgrim practice of government by consent of the whole people and the direct election of governors left a permanent imprint on American history. The simple heroism and idealism of the Pilgrim Fathers was never forgotten by succeeding generations, and certain episodes in their quiet history, such as the story of Priscilla and John Alden, became part of the folklore of the American people.

THE PURITANS

New England might have become the domain of a landed aristocracy if the plans of Sir Ferdinando Gorges had succeeded. He obtained control of the Virginia Company of Plymouth, and, after the failure at Sagadahoc, spent a fortune on numerous expeditions to the New World. In 1621, he obtained from the King a new patent authorizing him and forty other noblemen and landed gentlemen to incorporate themselves as the Council for New England and to take over the territory of the Virginia Company of Plymouth. Grandiose plans were drawn to divide the land among baronies, lordships, and manors, whose owners should enjoy feudal privileges, the whole to be ruled by an autocratic governor and a bishop. Visible in the scheme was the purpose of Royalists to recover in the New World some of the position they were losing in England.

The Council began to issue patents to settlers of a very different character from the pious and sober Pilgrims. Probably Captain Wollaston held such a patent when he led a party of several gentlemen and many servants to the present site of Braintree, Massachusetts, twenty-five miles from Plymouth. One of the group was Thomas Morton, Gent., a lawyer and a singularly gay fellow. He named the settlement Merry Mount and organized scandalous revels in the wilderness, as if to torment the neighboring Pilgrims. For days on end drinking and dancing around a maypole, dalliance with Indian women, and feasting occupied Morton and his crew. A rimester like any other English gentleman of the day, Morton composed ribald jests in verse at the expense of the pious Pilgrims. In 1628, goaded by his trade in guns with the Indians, as well as mortified by his impious revels, the Pilgrims sent Captain Miles Standish to disperse the settlement. Morton surrendered and returned to England. Merry Mount provided a glimpse of the future New England if the plans of the aristocratic Council had succeeded. But the only direct effort of the Council to settle the country, an expedition under Sir Ferdinando's son Robert to the present site of Weymouth in 1622, failed within six months. The profit and aggrandizement of a few provided no sufficient incentive

to the settlers who had to do the work and endure the hardships of a new colony.

As in the case of Plymouth, so in the founding of the Massachusetts-Bay Colony, a religious ideal provided the impulse for colonization that proved successful. The Puritans were Calvinists who wished to reform the Church of England, to "purify" it of all relics of Roman Catholicism in ritual and organization. They were scandalized by the frivolity and corruption of the Anglican clergy and wished to carry the Reformation to its logical conclusion. They did not lose hope that they might succeed without disloyalty to the King and the Establishment until King Charles I and Bishop Laud tried to purge the church of Lutheran and Calvinist elements. Clergymen of Puritan tendency were silenced and deprived of their incomes; Puritan writings were burned; and in many parishes the Word of God was preached only secretly by "lecturers" who were subject to punishment. Under these circumstances, the professions of loyalty to the Established Church by the Puritans who migrated to New England were only nominal; in practice they became Separatists.

Many merchants and landowners of England turned to Puritanism during the 1620's and 1630's, and even some members of the nobility were sympathetic. Plain fashions in dress were an outward expression of the strict morality that Puritans opposed to the frivolities and luxuries of the nobility and court. Thrift and careful attention to money-making, so long as wealth was justly acquired and used, had a significance for Puritans that went beyond their ordinary meaning: material success and possession of the economic virtues encouraged the Puritan to believe that God had ordained him for Heaven. Puritans looked upon the absolutist tendencies of Charles I as more dangerous to their faith than the persecutions of Laud himself, because Laud was only an instrument of the King. Many leading Puritans began to dream of a City of God in the American wilderness, where they could escape the authority of the King and establish a commonwealth ruled by the elect according to God's design.

The project seemed hopeless so long as Gorges and the Council for New England reserved the territory for Royalists and Anglicans. But Puritan leaders of exceptional intelligence outwitted the Council. A group of Dorchester men with Puritan tendencies attempted in 1623 to establish a fishing station at Cape Ann under patent of the Council. The project did not prosper, and the remnant of settlers under the leadership of Roger Conant moved to Salem. Conant appealed to friends in London to save the experiment by obtaining aid from such men as wanted a religious refuge. A number of Puritans of wealth, who had friends among the nobility, obtained from the Council a charter to establish the New England Company and settle territory between the Merrimac and Charles Rivers. John Endicott was sent over in 1628 as Governor of the struggling Salem community. He was ordered to make preparations for a great enterprise that was forming in the minds of the outstanding Puritans of England.

The Massachusetts-Bay Colony

With the help of the Earl of Warwick and other sympathetic noblemen, the Puritan leaders in 1629 by a shrewd maneuver obtained from King Charles I a charter granting to a new corporation, the Massachusetts-Bay Company, the land patent of the New England Company. This charter violated the rights of the Council for New England, not only in giving the new company land rights, but also in granting it political authority to govern its territory. In many respects the new

charter was irregular, and the Puritans concluded that they could ensure
the success of their scheme only if the officials of the company moved
with the charter itself to America. Then neither king nor company could
interfere with them. The Puritans would make the charter into the constitution of a self-governing holy commonwealth. This audacious scheme
they carried out with efficiency and dispatch. The strange sequel was the
establishment of an independent religious and political community in
America by the very party to which Charles would yield nothing at
home. Apparently the King was willing to see the Puritans of England
weakened by a mass migration.

The Puritans poured their money into the new enterprise. Hundreds,
eventually thousands, sold their properties in England and moved to
America with many things—such as fine silver and furniture, ample
provisions and tools—that earlier settlers had lacked. The region of East
Anglia, the "Cradle of Puritanism," yielded many migrants, most eminent
of them being John Winthrop, lord of the manor of Groton, lawyer,
matriculate of Trinity College, Cambridge, and justice of the peace, who
was elected Governor of the company before it moved to America.
Landed gentry, well-educated professional men and ministers, and successful merchants were numerous in the Great Puritan Migration of the
1630's. In their combination of intelligence, knowledge of the world and
its business, classical and professional education, theological preoccupations, religious and social idealism, and wealth, perhaps no colony in
the world's history could match the settlers of Massachusetts-Bay.

Seventeen vessels sailed to New England in 1630, among them the
Arabella carrying Governor Winthrop and the charter, and for thirteen
years each summer saw another fleet cross the ocean. Charlestown was
the first site of the government, but settlers quickly scattered throughout
the Boston region and established towns. Clergymen were numerous
among the migrants and became the unofficial rulers of each community
and of the colony as a whole. Winthrop had promised before he left
England that the colony would not set up a church separately from the
Church of England. But it was a "purified" Church he had in mind, and
these Puritans recognized no authority over them but God.

The churches and the town and colony governments of Massachusetts-
Bay were organized according to a Puritan addition to Calvinist doctrine that differed very little from the covenant idea of the Separatists.
The Puritans as Calvinists retained the important distinction between
the elect and the damned. They admitted that in individual cases it
was not always possible to detect in a virtuous life and material success
the "outward signs" whereby God's elect manifested their heavenly
destiny. Therefore they recognized two covenants: the invisible Covenant
of Grace, which joined God with his saints and was known only to Himself; and the visible Covenant of the Church, which was composed of

those who by outward signs seemed destined for Heaven and therefore entitled to join in the government of the Church as full-fledged members with voting power. In early Massachusetts others might, indeed they must, support the Church and attend its services, but they stood anxiously outside the circle of the elect, without a voice in the government of the Church or in determining their own admission to its Covenant.

Massachusetts is often called a theocracy because Church members, led by their ministers, effectively ruled in the civil as well as the religious sphere. But the Puritan theologians recognized a third or Civil Covenant, between political officials with Church members who had a vote in their election, and the people as a whole. Therefore the political government was theoretically distinct from the religious, even though, in practice, the will of the clergy became the law of the colony. Formerly, "freemen of the company," that is, stockholders, had elected officials. In Massachusetts a transformation took place in 1631 whereby the elect of God acquired the privilege of freemen. Under this dispensation there was a rough correspondence between social and economic position on the one hand, and political and religious position on the other. Massachusetts was very far from being a democracy, a form of government for which the Puritans could find no authority in the Bible. It was a religious oligarchy.

The unprecedented transformation of the Massachusetts-Bay Company into the government of the religious commonwealth of Massachusetts occurred in the following way. The charter called for elections by the freemen of the company of a governor, deputy governor, and court of eighteen assistants or magistrates. The freemen were to meet in general court, or legislative assembly, four times each year. Very few of the settlers were stockholders of the company. Therefore, in order to fulfill the requirements of the charter, Winthrop called a mass meeting soon after he arrived, and asked all those who wished to be freemen to raise their hands. This informal procedure, however, opened the possibility that some who were not in sympathy with the religious aims of the leaders might gain influence in the government. At a general court in May 1631, it was voted that Winthrop should continue as governor. He thereupon required all who wanted to qualify as freemen to take an "ironclad oath" that none but Church members would be "admitted to the freedom of this body polliticke." Thenceforth a freeman was not necessarily a stockholder of the company but a person recognized in his congregation as one of the elect of God.

At first Winthrop and the magistrates tried to rule arbitrarily. They distributed lands and settled issues in their own way. But when they laid taxes on the towns without their consent, a "revolt" occurred which ended in concessions by Winthrop and led to the establishment of a representative form of government. It was decided in 1634 that the freemen of each town should elect delegates to represent them in meetings of the General Court, and that this body should have legislative authority. The freemen retained their right to elect the governor and magistrates by direct vote. They celebrated their victory over Winthrop by electing Thomas Dudley as Governor. Ten years later the question whether the governor and magistrates could veto an act of the deputies was settled by decision against the veto. Gradually a system evolved which added an important precedent to the one already set by the establishment of the House of Burgesses in Virginia: a governor who received office by direct election.

The rule of the Massachusetts oligarchy was continually opposed by settlers who were excluded from church membership; it was fought outright by sectarians of other faiths; and sometimes even the elect resisted leadership which they found arbitrary and autocratic. Furthermore, the Puritan oligarchs allowed to grow up almost unnoticed a form of local government, the town meeting, which was purely democratic.

The town system originated in the method of distributing land. A group of settlers, usually numbering about sixty, could obtain from the government a land grant for a new town amounting to 36 square miles on the western fringe of settlement. At a suitable location in the new tract a village was laid out. Common lands, pasture and woodlot, were set aside and each head of family received a village plot for his house and a share of the surrounding farm lands. Thus each family started out on a roughly equal economic footing with its neighbors. A meeting-house to serve as church and town hall was erected on the village green. At least once a year all the property owners of the town met to vote on all matters of local interest, including education and defense, and to elect selectmen and other town officials. Thus the legislative authority was vested in virtually the whole body of citizens. The chief concerns of a farming population were local, and the town meeting was a democracy for which perhaps there had been no precedent since that of Athens in the fifth century, B.C. It developed a citizenry that was skilled in self-government and jealously watchful of the rights of the people. The New England town meeting was one of the seedbeds of modern American democracy.

The method of town settlement was conducive to religious unity. So long as the population of the town clustered in medieval style around the village green, the minister could handily control his flock. Later in the seventeenth century, settlers tended to live on their farms rather than in the village, and this removal from the guardian eye of the minister helped to undermine the authority of the Puritan oligarchy. Still to this day, the New England village of simple but comely houses drawn up in friendly ranks around the village green and dominated by the church spire is a symbol of equalitarianism, as well as a masterpiece of town planning.

Next to religion, education was of highest importance to the Puritans. Many of the leaders were graduates of Emmanuel College, Cambridge. They were determined that their children in America should not be deprived of educational opportunity, and that new generations of learned clergymen to lead the people should be assured. Moreover, the Puritans were concerned that everyone should be able not only to read the Bible but to interpret it with some of the subtle insight of the Calvinist theologian. They were not "primitive" Christians. They believed that learning, like wealth, was a sign of God's grace. In 1647, the General Court decided that in order to foil "that old deluder Satan," who wished to deprive men of knowledge of the Scriptures, each town of fifty households must provide a teacher of reading and writing for its children, and each town of a hundred must also provide a Latin grammar school. This was the first American law establishing a free public school system.

To provide training for the ministry, the General Court in 1636 established Harvard College, the first institution of higher learning in the present territory of the United States. Harvard offered the same course of instruction as Oxford and Cambridge universities. Scholarships were provided for talented poor boys, and tuition payments were often made in farm produce. Most of the graduates entered the ministry and were called to frontier towns, where as teachers and preachers they set remarkably high cultural standards for New England. It was not unknown for a farmer graduate of a Latin grammar school to prepare his boy for Harvard in Hebrew, Latin, Greek, and mathematics in the kitchen of their remote farm home. New England Puritanism is a chief source of the modern American ideal of some education for all and advanced education for the talented without regard to wealth.

The Great Migration ended when the success of the Puritan Party in England in 1646 removed the religious incentive for migration. Later immigrants were less homogeneous in character. Many of them came to New England without sympathy for the rule of the Puritan clergy and magistracy, and they helped to overthrow it. In the meantime, the rigidity of the oligarchy resulted in the founding of a new colony, Rhode Island, by refugees from religious tyranny.

RHODE ISLAND

Roger Williams, the founder of Rhode Island, was a minister and a graduate of Pembroke College, Cambridge, who came to New England in 1631. He was a theologian and political scientist far in advance of his time. He carried the revolutionary doctrines of seventeenth-century England to their logical "modern" conclusions. He would not compromise his theories in favor of "practical necessities," therefore he was execrated as a troublemaker. But his successful experiment in state-building proved that he was also gifted in practical affairs.

Williams refused a pulpit in Boston because he regarded the nominal loyalty of the Puritan Church to the Anglican as dishonest. The Salem church members were more sympathetic to Separatism and made Williams their pastor. From the Salem church he launched bitter attacks against the Puritan unity of Church and State, which he called a heinous mixture of "Christ and the World together." He demanded, not toleration of religious differences, because toleration implied superiority in one religion and inferiority in others, but the treatment of all religions as equal by the civil government. Thus he anticipated the modern American solution of the relations between Church and State. Another of his sins was that he denied the right of white men to take Indian lands. His diatribes were too much for the Salem congregation, so, undaunted, he separated from it and conducted religious meetings for a handful of adherents in his own house. In 1635, the General Court banished the rebel. Williams planned to lead a group of his followers to Narragansett Bay. The magistrates tried to arrest him, but he escaped through the woods, deep in winter snow, to Rhode Island, where the Indians befriended him. Then he set about drawing up a form of government for a new colony (1636) according to his principles of religious liberty.

At this time the methods of the Puritan leaders were under attack in England. Pointed questions were asked as to whether the charter justified their independent and despotic course; the Bay Colony was in danger from the French and Indians; and, worst of all, the Antinomian heresy was winning converts in Boston and threatening to destroy the theological unity of the commonwealth. The leader of the Boston heretics was Anne Hutchinson, the mother of fourteen children and possessor of a brilliant mind and fearless character, who refused to follow the Puritan prescription that a woman should obtain her ideas of God "from the contemplation of her husband's excellencies." She organized a group of followers to whom she preached in her home that the Puritans were guilty of "legalism," that is, they mistook outward signs for evidence of inward grace. She denied the validity of the Church Covenant with its requirement that "works" (the performance of prescribed religious duties) must precede admission to membership in the Church. She taught that the Covenant of Grace comprised all believers, that each individual need only listen to the inner voice of God to be saved. This doctrine, called Antinomianism, threatened to destroy the theological foundations of the Puritan Church since it wiped out the distinction between the elect, who were entitled to leadership, and the rest of mankind, who were required to obey. It even threatened to make ministers unnecessary altogether. It was similar to the doctrines of Quakers, Anabaptists, and all the radical Pietist sects. It became dangerous to the rule of the oligarchy when it was embraced by a large share of the Boston church members, including the Reverend John Wheelright and Governor Vane.

The issue was settled in the fiercely contested elections of 1637. Vane was defeated, though by rather high-handed methods. A meeting of ministers followed and, after twenty-four days of theological debate, 82 heresies were condemned. The leading heretics were then banished. Anne Hutchinson was subjected to a theological "trial." When she declared that her doctrines were "an immediate revelation" by God, she was banished on the ground that, since Puritanism was itself a revelation by God, contrary doctrines must be inspired by Satan. The Puritan commonwealth was strengthened by this purge of heretics and faced its external enemies with greater unity. But tyranny was also confirmed as the method of obtaining unity. The oligarchy went to even greater excesses against Quakers—adding to the penalties whippings, mutilations, and death for those who returned after banishment. The mass of settlers gave in to apathy as the safest attitude towards religious matters. In the long run this undermined the rule of the oligarchy as effectively as opposition.

In the Rhode Island of Roger Williams, seekers of liberty found a refuge. Anne Hutchinson and many other exiles from Puritan wrath joined him there. Williams bought land from the Indians and divided it among the settlers. They erected a government under a compact that it should have jurisdiction only over political matters and should do nothing to coerce any individual's conscience. Liberty of religion was extended to non-Christians, and one of the first Jewish communities in America was subsequently established at Newport. Williams lived up to his own principle of absolute religious freedom. He opposed the Quakers in theological matters but invited them to dwell in safety in his colony.

The Rhode Island settlements prospered by means of farming and raising cattle. Williams obtained from Parliament in 1644 a charter legalizing "Providence Plantations" as a separate and self-governing colony. An extremely democratic system of government left legislative authority largely in the hands of town meetings, while the central executive officers, a president and four assistants, were elected by freemen of the towns. In 1663, King Charles II confirmed the charter of Rhode Island, and it remained in force until 1842. Its longevity constitutes a remarkable tribute to the advanced character of the ideas of Roger Williams.

Rhode Island attracted all manner of heretics and discontented elements from Europe and other colonies. Dissensions naturally resulted from the heterodox character of the people, and the little haven of individualism seemed to conventional observers of the seventeenth century a nest of anarchy. Neighboring colonial governments looked upon Rhode Island as an eyesore and in petty ways persecuted its inhabitants when they came within reach. But the experiment weathered all trials and stood as a first proof that separation of Church and State, absolute religious freedom, and democracy might be the guiding principles of a successful body politic. Roger Williams was an idealist who brought his dream to realization in America.

CONNECTICUT

Rhode Island, Connecticut, and New Hampshire were all early offshoots of the settlements in Massachusetts. They illustrated a rule of American expansion: as soon as one district was settled, discontented elements with hope in their hearts to improve their economic, social, political, and religious condition set forth into the wilderness to settle new areas. Fur traders often acted as the scouts for such movements. They spied out new territories and brought back reports of fertile lands. Trading posts became the sites of towns and the trails of traders through the forests became roads of migration.

The Connecticut River Valley is the most fertile strip of land in New England. The Dutch of New Amsterdam in 1633 established a trading post, the "House of Good Hope," near the site of Hartford. Indians carried news of this "invasion" to the English at Plymouth and Massachusetts-Bay. Soon English traders had posts on the river north and south of the Dutch. News of level fields and deep soil excited settlers who were discouraged by the thin, stony soil of eastern Massachusetts. The territory was claimed by both the Massachusetts-Bay Company and by Lord Saye and Sele and Lord Brooke by patent from the Crown. The latter sent over from England in 1635 John Winthrop, Jr., as "Governor of the river Connecticut" and surrounding areas. Young Winthrop and a group of wealthy Puritans built a fort at the mouth of the river and this became the center of Saybrook plantation.

The Reverend Thomas Hooker and his congregation at Newtown (Cambridge), Massachusetts, saw in Connecticut an opportunity. They were orthodox Puritans, and claimed that they wished to emigrate only to find better land, but they also had in mind independence from the Massachusetts oligarchy and a freer system of government. They sold their homes to immigrants from England and set out for the Promised Land on foot, driving their cattle before them. This first mass migration in American history set the pattern for many a future trek.

Hooker and his followers founded Hartford. Other groups from Massachusetts founded Wethersfield and Windsor. In 1637, the three settlements, ignoring the claims of Massachusetts and the backers of Saybrook, organized the self-governing colony of Connecticut. The form of government was an imitation of the Massachusetts system, with one important difference: church membership, that is, "election" by God, was not required in order to enjoy the right to vote for civil officials. In 1639, a constitutional convention in Hartford drew up the Fundamental Orders of Connecticut, the first American constitution providing in detail a form of government. Its authors had been inspired by a famous sermon in which Hooker declared that the power of government resides in the people. Still Connecticut was not a democracy, because religious orthodoxy, adherence to Calvinistic Christian belief, was required of voters. Hooker's colony stood somewhere between the conservatism of Massachusetts-Bay and the radicalism of Rhode Island.

The Connecticut settlements prospered from the fur trade and farming. Fearful lest Connecticut depart too far from strict Puritanism, the Reverend John Davenport in 1638 led a band of settlers to found New Haven on Long Island Sound. Theophilus Eaton, a former London merchant, shared the leadership, and New Haven became an important trade center. Davenport organized a government even stricter than that of Massachusetts. Nothing but Old Testament precedent was respected. Such an English right as trial by jury, which was recognized in Massachusetts, was denied in New Haven. For generations after its removal to the town in 1703 Yale College (founded in 1701) continued the tradition of outdoing Boston itself in Puritan orthodoxy. But the Connecticut River towns refused to be swallowed up by orthodox New Haven. In 1662, they applied to the King for a charter recognizing their government. John Winthrop, Jr., supported the petition and it was shortly granted. New Haven and its surrounding settlements were then placed under the government defined by the Fundamental Orders. Thus Connecticut was firmly established as a third self-governing colony in New England.

New Hampshire and Maine

Settlers in present-day New Hampshire and Maine did not so easily escape the control of Massachusetts. The Council for New England granted these territories to Sir Ferdinando Gorges and Captain John Mason. They divided the area between themselves, Gorges taking Maine and Mason New Hampshire. But they were not successful in colonizing their domains. Actually, the first settlements were made by sundry unauthorized groups, some of them refugees from Massachusetts. The Antinomian Reverend John Wheelright and a handful of followers founded Exeter, New Hampshire, in 1638. The coastal towns of Portsmouth, Dover, and Rye were founded by English Anglicans. The settlers set up their own government on lines very similar to that of Rhode Island. But in 1641 Massachusetts took advantage of the Civil War in England to extend its rule over New Hampshire. After the Restoration, the New Hampshire towns reasserted their independence and in

1679 obtained a charter as a royal province, under which they were ruled by an elected legislature and a governor appointed by the king. Massachusetts won a complete victory in quarrels over Maine, which was ruled from Boston until 1820.

INDIAN WARS

Within a few years after the first settlements on the coast of New England, the Massachusetts-Bay Colony had shown marked expansive power. The rapid advance of settlement struck fear and dismay into the hearts of the Indians of the region. The Puritans, unlike the Pilgrims and Roger Williams, did not repay the Indians for their friendly advances and indispensable aid to the first settlers. The Puritans professed the aim of converting the Indians to Christianity, but harshness stemmed from the conviction that only they themselves had truth, all differences from them being the product of Satan which the "saving remnant," God's chosen few, must destroy. Consequently, their conduct towards the original occupants of the land was marked by extreme brutality. They tried to enslave Indians and force them to labor, but the proud redmen, bred to hunting and fighting, looked upon ordinary labor as women's work and would not submit to it. The view became common among the settlers that Indians were children of the devil, wherefore the part of virtue required their extermination. The Reverend John Eliot believed that Christ intended even Indians to be saved, and he did what he could to convert them and save them from the wrath of the colonists as well as that of God. But the government of Massachusetts-Bay refused to admit that Indians held any legal title to the land, and this made conflict inevitable.

The Pequots were the weakest of the New England tribes. They had been defeated by the Iroquois and pushed into a narrow strip of land along the Mystic River where they were flanked by the Rhode Island and Connecticut settlements. They killed a Boston trader in 1636. The Massachusetts authorities sent an expedition to burn their villages, and the Pequots in desperation declared war. In 1637, Captain John Mason led a small force in a surprise attack and not only defeated the Pequot warriors but also massacred all their women and children, wiping out the tribe.

Other tribes waged sporadic warfare against the frontier settlements. To strengthen measures against them, and also against the French in the North and the Dutch in the West, the Puritan colonies in 1643 organized the New England Confederation. This was the first attempt of American colonies to unite, and their motive, defense against external dangers, inspired all subsequent attempts. A board of commissioners was established to concert measures of defense. Quarrels among the colonies over boundaries and runaway servants were also dealt with by the commissioners.

Settlers in Connecticut wanted the confederation to expel the Dutch from New England, but Massachusetts refused to take part in such a war. The Dutch were nevertheless eliminated as trade rivals by the English conquest of New Netherland in 1664 and its conversion into the royal province of New York. The French were pushing westward from the Saint Lawrence into the Great Lakes country, and New England was temporarily spared trouble from that quarter. But the Indian tribes of New England, harried by the rapid establishment of tier after tier of towns, decided to meet unity with unity. With them the question was not merely that of holding on to their lands. Fur traders had given them guns and "firewater," and such products of civilization made them dependent on the whites. Settlers who followed the fur traders attempted to withhold guns and rum from the Indians. The Indians chose to fight rather than allow themselves to be disarmed preliminary to the seizure of their lands. Thus it was that they fought for the products of the civilization that destroyed their own way of life.

King Philip, sachem of the Wampanoags who lived east of Rhode Island, refused to accept a disarmament treaty offered by the Plymouth and Boston authorities, and his warriors raided the Plymouth frontier in 1675. This might have remained a local affair, but Massachusetts-Bay seized the opportunity to strike a blow at Rhode Island and gain control of lands in that neighborhood by sending an army against the Narragansett tribe. This invasion led all the New England tribes to unite under the leadership of King Philip. The bloodiest war of New England's history followed. Exposed frontier towns like Deerfield, Massachusetts, were raided, and each side massacred men, women, and children and burned villages without mercy. A Massachusetts army of a thousand men destroyed the Narragansett tribe by slaughtering all of its members except some warriors who escaped to the frontier. The whole belt of English settlements beyond the seacoast was practically deserted and Boston prepared fortifications in fear of the other tribes.

Victory by the whites was almost accidental. In 1676, they followed up a local success by burning Indian cornfields in the Connecticut Valley. The main body of Indian warriors suddenly gave up the fight because they feared starvation the next winter. They were easily driven into the mountains of New Hampshire, and King Philip was captured and shot. Indians remaining within reach were slaughtered or sold into slavery, their lands being awarded to veteran soldiers. Massachusetts and Connecticut agreed to establish a ring of frontier posts beyond their limits of settlement, and local Indians never again menaced the advance of this frontier. The New England Confederation, having served its purpose, fell into disuse.

CODFISH AND WITCHES

After 1650, New England grew prosperous. Its economy was based on the fur trade, forest products, agriculture, and the codfish which were caught in huge numbers and exported—especially to the Catholic countries of Europe. Shipbuilding thrived as trade grew with all parts of America and Europe, and eventually with Africa as the slave traffic developed. Fisheries, shipbuilding, and commerce were the chief sources of New England's prosperity, but even the farmers eked out a fair living from the less stony fields. Diversified crops for subsistence were the standard practice, and surplus wheat, corn, pork, and beef were sold for export. The forests yielded timber to the farmer who turned woodsman during the winter months. Farmers learned to make most of their own tools and clothing, built neat houses and good barns with the help of neighbors, and saved their money for the essential imports and a few luxuries.

In the coastal towns, merchants who acted as middlemen between the interior and the far ports of the world began to grow rich. They invested surplus capital in ships and extended loans to less fortunate businessmen. These merchant-shipowner-bankers became a new aristocracy, living in beautiful houses furnished with imported luxuries. They rivaled the Puritan clergy in influence and power. Luxury for the few did not contradict Puritan principles. In fact, it was provided for in Massachusetts laws which authorized laces, ribbons, and ornaments for the upper class and forbade them to the "meaner sort." But in the later seventeenth century, Puritan gentlemen took up such an English court fashion as the full-bottomed, curled, and perfumed wig, and this was eloquent of the worldliness that came with prosperity. Contacts with the outer world through trade broadened the Puritans' outlook and made the ideal of an isolated wilderness Zion seem provincial. Ministers preached in vain against the growing indifference to religion. The oncoming generation that had been born in America had not the zeal of their fathers who had known persecution for Christ's sake in England.

At the frontier, too, the original zeal was dying. This was due in part to a change after 1650 in the system of town settlement. Anxiety to speed the process of settlement in order to erect barriers against the Indians led the General Court to grant towns to speculators and absentee owners who promised to finance actual settlers. Such proprietors held the best lands for themselves, to be sold later at a profit. Proprietors were careless of the religious orthodoxy of the settlers, and the western towns became hotbeds of heresy. Quakers, Antinomians, Baptists, Anabaptists, and members of many other sects found refuge at the frontier in Massachusetts as elsewhere in America, and as they grew in numbers they built up rough democracies which struggled, sometimes violently, against the rule of the conservative East.

Still the Puritan stamp on New England was so firm that it was modified only in the course of many generations by growing worldliness, religious dissent, and democracy. The "New England conscience," famous for its habit of anxious examination of personal morals—those of neighbors as well as self—and insistence on righteousness, were perhaps the most enduring Puritan legacies. Long after the Massachusetts oligarchy had been overthrown, New England continued to live by high standards of personal probity. The Puritan ideal of self-improvement was also a peculiarly valuable bequest because it included the ideal of mental culture and learning. In Boston it was necessary for a gentleman to be more than wealthy; he had to be educated, preferably at Harvard. Conversely, the person of talent, although he might lack wealth and family position, was honored in New England as nowhere else in America.

Hysteria in Salem

The darker side of Puritanism, its harshness towards dissent, produced its own corrective. The excesses of the oligarchy in the last decades of the seventeenth century produced a reaction which contributed greatly to its overthrow. This is the broad meaning of the notorious witch trials at Salem and elsewhere in 1692. This episode must be placed against the background of the political and religious situation of the time. The oligarchy was under attack from England and from "unruly spirits" in the colony. Indifference to religion was perhaps the most effective weapon of Satan against God's commonwealth. The clergy turned to desperate measures to revive the zeal of the fathers in the hearts of the sons. In sermons they insisted that hell-fire awaited their listeners. Poetry was enlisted in the cause. Michael Wigglesworth's terrifying epic of the Last Judgment, *The Day of Doom* (1662) became the most popular poem in New England, and children were required to memorize its stanzas, including one in which the doctrine of infant damnation was moderated only by God's assurance that unbaptized infants would be allowed to enter "the easiest room in hell." Increase Mather in his *Essay for the Recording of Illustrious Providences* (1684) gave examples to prove that God and Satan daily intervened in New England, and that Satan sent demons who functioned in the persons of witches to corrupt Zion.

The literature of superstition caught hold of people's imaginations, as it did in Europe at this time. Even in easy-going Virginia, "witches" were persecuted, although none was executed. In Europe and England, executions were common. That Massachusetts-Bay fell victim to the mania is not surprising in view of its attempt to apply literally the injunctions of the Old Testament. "Thou shalt not suffer a witch to live" was incorporated in the colony's "Body of Liberties." Mistaking public fascination by the literature of superstition for religious sentiment, the Puritan clergy strengthened the potion. Cotton Mather, son of Increase, took accused witches into his house for observation, and published his horrendous findings in *Memorable Providences Relating to Witchcrafts and Possessions* (1689).

Public hysteria followed. The pattern of demagogic appeals to fears, resulting in mob action against the innocent, was to be repeated often enough in American history, and in this early case the responsible officials of the government satisfied the mob's demands for blood. Harmless eccentrics, especially old women, were targets of weird accusations. The clergy, led by the Mathers, urged the courts to speed trials and execute ruthless punishments. Reasonable rules of evidence went by the board. Refusal to confess guilt was regarded as proof that Satan possessed the accused. Hundreds were jailed, many were hanged, and one person was pressed to death in medieval style. Even those of high standing in the community were not exempt, and it was this perhaps that gave rise to doubts among the leaders. The panic subsided quickly in 1693. Judge Samuel Sewall publicly confessed error and repentance for his part in the trials. An eminent merchant, Thomas Brattle, spoke out boldly against the ignorance of the clergy. The clergy in general refused to recant, and they never fully recovered from the blow to their prestige.

Strangely, the Mathers themselves did as much as anyone to rout superstition and promote scientific studies in New England. Cotton Mather advocated inoculation for smallpox and was persecuted for his advanced views. In 1682, Increase organized a scientific society in Boston. He made reports to the Royal Society of Science in London and was elected a member. Learned men of New England studied the new physics of Sir Isaac Newton, and such influences destroyed superstition and substituted a rational view of nature. Thus the Puritan devotion to learning corrected Puritan religious extremism. The decisive blow that overthrew the oligarchy, however, did not come from inside the colonies but from England, in the course of a general organization of the Empire.

CHAPTER 5

Organization and Development of the Empire

THE FOUNDING OF THE ENGLISH COLONIES IN THE FIRST half of the seventeenth century was a rather haphazard affair. No over-all plan for an empire existed, and the promoters and settlers were allowed almost free rein in carrying out their ideas. The first colonies received no aid from the home government beyond permission to settle on land claimed by the Crown. The grants and charters were issued carelessly, the same land was sometimes bestowed on half a dozen persons and companies, and this caused endless trouble. Neglected by their home government in a period of domestic conflicts in England, and dependent on their own plans and efforts for success, the settlers soon showed a spirit of self-reliance and independence.

But in 1660 the English government began to show an interest in organizing the patchwork of colonies into a coherent system and planning a centralized empire. The government of Charles II sought to assert the royal prerogative in many spheres and adopted to some extent the absolutist doctrines of the French government which the King had learned to admire during his exile in France. Thus the Restoration of the Stuarts led to an attempt by England to install a mercantilist colonial system modeled in certain respects after the policies of Spain and France. English merchants and economists had advocated a consistent colonial policy since early in the century. A few general measures had been enacted by Parliament, but the policy was not adequately implemented by laws and administrative agencies until Charles II took power.

Merchants and officials saw definite benefits which a mercantilist empire would bring to England. The money now paid to Scandinavia for naval stores, to Portugal and the Dutch for spices, to the French for wine, might be kept in English hands if the colonies could be encouraged to produce these and other commodities that were now imported.

English manufactures would thrive if the colonists were forbidden to buy foreign articles. English trade would increase if the colonies were forced to send all their produce to England, not only what England consumed but also what foreign countries would buy; it should be handled by English merchants and carried in English ships. All this would make England richer and more powerful in peace and in war. The colonies would gain some advantage, but not to the injury of the mother country: they should exist not for the benefit of their inhabitants but for the greater wealth, power, and glory of the Empire in general and the mother country in particular. Such a program had important political implications for the colonies, because self-willed proprietors, local legislatures, and charter governments could not be allowed to interfere with imperial regulations.

The program also involved strategic considerations which led to planned extensions of settlement in America. For defense against Spain, buffer colonies were established in the Carolinas between Virginia and Spanish Florida. New Netherland was taken from the Dutch to unify control of the coast. New Jersey, Pennsylvania, and Delaware were settled to complete the occupation of territory from north to south. The abortive Dominion of New England was organized to strengthen northern defenses against France. All the new colonies were handed over to proprietors who, it was hoped, would carry out imperial policy more faithfully than companies with privileges of self-government.

The program had material value for the colonies in that it encouraged certain types of economic prosperity, furthered the expansion of settlement, and strengthened colonial defenses. English imperialism and mercantilism were never worked out with the logical and oppressive rigor of the French or Spanish system. The English colonists for a century shared in the patriotic elation of membership in a great new empire. But the program nevertheless contained germs of trouble because the English colonists were even more devoted to unlimited mastery of their own fate than they were to imperial glory.

THE NAVIGATION ACTS

In 1651, a Navigation Act had been passed by the Cromwellian government, chiefly to drive Dutch shipowners out of the English carrying trade. This was confirmed by the Act of 1660, under the Restoration, and supplemented by the Act of 1662. These laws forbade the bringing of cargoes to England from Asia, Africa, or America in foreign ships, and the taking of European cargoes to America in the ships of any nationality except England or the European country that produced the cargo. The laws created business for the English merchant marine, including American-owned vessels. They strengthened the English Navy, which could draw in time of need upon the merchant fleet for trained sailors and on the shipyards for warships. Another part of the Act of 1660 was directed at the colonies as sources of raw materials. Enumerated commodities— sugar, tobacco, ginger, indigo, and dyewoods to begin with—might be shipped from a colony only to England or some other English colony. Rice, naval stores, and other articles were added later. Thus tobacco planters could not sell to Europe directly, but only to English middlemen who took a profit when they resold to Europe. At first, the banning of Dutch ships and the closing of Dutch markets worked a hardship on Virginians, but this law forbade the growing of tobacco in England and the purchase there of tobacco grown in non-English colonies, so that a market was assured to the American planters. This market grew and English taste to this day is for pure "Virginia" tobacco.

In 1660, mercantilist purposes became clearer when the King created a planning committee best known as the Lords of Trade and afterwards superseded (1696) by the Board of Trade. Its duties were to supervise the trade of the Empire and to recommend laws and policies to Parliament and the Privy Council.

The Navigation Act of 1663, called the Staple Act, regulated imports into the colonies just as the Act of 1660 had regulated their exports. Colonists were forbidden to buy European products directly, with a few exceptions, such imports being required to pass through England and the hands of English middlemen. The profit taken by the latter and increased shipping costs raised the prices colonists had to pay for European goods. This provision was intended to create a lower relative price for English manufactures in the colonies so that England would benefit either way: if the colonists bought European products, English merchants profited; if they wished to buy more economically, English industry could grow. The English government, unlike the French and Spanish, did not intend to obtain revenue for itself from foreign goods sold to its colonies, hence it allowed drawbacks or rebates of duties when European goods were sent from England to America. The Navigation Act of 1672 was designed to prevent evasion of the Act of 1660. It required that a duty—the so-called "plantation duty"—be paid on the enumerated commodities before they left the colonies unless the ship captain gave financial surety that he would not evade the law by carrying cargo to some other country than England. Customs collectors were sent to America to enforce the laws. Further administrative machinery was set up later by the summarizing Act of 1696.

The Americans, by illicit trade with the foreign West Indies and other devices, generally avoided the injuries the Navigation Acts might do them, while taking full advantage of the favorable clauses of the laws. In New England especially, the colonists opposed the efforts to subordinate their interests to imperial aims, and they gave the customs collectors a hard time. From the imperial point of view this opposition was one of the evil effects of the self-governing institutions which had taken root in the colonies. The English government concluded that if colonial economic life was to be made subordinate to England, then political institutions must be made subservient to the home government. This led to drastic action on one side and strong resentment on the other.

NEW PROPRIETARY COLONIES

The Restoration government's regulations of trade were paralleled by its encouragement of new settlements. We have already seen that New Netherland was taken from the Dutch in 1664 and developed as a prosperous colony. The purpose of gaining tighter hold on the American colonies was apparent in the grant to the Duke of York, brother of King Charles II, as proprietor of the regions claimed by the Dutch. It was he who had organized the expedition of 1664. New Netherland was renamed New York for him, and he furthermore made subgrants of New Jersey to John Lord Berkeley and Sir George Carteret, and of the Dutch and Swedish settlements in what is now the state of Delaware to the Penn family.

New Jersey

Proprietors were entitled to rule in any way that did not conflict with English law, and their motive was usually the simple desire to obtain revenue from land sales, quitrents, and taxes. But they found it expedient to make many concessions in order to attract settlers. Berkeley and Carteret in 1665 provided for freedom of conscience, a representative assembly, and cheap land in their "Concessions and Agreements." In 1674, Berkeley sold his share in New Jersey to Quaker proprietors who presently added William Penn to their number. This part became known as West Jersey, while Carteret held East Jersey. On his death in 1680, his heirs sold this also to Quakers, including Penn. The latter's influence was visible in further concessions to settlers. In 1701, the two districts were united as a royal colony, but proprietors continued to hold land rights, and confusions of title vexed New Jersey until all vestiges of the proprietors' rights were abolished in the American Revolution. New Jersey lacked a favorable seacoast for trade. Small farming prospered, but the cream of its economic prosperity was drained off to New York in the northeast and Philadelphia in the west.

The Carolinas

Rational planning for the organization of the Empire was more fully carried out by the founding and settlement of Carolina. The area between

Virginia and Florida invited the erection of a buffer colony to protect the English settlements from the Spanish in the far south. It was believed that the semitropical products of the region would be ideally suited to mercantilist aims because they would not compete with English crops and would enable the home country to stop buying such produce from foreign countries. A group of courtiers saw in this situation an opportunity to make themselves lords of profitable estates, and Charles II was pleased to encourage their devotion to aristocratic principles as well as imperial interests. In 1663, he granted to a group of eight, including Sir Anthony Ashley Cooper (later Earl of Shaftesbury), the Earl of Clarendon, the Duke of Albemarle (General Monck), and other outstanding nobles, the region between Virginia and the present northern boundary of Florida, and westward to the "South Seas." Sir Anthony Ashley Cooper commissioned John Locke to draw up the Fundamental Constitutions for the colony in 1669.

This document was a strange mixture of feudalism and utopianism, reflecting the hope of the Restoration era that aristocracy and colonial profits were not incompatible. It called for a fantastic hierarchy of ranks with proportionate land holdings, ranging from palatines (the proprietors) in England to freeholders in the colony with the 50-acre share required for voting, and in between were landgraves, *caciques,* and lords of manors. The bulk of the population would be nonvoting tenants, serfs, and slaves. The hierarchical experiment never got started. Tenants and serfs were unavailable. No manors were erected and the few landgraves and caciques that were created died out. After more normal settlement had begun, the proprietors modified Locke's scheme (1682) but the colonial assembly would have none of it.

So many small farmers and runaways from indentured service had already settled in the region of Albemarle Sound below the Virginia line that the proprietors recognized the area in 1691 as the separate province of North Carolina. The relatively inaccessible Albemarle district became a region of tobacco culture, but its agriculture was on a lesser scale than in Virginia. The Cape Fear district in the present state of North Carolina was settled in the early eighteenth century, and Wilmington became an important port for naval stores. The inland country became the home of small farmers with strong dislike for the slave-owning aristocracies and the religious and political institutions of their neighbors to the north and south. As early as 1677, settlers in the Albemarle region staged a revolt against the proprietors known as "Culpeper's Rebellion," and a century later the "regulators" in the Piedmont carried on the tradition of hostility to authority. North Carolina was the Rhode Island of the South, the least aristocratic and most individualistic colony of the region.

The coastal area of South Carolina was extremely well suited to staple productions. The Lords Proprietors sent out an expedition of Englishmen

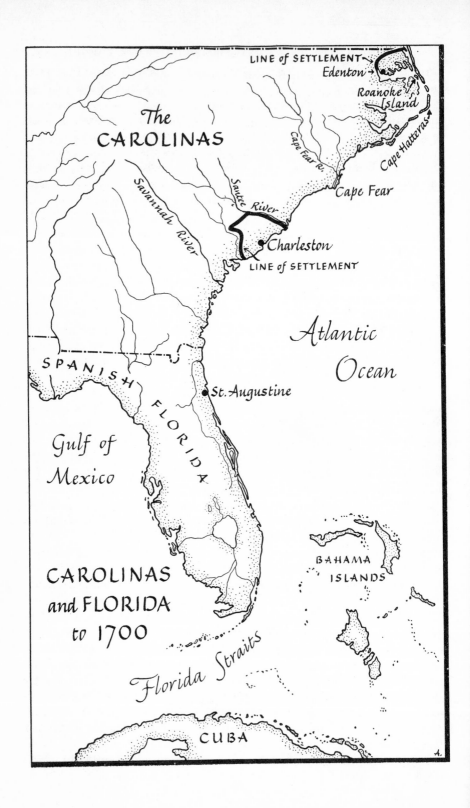

LINE of SETTLEMENT
Edenton →
Roanoke Island

The CAROLINAS

Cape Fear R.

Santee River

Cape Hatteras

Cape Fear

Charleston
LINE of SETTLEMENT

Savannah River

Atlantic Ocean

SPANISH

FLORIDA

St. Augustine

Gulf of Mexico

CAROLINAS and FLORIDA to 1700

BAHAMA ISLANDS

Florida Straits

CUBA

A.

and Barbadians who founded Charlestown (later Charleston) in 1670, at the junction of two rivers, which were named the Ashley and the Cooper. After a considerable period of experimentation with a variety of crops, rice, which was afterwards supplemented by indigo, became the basis of South Carolina's prosperity and of her plantation system. French Huguenots added their admirable qualities to the population before the end of the century. The excellent harbor of Charlestown invited trade and shipping, while along the coastal inlets and rivers huge plantations were built up. Connections with the West Indies were close, and Negro slaves were probably introduced from Barbados in the first year of settlement; they were specially useful in this climate and economy. By the end of the seventeenth century, Negroes outnumbered whites, as they continued to do until recent times. As in Virginia and Maryland, landowners who could afford to buy slaves engrossed the best lands and made themselves into a plantation aristocracy before the middle of the eighteenth century. Merchants invested their profits in plantations, and in South Carolina a fusion of merchants and landowners produced a ruling aristocratic class which was less challenged by small farmers through the generations than the comparable group in Virginia was.

The original proprietors of Carolina had lost interest when the colony failed to provide quick profits for themselves. They made little effort to carry out Locke's plans and allowed the settlers to establish a legislature which was only nominally subordinate to a governor appointed by the proprietors. Quarrels between settlers and proprietors resulted in the conversion of the grant into two royal provinces, South Carolina in 1721 and North Carolina in 1729. The Anglican Church was established in both of them, firmly in South Carolina where the Huguenots generally joined it, and rather feebly in North Carolina, where radical sectarians found refuge from other colonies.

North Carolina was afterwards described as "the valley of humility between two mountains of conceit." The planting aristocracies of Virginia and South Carolina were similar in many respects, but they were differentiated by the fact that the latter colony had an urban center, Charleston, to which wealthy landholding families escaped from their plantations during the summer malaria season. There in the course of time they built town houses surpassing in luxury anything in America and supported a social season which was a provincial replica of fashionable life in London. If the Virginia planters took the English country gentry as their models, the South Carolinians looked to the English capital and nobility for their pattern. They assumed the style and prerogatives of an ordained ruling class. Despite the collapse of Locke's fantasy, aristocracy was more real in South Carolina than in any other English colony on the mainland. The sense of public responsibility which

so strikingly characterized Virginia's planters in the eighteenth century
and bore such rich fruit in later statesmanship, was less keen among
the leading South Carolinians. They were notable in colonial times as
patrons of the arts, but were little concerned with education beyond
providing schools or tutors for their own children and sending them
to England for higher education. Their responsibility to protect the
frontier against Spain and the Indians was fairly easily discharged, and
after 1733, when Georgia was founded, that colony assumed the burden.
Secure and prosperous, the planters who flourished amid the luxuriant
vegetation of the Low Country did reflect the aristocratic-utopian hopes
of the founders. Only enterprising men could have established and maintained an English society in this far-southern region, but their historic
role was to be predominantly, and in the end passionately, conservative.

Pennsylvania

Visions and results of another sort marked the founding and early
history of Pennsylvania. Charles II in 1681 granted to William Penn
the vast and fertile region between New York and Maryland. Its indefinite
boundaries led to endless disputes. The charter made Penn and his
heirs proprietors, but the increased tendency towards imperial control
was shown in the requirement that Penn enforce the Navigation Acts
and submit to the Privy Council all laws passed in his colony. The new
colony would fill the gap between northern and southern settlements
and complete England's control of seacoast and frontier from New England to Florida. Troubles with proprietors made the English government
reluctant to create another colony of this sort. It did so only because
William Penn skillfully exploited the indebtedness of the House of
Stuart to his eminent father, Admiral Sir William Penn, for whom the
new colony was named.

No colony represented more faithfully than Pennsylvania the ideals
of a single man. Penn had been expelled from Christ Church College,
Oxford, for his nonconformist religious opinions, and he was afterwards
converted to Quakerism, the most radical religion of the period. George
Fox, the great founder of the Quakers (more properly called the Society
of Friends), rejected all external authority, even that of the Bible, over
the individual conscience. The individual was responsible only to the
voice of God speaking to his soul. Every man was his own priest, as is
exemplified perfectly in the religious services of the Friends; these consist merely of meeting together to listen to whatever persons feel impelled
by the Inner Voice to say. The merciful and loving Jesus of the New
Testament, rather than the angry and vengeful Jehovah of the Old Testament dominates the Quaker spirit. Nevertheless, the latter-day notion
that the Friends were invariably meek and mild is incorrect: the early

members of the group earned the name "Quakers" by their outlandish manner of preaching, and they were aggressive and fearless in proclaiming their doctrine to hostile audiences. In deliberate defiance of the Puritans, Quakers sought martyrdom by shouting anathemas on the streets of Boston. Thousands of them were imprisoned in England during the first years after the Restoration, but they could not be crushed.

William Penn dreamed of a colony in America where not only Quakers but members of any faith might enjoy religious and political liberty. In 1669, while imprisoned in the Tower of London for writing one tract, he composed another and more famous one, *No Cross, No Crown.* The next year he was tried for preaching, but the jury freed him. He made missionary journeys into the German Rhineland, where he met radical sectarians of similar views and broadened his conception of a colony to include the idea of refuge for the persecuted of all nations. That such a man should have obtained from Charles II the grant of Pennsylvania to try out his unorthodox scheme is a tribute not only to his power of persuasion but also to the basic tolerance of the English government, even under the Stuarts.

His proprietary grant was not quite virgin territory in 1682 when Penn arrived in the ship *Welcome.* Fur traders and farmers were scattered here and there. Swedes, Finns, and Netherlanders lived on the lower banks of the Delaware River and small groups of Englishmen could also be found. The Three Lower Counties (later the state of Delaware) were most thickly settled. Penn took charge of the existing settlements there, though his title to the government was uncertain. Penn's first Frame of Government for his province (April 25, 1682) asserted the "native goodness" of all men, and he established the most liberal form of government to be found in any proprietary colony except the one in West Jersey for which he was also responsible. Penn or his deputy was governor, but the members of the Governor's Council as well as the Assembly were elected by the freemen. All Christians were guaranteed liberty of religion, and all settlers were assured of the fullest measure of English personal liberties. Penn, like Roger Williams, recognized the Indians' ownership of the land. He treated them as brothers and in a series of treaties established peaceful relations which long continued.

Penn conducted a vast international publicity campaign to attract settlers to his "Holy Experiment." It was immediately successful in bringing to his province Welsh and Germans (who settled Germantown), besides many Englishmen. Palatine Germans and Scotch-Irish poured in during the early decades of the eighteenth century and moved on to the fertile lands of the interior. Pennyslvania became the country's first "melting pot." The American of mixed ancestry emerged as a notable type in this "keystone" colony, which had a strategic location in relation to the expansion of the frontier. From the Swedes and Finns the settlers

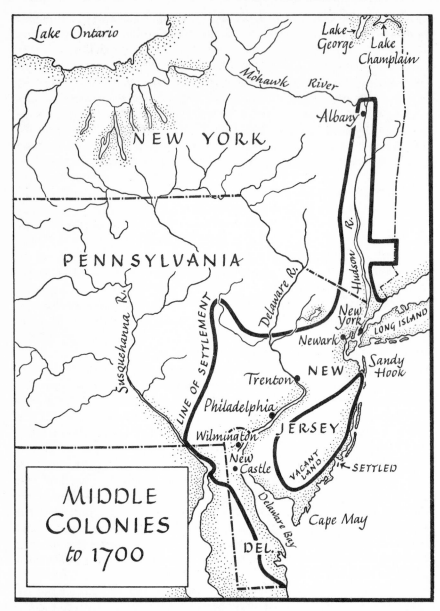

Lake Ontario

Lake George Lake Champlain

Mohawk River

NEW YORK

Albany

PENNSYLVANIA

Susquehanna R.

Hudson R.

Delaware R.

LINE OF SETTLEMENT

New York

LONG ISLAND

Newark

Trenton

NEW

Sandy Hook

Philadelphia

JERSEY

Wilmington

New Castle

VACANT LAND

SETTLED

MIDDLE
COLONIES
to 1700

Delaware Bay

Cape May

DEL.

learned the art of building log cabins. These strong, cheap houses were
ideally suited to the requirements of frontiersmen. They sprouted
wherever trees grew in America and became a symbol of pioneer life.
Penn laid out Philadelphia, the "City of Brotherly Love," between the
Delaware and the Schuylkill rivers in a rectangular pattern which became the model for planning many later American towns and cities.

Pennsylvania was settled rapidly not only because the proprietor offered liberal government and religious freedom, but also because this colony contained the largest tract of rich and arable land on the eastern seaboard, which Penn offered to the poorest comer under a 50-acre headright system. Penn furthermore paid little attention to mercantilist notions of proper colonial economic activities. He encouraged family farms raising diversified food crops. Soon the farmers of Pennsylvania were producing surpluses of corn, wheat, pork, and beef which they exported. This colony became the granary of the British West Indies. Penn also offered great estates to those who could afford to buy land, but the family farm became the typical unit. Many craftsmen came to Pennsylvania, and trade and shipbuilding thrived. Philadelphia became the largest city in the country by the time of the Revolution.

Freedom, bountiful resources, and hard work by plain people were the secrets of Pennsylvania's success. Still the anomaly that this colony should be the private possession of one man led to disputes between Penn and the settlers. The efforts of the proprietor and his descendants to collect quitrents caused much trouble, especially among the Scotch-Irish on the frontier. The issue was finally settled only after the Revolution when the state government cancelled the claims of the Penn family by paying the heirs a lump sum.

Penn was absent from the colony between 1684 and 1700. His deputy governors lacked his great tact and got embroiled with the Assembly. Meanwhile, the overthrow of the Stuarts in England placed Penn under a cloud because of his intimate associations with them, and for a time he went into hiding. In 1689, William and Mary made Pennsylvania a royal province in line with the general program for the Empire. But Penn succeeded in making his peace with the new monarchs and in 1694 regained ownership of the colony. In 1700, he returned to Pennsylvania, hoping to stay and enjoy the splendid estates he had built for himself, but soon he returned to England to defend his rights. In his famous Charter of Privileges (1701) he modified and liberalized the government, making the Council appointive but merely advisory and leaving the unicameral legislature virtually supreme. At the same time the suffrage was extended and a separate legislature was promised Delaware.

Penn paid most of the administrative expenses of the provincial government and of his incessant efforts abroad in the colony's behalf. He lost heavily by his Holy Experiment. During his last years he spent time in debtors' prison in London. The people of Pennsylvania showed little practical appreciation for what he did for them, but he did not much complain when, after having encouraged the spirit of liberty among the colonists, he himself was made to feel its pinch.

Pennsylvania became a colony that was formally proprietary but almost wholly self-governing, the well-to-do Quakers being generally in effectual control. Neighboring colonies resented the liberties of her people, especially because settlers left other colonies to share them and because the pacifist Quakers did little to co-operate in wars against the Indians and the French. Imperial regulations were mostly ineffective in Pennsylvania. The people of the colony were guilty both of refusing "to gird on the carnal sword" and of harboring pirates as "honest men for bringing money into the country and encouraging trade." Bitter controversies raged in the Assembly between the proprietors' supporters and the antiproprietary party. The latter usually won.

Pennsylvania developed not only a rich mixture of ethnic and religious groups but also diverse social experiments and the most advanced scientific learning in eighteenth-century America. Crimes statutorily punishable by death in England were sharply reduced in number in Pennsylvania. The Quakers' humanitarian idealism was early expressed in such institutions as hospitals and orphanages. They were the first Americans to raise their voices loudly in protest against slavery. Education was provided publicly or privately for most children. Classical learning was not scorned, but emphasis was laid on the useful arts. Penn suggested that the old and the new in education might be combined by writing textbooks for mechanics in Latin! The colony gave land and liberty to many experimenters (chiefly from Germany) in austere religious and social doctrines: Mennonites and Moravians, Dunkards, Ephratists, River Men, the Society of the Woman in the Wilderness, the New Mooners, and many others.

Excellent education in the useful arts and crafts provided a foundation for advances on the frontiers of science. It was in this congenial environment that Benjamin Franklin of Boston found scope for his astonishing array of talents. The second generation of Quakers with growing prosperity relaxed their fathers' fanaticism and learned to indulge a decent appreciation of worldly pleasures, but they rarely lost their lofty ethical idealism, so that Quaker integrity and benevolence are bywords to this day. If liberty, plenty, progress, and civic virtue were tests, Pennsylvania was indeed the land of promise that its swelling crowds of immigrants sought. No colony was more directly responsible than Penn's for the character of later American life and institutions.

The West Indies

Georgia was founded in 1733 by James Oglethorpe for a combination of imperial and philanthropic purposes somewhat comparable to Penn's. It was the last new colony to be established on the mainland and will be described in the next chapter. Meanwhile, expansion and organization of colonies in the West Indies had proceeded on the same principles as those governing the mainland to form one integrated empire. The Bermuda Islands had been settled as early as 1612, and various adventurers and proprietors competed with Frenchmen for possession of islands of the Lesser Antilles which the Spaniards left unguarded. Cromwell was responsible for the addition of Jamaica (1655) to the English holdings. Prosperous English colonies developed on Barbados, Trinidad, St. Kitts, and other smaller islands. The rich soil and numerous Negro slaves were engaged in the production of sugar cane and other tropical or semitropical crops. Colonial Americans often combined holdings in both the mainland and the islands. Islanders developed their own assemblies with due care for the rights of Englishmen. West Indian settlements became important for New England traders, who found there a valuable market for foodstuffs from the continental colonies to feed the slaves, and ready cargoes of molasses to distill into rum in New England. Exchanged for Negroes in Africa, this became the key of the famous triangular routes. To maintain their trade with the British West Indies the Americans struggled persistently long after the Revolution. For England, the islands were more valuable than the northern mainland colonies because their products and needs fitted perfectly into the mercantilist system. For the planters, whether they lived in the islands or spent their profits on luxury in London, the West Indies were utopian. Negro slavery was more extensive and probably more exploitative than on the mainland. Americans hoped that the British islands would join them in revolt against the mother country in 1776, but contented planters and a population chiefly composed of slaves discouraged such a possibility.

THE RESTORATION AND THE GLORIOUS REVOLUTION

The organization and growth of the empire did not proceed without severe strains. These resulted from both internal colonial and external English causes. Culpeper's Rebellion in North Carolina has been mentioned. A similar but much more important outbreak occurred in Virginia exactly a hundred years before the Declaration of Independence.

"Bacon's Rebellion"

After the Stuart Restoration of 1660, Sir William Berkeley, the royal Governor of Virginia, took advantage of reaction in England to impose arbitrary rule. In the 1670's, overproduction of tobacco resulted in the collapse of prices, and Indian troubles contributed greatly to popular unrest. Berkeley refused to take strong measures to protect frontier settlements against Indian massacres, and the frontiersmen thought it was because he feared Indian reprisals against his personal fur-trade interests. The settlers decided in the spring of 1676 to take matters into their own hands. They organized a little army, chose as their commander Nathaniel Bacon, a planter and member of the Council well noted for his popular sympathies, and defeated the Indians. Furious at this assertion of provincial self-reliance, Berkeley sought to arrest Bacon, but support of the rebels was so widespread that he reluctantly consented to call an election for a new Assembly. Before this could convene, Bacon, still without commission from the lordly Governor, attacked the Indians again. When he came to Jamestown he was denied a seat in the Assembly and seized by Berkeley, but, being finally released, he escaped to lead a body of irate supporters back with him. The Governor was now forced to grant him a military commission, and reform measures were voted by the Assembly, but civil strife was renewed when the obdurate Governor proclaimed Bacon a rebel. In the course of the confused conflict Berkeley had to flee to the Eastern Shore of the Chesapeake, but he returned while Bacon was away on another Indian expedition. Bacon then marched on Jamestown, which he burned, and again forced the Governor to flee.

The rebellion suddenly collapsed when Bacon died in October 1676. It was most notable as a violent colonial conflict with stupid and tyrannical English authority, anticipating the greater one a century later. Berkeley executed remaining leaders of the rebellion, going to such extremes that Charles II is reported to have exclaimed: "That old fool has killed more men in that naked country than I have done for the murder of my father." A more moderate governor was sent out to take Berkeley's place, and the victory of Parliament in the Glorious Revolution of 1688 strengthened the position of the Virginia House of Burgesses. Largely controlled by the eastern planting gentry, this became a great arena of peaceful opposition to the governors.

Discontent in Maryland

In Maryland the frontiersmen had more serious grievances than in Virginia, and anti-Catholic sentiment increased with the growth of Protestant settlement. Josias Fendall, formerly Governor of the province, led abortive revolts against the proprietary rule of the Calverts and in 1681 he was banished. Associated with him was John Coode, an adventurer who later seized upon the opportunity provided by the Glorious Revolution. When the Maryland officials in 1689, more Jacobean than the English Parliament, refused to recognize William and Mary as their new monarchs, Coode led a band of militiamen of the "Protestant Association" to the provincial capital, St. Mary's, and seized the government. He called together an assembly that petitioned the King to make Maryland a royal province. The King did so in 1691, and within a few years the Church of England was established in the province and the capital moved to Annapolis, a Protestant settlement. When the Calverts were finally restored as proprietors in 1715, after they had become Anglican, the Maryland legislature had entrenched itself sufficiently so that the proprietors were unable to assert much authority. But in Maryland as in Virginia, legislative powers were exercised chiefly by the eastern planters.

New England against the Stuarts

Stuart reaction reached its American climax in New England. Economically, that region was relatively unimportant to mercantilists because few of its products were useful to the Empire. Indeed New England and to some extent the middle colonies were economically dangerous to the success of mercantilism, because in their energetic search for prosperity they embarked on manufacturing and agricultural activities that competed directly with those of the mother country. The New England colonies furthermore developed religious and political institutions which were highly distasteful to Royalists. The Puritan oligarchs defiantly refused to tolerate Anglicans after the Restoration. Their governments, especially that of Massachusetts-Bay, promised to perpetuate in America the anti-Royalist principles which had been overcome in England with the collapse of the Commonwealth. Massachusetts showed dangerous "imperialist" tendencies of her own by absorbing New Hampshire and Maine. New Haven harbored the regicide judges, Whalley and Goffe, whom the agents of Charles II hunted in order to punish them for the execution of his father. In 1662, after a year of obedience to a royal order that persecution of Quakers be stopped, Massachusetts-Bay re-enacted its law inflicting corporal punishment on them. Royal commissioners in 1665 reported to England the many contumacies of the Puritan colonies, and the King commanded that representatives come to England to answer charges, but the General Court refused to send them.

During the desperate fighting of King Philip's War, (1675-1676) New England was not harassed by the home government, but in 1676 a new royal agent, Edward Randolph, reported damning evidence that Massachusetts failed to enforce the Navigation Acts, executed English subjects for their religious views, denied the right of appeal to the Privy Council, and refused the oath of allegiance. Further hostile reports stressed the colonists' defiance of the Navigation Acts. In 1679, a royal commission separated New Hampshire from Massachusetts, and proceedings in the Court of Chancery resulted in 1684 in the annulment of the charter of Massachusetts-Bay on the grounds that it had been stretched out of all recognition and violated.

There was much evidence for these charges. But the remedies devised by imperial planners under James II, who ascended the throne in 1685 and attempted to revive the Divine-Right rule of his ancestors, bore hard on the rights and liberties of colonists in new ways, even while the severities of Puritan rule were being mitigated. Imperial planners designed a consolidation of all the northern colonies from Pennsylvania to New England for better military defense and enforcement of the Navigation Acts, calling this the Dominion of New England, and sent out Sir Edmund Andros in 1686 to organize it and be Governor of Massachusetts, Maine, and New Hampshire. Andros incorporated Rhode Island and assumed the government of Connecticut as well, although the charter was successfully withheld from him in the famous episode of the Charter Oak. Andros gave the Americans a sharp experience of reactionary government. He abolished assemblies, violated charters when courts were too slow, demanded payment of quitrents by freeholders, suppressed town meetings, levied taxes without consent, and forced Puritans to turn over church buildings to Anglicans. All this paralleled and exceeded the rigors of the rule of James II in England itself. Revolt stirred in the colonies and at home.

The Revolution of 1688

When a son was born to James's second wife, Parliament in 1688 deposed the King rather than permit his Catholic son to become ruler of England, and invited his first wife's Protestant daughter, Mary, and her husband, William of Orange, to take the throne. The new monarchs were required to give consent to the rule of Parliament and to a comprehensive Bill of Rights which codified the traditional rights and liberties of Englishmen. This Glorious Revolution, the turning point in the history of English liberty and self-government, was entirely peaceful in England, but in America some violence occurred as the colonists eagerly exploited events at home to overthrow James's agents in America.

In Massachusetts, armed rebels jailed Andros and sent him and his councilors to England for trial. In New York a popular leader named Jacob Leisler seized control of the government. The Dominion of New England collapsed and the various colonies re-established their self-governing bodies. The Mathers and other Puritan leaders struggled to recover the old charter of Massachusetts-Bay, but the new Parliamentary government of England had no more taste for Puritan than for Stuart tyranny. A new charter made Massachusetts a royal colony in 1691. Its Governor was appointed by the Crown, the General Court elected a council, and both were subject to the governor's veto. Most significant, the religious qualification for voting was abolished and a property qualification substituted. Appeals were allowed from the colonial government to the Privy Council and royal review of legislation was provided. Plymouth Colony and Maine were recognized as parts of Massachusetts-Bay. The new charter broke the hold of the Puritan oligarchy, which was already losing its grip as a result of its excesses, the witchcraft trials having been the latest. Connecticut and Rhode Island, however, were allowed to retain their old charters and elect their own governors. In New York a royal governor reasserted control and Leisler was hanged.

The Glorious Revolution greatly advanced liberty and self-government in America as well as in England. John Locke's treatise *Of Civil Government,* which asserted the compact theory of government to justify as legal the overthrow of Stuart tyranny and the assertion of popular and parliamentary rights, became a handbook of colonial rights. The example of Parliament's triumph in England was used by Americans to justify claims of authority by their own legislatures. Such claims obviously contained the seeds of American opposition not only to royal prerogative but also to Parliament's authority to legislate for the Empire. But these seeds did not sprout so long as imperial regulations did not impinge too severely on colonial development. The events of 1688-1689 actually resulted in a new fervor of American pride in and loyalty towards the mother country because she now stood with the Bill of Rights, which applied to Americans as well as Englishmen, as the most sturdy protector of human liberty in the world.

The new government of England furthermore expressed the economic ambitions of colonists as well as Englishmen. After 1689, the pursuit of wealth superseded the pursuit of salvation as the chief purpose of government. The reduction of Puritan power in New England and the indifference of Anglicans elsewhere removed religion from the center of politics. The colonies entered a long period of internal peace, territorial expansion, and economic and cultural growth. Rich opportunities for the acquisition of wealth were left open by the mercantile system; colonists seized these and did not very much object to, although they often evaded, new measures for the consolidation of imperial control. In 1697, a system of Vice-Admiralty Courts was set up in America to enforce the Navigation Acts, as part of the machinery created by the Act of 1696. Obedience to the rule that no colonial law or policy should contradict English law or policy was strengthened by requiring all acts of colonial assemblies to be submitted to the newly-established Board of Trade for recommendation to the Privy Council for approval or "disallowance." Litigants in colonial courts were encouraged to appeal to the Privy Council for review of judicial decisions. The Board of Trade was continually active in surveying colonial affairs, drawing up instructions for the guidance of colonial officials and making recommendations on imperial policy and legislation.

The most important new laws forbade the colonies to develop manufactures which would compete with English factories and forbade them to depreciate the value of money. These measures came chiefly in the eighteenth century and completed the organization of the Empire. As the colonies entered a Golden Age of maturity and prosperity, few could foresee that the very growth of local liberty and wealth in the American colonies, despite the consolidation of imperial control, was creating foundations for the overthrow of British rule.

CHAPTER 6

Colonial Life in the Eighteenth Century

EXPANSION AND GROWTH WERE THE KEYNOTES OF colonial life in the eighteenth century. Between 1700 and the outbreak of the American Revolution the population grew, as the result of a high birth rate and immigration, from about a quarter of a million to about two and a half millions. During the seventeenth century little more than the seacoast and the shores of tidal rivers had been settled. By the time of the Revolution, the wider belt of territory between Tidewater or Low Country and the Appalachian range was filling with farms, and hardy traders and pioneers were pushing through gaps in the mountain barrier into the vast and fertile lands beyond. At the same time, coastal towns grew into thriving little cities, and interior settlements, especially those located at the fall line of the rivers, became important trade centers. Lacking agricultural machinery, the family farm of the eighteenth century was still small and methods of transportation were still primitive. The pioneer wagon, covered or uncovered, was not developed until late in the century. Meanwhile, the fortunate went on horseback into the new and trackless country while the others went on foot, often pushing crude and heavy-laden carts by hand.

SETTLING THE OLD WEST

During the seventeenth century, the eastern seaboard itself was a frontier territory. By trial and error the settlers acquired the techniques which made for success. They learned the peaceful and violent methods of handling the Indians, the ways of the fur trade, the forest arts of hunting, building log cabins, and preparing timber for market, skills in growing crops suited to the new land, and the business of marketing American products abroad. They learned how to attract immigrants by propaganda and by offering land and liberty to all comers. Negro slaves were coming to be used, however, to fill out the labor force when freemen found working for others unattractive. In the eighteenth century these techniques were used to conquer the next belt of territory, the "Old West." Explorers entered the wilderness and were followed in rapid order by fur traders, cattle drovers, pioneer settlers who cleared the fields, and farmers who raised crops for subsistence and for market. Organized government, churches, schools, and towns created civilization where Indians and wild animals had roamed.

The Southern Region: Georgia

This general pattern of frontier development was not invariable. In Virginia, for example, the work of pioneering was often performed by an overseer and a gang of slaves whom a planter had sent ahead to prepare for his occupancy lands that he had acquired by grant from the Governor and Council. The southern Piedmont was settled before the less hospitable hills of the North. Forts were built at the falls of the rivers, and from them exploring parties and fur traders moved into the wooded hills. A new chapter in the settlement of Virginia was started in the second decade of the eighteenth century during the governorship of Alexander Spotswood. He pacified the Piedmont Indians and led a party of explorers whom he called the "Knights of the Golden Horseshoe" into the beautiful Shenandoah Valley. There English from the East were to mingle with Scotch-Irish and Germans who came down from Pennsylvania. Spotswood had some success in his efforts to check the monopolizing of great tracts of lands by individuals who held them for speculative purposes, and to aid actual settlers in the outlying regions, though he gained large holdings for himself while Governor. He became embroiled with the Council, through which lands were granted and which consisted of wealthy planters. He vainly sought to remove from that body William Byrd, second of the name in Virginia, a great landowner and the elegant master of Westover. The greatest estate in the province was that of Lord Fairfax, in form a proprietorship which dated back to the time of Charles II. This extended from the Potomac to the Rappahannock rivers, covering what was known as the "Northern Neck." Here the lord proprietor granted the lands, and here were the homes of the Lees and George Washington. Among other great Virginia landholders were various Carters and Randolphs. Besides the acres they planted in tobacco, they characteristically had great holdings in the West. In the Carolinas, also, huge western grants were made to influential eastern planters, and Maryland's relatively narrow strip of western land was settled much as Virginia's was.

The speculator with his agents had much to do with the settlement of every new American frontier. The headright system, like the later Homestead Act, was to some extent nullified by the favoritism that provincial governments showed to influential persons. Farmers who improved their lands, only to find that these had been granted to speculators, staged a continual fight for their rights, which were often, so far as legal title went, more shadowy than those of the speculator. Out of this sort of struggle grew much of the antagonism between West and East. Some grantees attempted to hold their land while tenants farmed it, but slaves were the only laborers who could not easily avoid working for others. Inefficient surveying and overlapping grants vexed the actual settlers. The farmer who followed the pioneer had to pay for his title, sometimes several times over.

In the southern Piedmont the frontier did not advance in the orderly manner of New England, where as a rule a new tier of four-square townships was opened only when the preceding tier was settled. Large counties were the standard political units of the South, and farms were laid out in helter-skelter fashion. The scattered population was not unified by such an institution of local self-government as the New England town meeting. The backwardness of education among the people as a whole may be largely attributed to geographical conditions and to the intense individualism that prevailed in the region.

The western area of South Carolina was the scene of a long contest between French, Spanish, and English forces. The Indians were allied to one or another and the frontier was in turmoil. In the midst of the Natchez War (1729-1739) between the French and a coalition of Indian tribes fighting for the English, the colony of Georgia was founded to protect the southern frontier and at the same time to provide homes for debtors and other unfortunate persons. James Edward Oglethorpe, a wealthy young Englishman who has been aptly described as an "Imperial Philanthropist," obtained in 1732 a charter permitting him and others as trustees to settle the region between South Carolina and Spanish Florida, and he personally established the first settlement at Savannah. He built a ring of forts around it and at his instance the trustees forbade slavery in the colony, prohibited liquor to prevent traders from giving it to the Indians, and limited farms to 50 acres to insure compact settlement. The English government helped finance the Georgia enterprise for imperial purposes, and wealthy associates helped in the work for philanthropic reasons. The colony was made a proprietary domain under the trustees for twenty-one years, after which it was to revert to the Crown as a royal province. The paternalistic regime was exceedingly unpopular and it actually ended in 1751, a little ahead of time, after the trustees had been forced to repeal the liquor and slavery prohibitions, to relax the land laws, and finally to grant the settlers an assembly. The colony continued to be an expense to the British government almost until the

Revolution. It soon lost its character as a refuge for the unfortunate, but it served a real imperial purpose as a military outpost. Most of the present state of Georgia was still occupied by Indians, but a plantation economy like that of South Carolina developed in the coastal region around Savannah.

The Middle Colonies: Germans and Scotch-Irish

In the middle colonies, westward expansion was hindered by the mountain barrier which runs closer to the seacoast there than elsewhere. New York's great route through the Appalachians by way of the Hudson and Mohawk rivers was long closed to settlers by the refusal of fur-trading interests, with headquarters at Albany, to allow farmers to move into the western domain where Indians trapped and traded. Furthermore, the English who succeeded to Dutch rule maintained the patroon system and extended the similar English manorial system to the whole Hudson Valley. Huge speculative holdings were common. But farmers refused to work as tenants on the great Dutch and English estates, some of which were millions of acres in extent, and the fertile land was idle. In this situation the English government decided to take a hand.

Certain German Protestants, who had suffered religious persecutions and fallen into extreme poverty as a result of the devastating Thirty Years' War, were eager to go to America, and immigration and shipping companies began to make a business of organizing migration. The English government sent out a small party of Palatine Germans in 1708 to found the town of Newburgh on the Hudson. The next year thousands of Palatines descended on London, where the army housed them in tents while ships were made ready. Groups were dispatched to various colonies, the largest number to New York. They were settled in camps along the Hudson and fed at government expense while they produced naval stores. The enterprise was not a success and was abandoned in a few years. The Germans, who were allowed to go where they pleased, promptly defied the Albany traders and moved into the Mohawk Valley. Soon a line of neat German villages and thrifty farms pointed the way to New York's great and fertile interior valleys, though the full settlement of that region was delayed because of the Indians. Afterward the main movement of the Germans was into Pennsylvania, where they came to be called incorrectly the Pennsylvania Dutch (from *Deutsch*, meaning German), and through that province into western Maryland and the Valley of Virginia, whence they proceeded southward into the Carolinas and the eastern part of what is now Tennessee.

Proprietors' rights were largely ignored in New York and Pennsylvania. Settlers simply squatted on the land and defied the authorities to dislodge them. Out of their practice they boldly rationalized the theory of "squatters' rights." The Scotch-Irish were especially aggressive in advocating and practicing this doctrine. These hardy people were mostly Lowland Scots who had been sent to northern Ireland in the seventeenth century to subdue the Irish and create a Protestant counterweight to the native Catholic population. In Ulster they learned how to clear their fields and produce a crop while fighting off marauding Irish tribesmen. Despite their services to the English government, the Scots in Ireland were not allowed to prosper. Between 1665 and 1699, a series of laws restricted their trade; Presbyterians were placed under civil and religious disabilities in 1704; and the rents on their lands were increased a few years later. Stubborn in their determination to make their way in the world and full of hatred for England, the Scotch-Irish migrated to America in such numbers that they constituted about one-eighth of the population by the time of the Revolution and were the largest non-English group.

At first they thought that Calvinistic New England would be a congenial place to settle. The Puritans were willing enough to send the rough newcomers to the frontier as Indian fighters, and a number of them settled in New Hampshire and western Massachusetts and all along the northern border, as the town names show. But the land was poor, the Puritans forced them to support the established Congregational Church, which varied in organization from their Presbyterianism, and their turbulent ways and strange accents made them unpopular. The main stream of Scotch-Irish migrants turned to Pennsylvania. There they moved into mountain valleys, westward of the Germans. Thence many of them went southwards through the Great Valley of Virginia to settle the back country of the southern colonies. John C. Calhoun and Andrew Jackson were of this stock.

The Scotch-Irish defied landowners and rent collectors. They said it was "against the laws of God and nature, that so much land should be idle while so many Christians wanted it to labor on to raise their bread." They fought Indians with righteous zest and had little respect for the laws of England or of its colonies. No group was more nearly unanimous in support of the American Revolution or provided a larger percentage of tough fighters for Washington's Army. While they advanced the frontier in many colonies with unexampled vigor, the Scotch-Irish by no means abandoned their Calvinist love of learning. Wherever they went they established church schools and in 1726 they founded at Neshaminy, Pennsylvania, the famous Log College to provide training for the ministry. Classical learning was maintained in these frontier institutions, but the special genius of the Scotch-Irish was for practical affairs. In time their businessmen, lawyers, engineers, politicians, and soldiers displaced Quakers and other groups as leaders of the middle colonies. In every colony that had a frontier they strengthened the radical party in opposition to eastern as well as English rule, in favor of western farmers' rights and the overthrow of established churches. They typified the spirit of the Old West.

New Jersey and Delaware were hemmed in by other colonies and produced no important frontier development. Conflicting proprietary grants in New Jersey troubled that colony. It attracted a bewildering variety of settlers from Europe, England, and other colonies, who united only in demanding freemen's rights against remnants of the proprietors' authority. Agriculture, whaling, and trade thrived. The present area of Delaware was claimed by William Penn, and the Privy Council gave him the right to appoint a governor in 1703. Its people won a separate legislative assembly in 1704 and later made good their independence from Pennsylvania by the indirect method of declaring their independence from England. Delaware developed a placid rural economy and way of life which was little disturbed until the great industrial activities of the du Pont family in the nineteenth and twentieth centuries transformed it.

New England

In New England, the Old West was the hill country of New Hampshire, Vermont, and western Massachusetts. The downfall of the Puritan oligarchy at the end of the seventeenth century and the rise of a rich merchant class in the seacoast towns transformed the New England method of frontier settlement. Towns were still laid out in neat tiers and the town meeting persisted as a democratic instrument of local government, but land speculators skimmed rich profits from the work of the settlers. The colonial governments began in the 1720's to create new towns for the benefit of promoters, who were usually merchants looking for investments. Often the promoters established sawmills and other improvements in new town sites, gave away the first lots to settlers who would build roads, and then sold the remaining lots at enhanced prices. The worst evil of the new system came from the influence of absentee owners during the period of settlement. The speculative fever also created new towns faster than settlers could fill them, resulting in a weak frontier line and poor communications. The system gave rise to a bad situation in the present area of Vermont, which both New York and New Hampshire claimed. Governor Benning Wentworth of New Hampshire began in 1749 to give town sites in the "New Hampshire Grants" to speculators— reserving 500 acres in each for himself. Settlers found their titles disputed by agents of New York, and organized the famed "Green Mountain Boys" to fight off the Yorkers. Like the inhabitants of Delaware, the Vermonters tried to secure their independence from neighboring colonies by declaring independence from England, but the stratagem did not work so well. They were kept waiting for admission to the Union until 1791.

The New England pioneers rapidly penetrated the Berkshire hills and threatened to spill over into New York. The tenant farmers of the Hudson Valley welcomed them, hoping that the New England colonies might annex the region and make them owners of the farms they tilled, but the New York authorities obtained a Crown decree fixing the eastern boundary of New York 20 miles east of the Hudson River. Thwarted there, the New Englanders moved northward into Maine, New Hampshire, and Vermont. Some Connecticut groups also found outlets for the land fever of speculators and settlers in the Wyoming Valley of Pennsylvania.

Frontier radicalism was nourished in New England as elsewhere by the excesses of Eastern speculators. The frontiersmen became impatient of all law, restless in the search for independence which seemed to require remoteness from other settlers, supremely self-reliant and contemptuous of anything hinting of personal subservence, and equally fearless in facing the dangers and hardships of the forest and man-made dangers to their liberty and independence. In the Old West, cut off from Europe and the seacoast, the American as a new type of humanity first took form. Compounded of many nationalities, dependent on nothing but his axe and his gun, capable of turning his hand to anything from making his own clothes to building a house, given to hard drinking and wild, exaggerated humor, distrustful of theory but quick to invent and adopt new practical devices, intensely optimistic, fierce in enmity and generous in friendship, the Westerner was certain that he was indeed "nature's nobleman." He created in his own image a distinctive American civilization which was a mixture of European inheritances and frontier influences.

THE BROADENING ECONOMY

Commerce

Throughout the eighteenth century the eastern seaboard maintained closer contacts with Europe than with the new settlements in the western hills. Colonial merchants sometimes were agents of English mercantile houses, but as profits accumulated in colonial hands independent capitalists often took over the business of the colonies with the mother country. A favorite form of investment was in ships. Trade and shipping prospered as a result of rising prices for colonial produce in Britain and Europe. Higher prices directly affected the West Indies and the southern colonies, which produced the sugar, molasses, tobacco, rice, indigo, and other staples most in demand abroad. But the merchants, shipowners, and

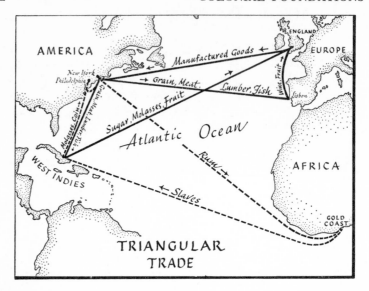

manufacturers of the northern colonies quickly learned how to obtain a share of the prosperity of their neighbors.

West Indian molasses was brought into the northern colonies and manufactured into rum. Parliament in 1733 passed the Molasses Act, imposing a prohibitory duty on foreign molasses and sugar, but the law was commonly violated in order to bring in the cheap products of the French and Spanish West Indies. Rum was carried from the New England ports to Africa where it was exchanged for slaves. The slaves were sold into the West Indies and southern plantations, where cargoes of molasses or other staples were taken aboard, thus completing the triangular trade on which colonial as well as English merchants grew rich.

Baltimore was founded in 1729 and became a leading site of water-powered mills which ground wheat into flour for sale to the West Indies, England, and Europe. Philadelphia remained pre-eminent in the grain and meat trade, while New York was the chief purveyor of furs to the world. The coast of New England from Connecticut to Maine was dotted with busy seaports. Fish and forest products were the chief articles of New England commerce, but the aggressive Yankee businessman followed his keen scent for profits into many a trade, triangular and quadrangular, which employed his ships and capital. The rice and indigo of South Carolina flowed through Charleston, making it the leading southern port, but in Tidewater Virginia and Maryland ships came up to the wharves of the plantations and the planters dealt directly with English factors or northern merchants, hence there were hardly any towns.

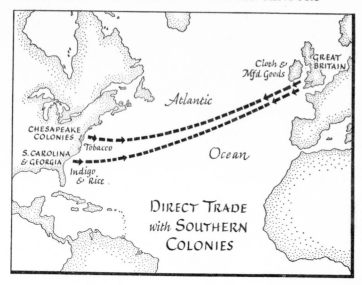

Crafts and Skills

Economic freedom in the colonies was considerably achieved in spite of imperial mercantilist laws. This was chiefly because of the ease of acquiring land and the laxity of English law enforcement. The prosperity of American trade, partially conducted in violation of English law, encouraged manufactures. Back-country conditions encouraged mechanical ingenuity and widespread cultivation of craft skills. "Kitchen manufactures" of tools, cloth, furniture, leather goods, and many other things thrived from the beginning. The English government forbade the emigration of skilled artisans with their tools to America, but they came anyway.

In America every farmer and his family practiced many crafts and American industry grew out of this vast reservoir of skills. Textile production was the earliest important manufacture. The governments of New England early encouraged sheep-raising by tax exemptions, special pasture privileges, and prohibitions against killing ewes. At first all the work of shearing the sheep, cleaning the wool, carding, combing, spinning, dyeing with the juices of plants, and weaving the cloth was performed by hand, much of it by the women and children. By 1700, New England was self-sufficient in the coarser grades of woolen cloth. In the other colonies woolen manufactures were also common, while linen made from flax and cotton goods were also produced. The textile industry was one of the first to be moved out of the kitchens into specialized mills. By the middle of the eighteenth century the most skillful craftsmen were spending their full time in performing one or more of the processes for their neighbors, and from this system factory production gradually grew.

Manufactures of wood had a similar history. At first every settler turned his hand to carpentry and the fashioning of tools and furniture. Wooden tools were almost universal except for axes and tips of plows. Wooden pegs substituted for nails and mauls for hammers. Sturdy furniture in simplified imitation of the Jacobean styles of England was one of the earliest and best products of American craft. In the eighteenth century the carpenter's trade became important as a special vocation. Ship-carpenters were the earliest professionals, and their skill advanced so rapidly that along the seacoast houses and furniture like the "Cape Cod cottage" and the "captain's chair" were often built according to sea-going techniques. While the wealthiest began to insist on mansions of brick, which was sometimes even imported from abroad, and a few, especially in eastern Pennsylvania and among the Dutch in New York, built with stone, the characteristic building material in early America was wood. In forest clearings the log cabin became standard. Prosperous farmers and most townsmen built with boards supplied by local sawmills. The most pretentious of these houses displayed wooden imitations of current European styles of ornament. The typical "architect" of the colonial period was a carpenter with a well-thumbed European builder's manual.

Ships were the greatest of the colonial manufactures of wood and in this craft New England, with ample timber, numerous craftsmen, and maritime ambitions, surpassed the other colonies. Governor Winthrop had the first American ship, the *Blessing of the Bay,* built in 1631. After 1700, the numerous shipyards of the New England towns, some of them far inland on rivers, not only supplied local owners but sold ships to the other colonies, England, and Europe. During the colonial period it was the cheapness of materials that gave American shipyards their advantage; but superiority of design and construction maintained it. The middle colonies had some success in shipbuilding, but the southern colonies failed to develop or attract shipwrights despite bounties.

Iron manufacture was the first metal trade practiced in British America. The need for tools, kettles, and hardware stimulated many efforts to exploit the readily available deposits of bog-iron. In this, too, New England excelled. The first American furnace for smelting iron ore and forge for beating it into hardness and fashioning useful shapes were erected at Lynn, Massachusetts, in 1643. In the seventeenth century, Connecticut vied with Massachusetts in developing iron industries, but by 1750 Pennsylvania had won the supremacy which she has never lost. The chief product of the mills was bar iron and steel which was distributed to local blacksmiths for working into finished articles. Few families by the end of the colonial period could afford to buy much domestic metalware because even the simplest nail required special forging of the head to the shank. An iron kettle, iron plow-point, an iron axe head, and the indispensable gun were the extent of the average farmer's metal equipment.

American skill was notably displayed in the development of the Pennsylvania rifle, later called the Kentucky rifle, from a German prototype. Its elongated barrel was the secret of the frontiersman's famous accuracy in bringing down game or more formidable quarry. New England ingenuity survived Pennsylvania's supremacy in heavy metal manufacturing, as it retained its lead in the production of hardware. The scarcity of metal was solved in the case of clockworks by the ingenious use of wood. By the middle of the century, other metals than iron were coming to be used. Lead for bullets and pewter was scarce and mostly imported, as was silver for the advanced craftsmen—like Jeremiah Dummer, John Coney, and Paul Revere. The future of metallurgical industries in America was visible, however, by the end of the colonial period in the fact that in 1775 the colonies produced one-seventh of the world's pig and bar iron.

Sawmills using the straight saw, and grist mills whose stones were turned by oxen or by water-wheels, were the most common colonial "factories." Sawyers and millers were the first manufacturers in every new settlement. Rum distilleries were probably the most profitable of all colonial factories. Shoemaking which many farmers practiced in the kitchen was gradually developed into a specialized trade. In the Old West, home processing of grain into whiskey and of wood into potash and pearl ash solved the problem of poor roads by reducing bulky materials to forms which justified costly transportation.

Dominance of Merchants

Manufacturing, whether at home or in specialized mills and shops, remained throughout the colonial period subordinate to the merchant. No manufacturer produced enough to undertake distribution himself beyond his own locality. Interchange of goods between localities was in the hands of merchants who bought the productions of many localities and sold them elsewhere in the colonies or abroad. The most successful merchants made their headquarters in the seaports of the northern colonies. They owned their own ships to ply the coasts and rivers and cross the ocean, and even functioned as bankers, extending loans at interest to lesser merchants and to manufacturers. Their strategic position enabled them to dictate low prices to the farmers and millers from whom they bought and high prices to consumers. Engrossing the markets, that is, establishing monopoly control by encompassing the total supply of a particular commodity, although forbidden by English law which colonial governments frequently affirmed, became a common practice.

From Massachusetts to Pennsylvania the merchants dominated colonial society. Their influence was felt in the South, which developed no strong merchant class of its own, although it accounted for more than two-thirds of all colonial exports and imports. The northern merchants were themselves subordinate to English merchants, for whom they often acted as American agents. Some English mercantile houses specialized in the southern trade and sent ships with English goods direct to the wharves of Tidewater plantations and picked up cargoes of tobacco. The northern merchant possessed market power of his own, but the southern planter could not avoid dependence on northern or English middlemen.

The consequence was that the northern merchant outranked all other Americans in ready wealth and steadily made headway even against his English competitors. By developing intercolonial trade, encouraging manufactures, invading the southern market, and ingeniously exploiting loopholes in the imperial trade walls, notably the triangular routes to the West Indies and Africa, he emerged as the controlling figure in the American economy. But at the end of the seventeenth century the English government began a new series of attempts to restrict the growth of American mercantile independence.

Cultural Developments

Rising prosperity after 1700 was accompanied by a new emphasis on worldly culture. Northern merchants and southern planters enjoyed comfortable living and cultivated the arts and graces. Rows of elegant mansions in the port cities, and plantation houses matching the splendor of English manors, were visible symbols of economic status. While the poorest family used homemade pine furniture, American cabinet makers learned to reproduce for richer clients the mahogany styles of England in native cherry, and the wealthiest imported the original articles. Fine silverware, porcelain, and glass displaced for the few the woodenware and pewter of common use. It became possible for a painter to support himself in America by turning out portraits of colonial worthies which bespoke wealth and status in the glow of silken garments, the pride of facial expressions, and the softness of hands.

Education

Mental cultivation was an ideal with more than ornamental meaning for the colonial merchants and planters. They collected libraries of ancient classics, the latest English publications, and a growing number of colonial imprints. In education the northern colonies maintained the lead which Massachusetts had early won. William and Mary College (1693) at Williamsburg, the capital of Virginia, whose reconstruction in our day provides an image of the golden age of the colonies, remained the only southern institution of higher learning during the colonial period. Yale College (1701) was followed by the College of New Jersey at Princeton (1746), which provided Presbyterian seminary training for the

Scotch-Irish in succession to their Log College. The University of Pennsylvania, nonsectarian, was founded in 1749 and King's College (now Columbia University) in 1754 as an Anglican institution. The Baptists educated their ministers at the College of Rhode Island (now Brown University), founded at Providence in 1764, and the Dutch Reformed Church established Queen's College (now Rutgers University) in 1766. Even the wild frontier of New Hampshire was provided with a college, Dartmouth at Hanover, established in 1769, partially for the benefit of Indian youths. Wealthy colonists, Southerners especially, went to England for professional education in law or medicine or for broadening travel. The latest fashions in ideas, the arts, and amusements quickly found their way to America, and little courts in imitation of the royal court clustered around the colonial governors. Frosty religious attitudes towards the theater, dancing, and other frivolities gradually melted in the face of the worldliness that accompanied growing wealth. Gambling, horse racing, and tavern drinking were popular diversions indulged in by those who could not as well as by those who could afford them.

Religion

The religious fervor of the earliest settlers gave way along the seaboard to decorous forms of worship and relative indifference, especially among the southern planters. The latter maintained nominal adherence to the Anglican faith as a kind of civil responsibility. The spiritual quality of the Anglican clergymen was not high. In Virginia they became famous for short and pallid sermons and long bouts of worldly diversion. They entered into the gay round of fox hunting, horse racing, and hospitality with the planters. Frontiersmen who liked their religion hot resented the attempt to make them help pay for the support of the Anglican establishment. All the Anglican churches in America belonged to the diocese of London, and the highest American official was a commissary of that diocese. Earnest Anglicans tried to improve the discipline and organization of the American clergy by asking the English government to create independent dioceses in the colonies, but local Anglicans as well as dissenters feared that it would lead to heavier taxes and successfully opposed the reform. The Anglican Society for the Propagation of the Gospel conducted missionary campaigns among the Indians and the colonists, but they were not so successful as dissenting evangelical preachers in arousing religious enthusiasm.

In New England increasing worldliness did not so easily overcome the religious spirit. The Puritan or Congregational Church remained the established Church everywhere except in Rhode Island, and dissenters were made to pay taxes for its support. There was a tendency among preachers to temper the rigors of Calvinism in favor of the mental comfort of their wealthier listeners, but it was dramatically reversed by the "Great Awakening." This religious revival got under way in several northern colonies in the 1720's and 1730's. Eventually it touched all the colonies and all the diverse religious groups in them with the exception of the negligible number of Roman Catholics. It caused splits in the older churches between enthusiasts and conservatives and led ultimately to the organization of a bewildering variety of new sects. The Great Awakening was a reaction against moderation and intellectualism in religion. Polite sermons by educated preachers failed to satisfy the mass of colonists, and they turned to preachers who excited their emotions. Revivalism was institutionalized and became a permanent feature of American religion.

The first great leader of the Awakening was Jonathan Edwards, a graduate of Yale and the Congregational minister of Northampton, Massachusetts. A famous revival began there in 1734 under his preaching. Edwards was a prose artist, something of a mystic, and an extremely eloquent orator. The tendency of his preaching was to strengthen the Calvinist conception of predestination and yet to encourage all men to behave as if they were elect by renouncing sin and striving to believe they were granted a share of Divine Grace. Edwards' evocations of the tortures of the damned made his hearers roll on the floor in physical agonies, but he thrilled them with hope that they might yet be saved, and the experience of conversion became the core of revivalist religion. His influence reached far beyond his parish by means of such publications as *A Faithful Narration of the Surprising Work of God in the Conversion of Many Hundred Souls in Northampton* (1737), which was widely reprinted in America and Europe. Revivalism spread like wildfire along the Atlantic seaboard and into the West during the following years. It was taken up by lay preachers, hysterics, and charlatans, as well as by many a sincere minister of the older churches. Conservative clergymen and their calmer followers held fast, and Edwards himself was eventually deprived of his pulpit. But in a series of penetrating theological works he developed a modification of Calvinism which placed emphasis on the capacity of every man for holiness and communication with God. He was the founder of the New England or Edwardean theology, which gave a new lease of life to Calvinism.

In England, John Wesley strove to bring invigorating emotionalism into the Anglican Church, and the movement he founded succeeded in turning large numbers away from their complacent religious leaders into the separate "Low Church," "Chapel," or "Methodist" communions. Wesley's English movement ultimately resulted in the Methodist Church in America, but its organization was long delayed. George Whitefield, sent out to preach in Georgia, was fired by Edwards' example, and in 1739 began his amazing career as itinerant revivalist preacher throughout the

American colonies. With Whitefield the Awakening literally burst forth from the churches, because no building could accommodate the crowds he drew. He could make himself heard by 20,000 people, could preach two sermons in one day, and ride many miles to repeat the performance the next day. Even the skeptical Benjamin Franklin could not withstand the eloquence of Whitefield. He went to hear him out of curiosity, decided presently that he might contribute a few coppers to the inevitable collection plate, and ended by pouring out the entire contents of his purse.

The Baptists and the "New Light" Presbyterians were the chief beneficiaries of the Great Awakening. These groups made conversion of sinners their chief objective, the revival meeting their chief technique, and extreme democracy their system of church government. In the East revivalism had less permanent importance than in the Old West. There it became not only the central religious activity but also an important means of social expression, mitigating the loneliness of frontier life and uniting the settlers in opposition to the established and more decorous religions of the seaboard. The broadest meaning of the Great Awakening is that it inaugurated the process whereby the conditions of American life which were conducive to individualism invaded the sphere of religion.

In the East a few of the most advanced minds developed religious attitudes precisely the opposite of emotional revivalism. They were influenced to move towards rationalism in religion by the rise of scientific inquiry into the laws of nature, heralded by the career of Sir Isaac Newton. The theology of Christianity became less important in their minds than the study of nature as a means of understanding God, "the Great Artificer." They rejected miracles and certain other articles of orthodox faith as superstitions based on ignorance of the immutable laws of nature. They conceived of God, not as a person intimately concerned with the doings of men, but as a "force," the "prime mover," more or less identical with the created universe. Such attitudes of the Age of Enlightenment gave moral and spiritual impetus to learning, particularly in the fields of the sciences, but they tended to reduce church-going to a rather empty formality. In extreme form these attitudes led to the rationalist, unorthodox religion of Deism. Many of the most intelligent colonists, including such later leaders as Benjamin Franklin and Thomas Jefferson, turned to rationalism in religion. Perhaps the best proof of their faith in reasonableness is that they did not personally break with the institutions of orthodoxy or attack the beliefs of others. But they strongly opposed the political claims of certain religious groups. The impulse that later resulted in the complete separation of Church and State was shared by seaboard intellectuals and frontier revivalists.

Rise of the Press

While science was displacing theology as the absorbing concern of the best-educated Americans, the press to some extent displaced the pulpit as the chief vehicle of popular education. The schools and colleges clung to older and safer notions, but the book and periodical press spread among Americans the latest and most dangerous political and philosophical ideas, imported and domestic. Without the growth of the press in the seaboard cities during the earlier eighteenth century, it is difficult to imagine that the Revolution, which required unity of minds and hands scattered along thousands of miles of coast and frontier, could have succeeded.

During the seventeenth century, colonial printing presses had turned out little besides religious works. The prolific and pedantic writings of the Mathers dominated the output of the most active printing center, Boston and Cambridge. The first attempt to establish an American newspaper in 1690 in Boston failed after the first issue because it displeased the authorities, but the Boston postmaster, John Campbell, successfully published the *Boston News-Letter,* beginning in 1704. The *Boston Gazette,* which began publication in 1719, was printed by James Franklin, half-brother of Benjamin. Two years later, James launched the *New England Courant,* in which certain of the traditional practices of American journalism were tried out. This newspaper promised "to entertain the town with the most comical and diverting incidents of human life," and it grievously offended the Puritans not only by its levity but by its severe attacks on the Mathers, Harvard College, and the Assembly. Young Ben Franklin served as printer's devil and writer for this paper, but he soon decided to go to Philadelphia to make his own way in its freer atmosphere. There he became printer-in-chief to the American people, disseminating books, tracts, almanacs, and periodicals, many of them written by himself, which made his presses the greatest engines of humorous common sense and political and scientific enlightenment the colonies possessed.

By 1765, there were twenty-five newspapers in the colonies. A famous victory for freedom of the press had been won in New York in 1735. John Peter Zenger was a Palatine German and the publisher of the *New York Weekly Journal,* which he made an organ of the popular opposition to the "court" party around the Governor. He published criticisms and jibes against Governor William Cosby which would not be considered remarkable if, today, they were directed against a President of the United States. But the colonies, like England, had severe libel laws and Cosby threw Zenger into prison. For many months the editor conducted his paper from a cell. His trial aroused excitement throughout the colonies. The great lawyer Andrew Hamilton of Philadelphia defended Zenger, arguing that the editor was innocent of libel because his criticisms of the Governor were true. Chief Justice De Lancey pronounced the English principle that anything "scandalous and ironical" was a libel even if it *was* true. Thus the issue was clearly joined on the question whether the press was free to print the truth. The verdict of the jury was that Zenger was not guilty of libel and he went free. This did not prevent further suppression of the freedom of the press before and after the Revolution, but it was a precedent of great importance which eventually prevailed.

CHAPTER 7

Colonial Politics
and a Cycle of Wars

JUST AS MERCANTILIST REGULATIONS MODIFIED BUT did not prevent independent economic growth in the English colonies, so the efforts of the Crown to systematize political administration were partially defeated by the lusty growth of colonial political skill and institutions. War usually requires a higher degree of centralized administration than peace, but even the participation of the colonies in four major wars against European powers, beside endemic war against the Indians, did not greatly alter colonial or imperial political development until after 1763. Internal colonial forces rather than any external influences were the chief source of political development. The character, ambitions, and ideals of the people provided the main explanation of colonial politics.

COLONIAL POLITICAL INSTITUTIONS

The type of colonial government favored by England after 1689 was the royal province. This form of government was not conducive to the establishment of new colonies, because it offered no incentives to competent leaders to risk investments of time and money. Therefore, almost all the colonies were founded by business companies holding charter privileges or by individual proprietors who received royal grants. It was after colonies had been successfully established that the English authorities wanted to transform them into royal provinces in order to gain more direct control over the policies and acts of their governments. Yet charters and royal grants were respected as vested rights in English law, and they could not be extinguished without court proceedings in which the government or some other suitor could show substantial cause why the Crown should be permitted to revoke them. The consequence was that not all the colonies were converted into royal provinces. Connecticut and Rhode Island kept their charters to the end and Maryland, Pennsylvania, and Delaware retained the proprietary form.

Governors

The essential distinctions among these three forms—charter or corporate, proprietary, and royal—lay in the degree of local self-government. All three were subject to the requirement that no colonial act should contravene English law, and to the review of their legislation by the Board of Trade, with the possibility of royal disallowance. The Privy Council was the highest court of appeal. A more immediate means of preventing undesired action by a colonial government, including action which did *not* contravene English law, was to install a Crown-appointed governor who was subject to instructions from the home government and armed with veto power over the colonial legislature. The royal governorship was the essential institution that differentiated the eight royal provinces from the proprietary and charter colonies. Governors were elected in Rhode Island and Connecticut, and in the proprietary colonies were chosen by the proprietor. In practice, after the Glorious Revolution, the proprietary governors were generally less severe than the royal because they learned from experience that the home government was eager to take advantage of disorder in proprietary colonies and convert them into royal provinces. Similarly, the charter governments of Connecticut and Rhode Island learned to avoid giving too much temptation to the English authorities. They retained their unusual rights of self-rule by keeping out of controversy.

Besides holding the veto power over the legislatures, the governors were the chief executives of the provinces. In the performance of their executive functions they were aided by a council, which was appointed except in Massachusetts, where it was elected by the lower house of the legislature. The council also served as an upper house of the legislature. It represented a cross between the Privy Council and the House of Lords in England, but in practice it often was hand in glove with the lower house of the assembly, which by the eighteenth century won the right to initiate legislation. Inasmuch as the governor himself was generally dependent on legislative grants or taxes for his salary, powers over local taxation and appropriations were crucial, and the assemblies had both powers. The threat of withholding his salary whipped many a governor into compliance even in matters over which the assemblies had no formal authority. In time of war the English government commonly laid requisitions on the colonies and these, too, were dependent on the consent of the assemblies. The power of the purse in the hands of the colonies caused the home government itself normally to exercise moderation in dealing with them. Today the exclusive right of the United States House of Representatives to initiate money bills is an inheritance of the most potent of all colonial legislative rights.

Bribery and corruption were common among government officials in eighteenth-century England and Europe and the system was not much criticized there. Public offices were handed out as favors without much regard for training or competence, and it was considered a normal exercise of privileged status for an administrator to enrich himself. But in America the corruption of royal officials was more palpable than in England, because many of them so obviously detested the colonies and accepted these offices only as a means of extracting plunder to take home. Furthermore, in the colonies, even the wealthiest classes identified themselves with other Americans as against court favorites from abroad. Some royal officials were able and honest, but criticism of most of them for their arrogance and malpractices was common throughout the colonial period.

Assemblies

The assemblies were generally made up of the leading men of each colony—as defined in terms of education, wealth, and social standing. In no colony was the franchise universal, but the ease of satisfying the property qualification for the vote—generally a 50-acre freehold, or a town lot with a structure on it, or property worth £40 or £50—was such that ordinarily only slaves, servants, tenants, and some artisans were disfranchised, besides young men who had yet to make their way. Large landowners were the earliest typical legislators. With the rise of trade and professional classes in the eighteenth century, lawyers became the typical representatives, though often they were also large landowners, especially in the southern colonies. Most lawyers identified their interests with the merchants or planters, but a few derived from their legal study doctrines of liberty which transcended class interests. Such "radicals" were the outstanding champions of colonial rights against royal privilege. The leaders of the last colonial generation of legislators were generally lawyers or planters versed in the law, and they became leaders of the Revolution. There has probably never been a revolution that displayed more legal and political skill, and this was a direct result of the long experience and training in self-government afforded by the colonial assemblies.

Political parties as such did not exist in colonial times, though factions were common. Voters and legislators grouped themselves around individuals without creating any permanent extragovernmental organization. Nevertheless, the germs of political parties were present in divisions created by issues, and as all issues tended to boil down to the one between colonial rights and English authority, with the great majority of assmbly-men on the side of colonial rights, governors had to contend with legis-latures controlled by what amounted to an opposition "party." The two were fairly evenly matched, the governor holding negative powers of veto and of dissolution, the colonials having power to frustrate the governor by refusing funds. But the governors were more reluctant to use their powers than the assemblies, so that prior to 1763, with minor exceptions, the assemblies made good their claim to sole jurisdiction over internal taxation and built up by steady accretions their authority over executive functions, such as the appointment of administrative offi-cials and control of the militia and armaments.

While the perennial struggle between governor and assembly was an excellent school of politics for the colonials, it also established a tradition of competition between the two branches of government which persists in the United States today and greatly differentiates American govern-ment from the English Parliamentary model. During the colonial period a lesser party division existed between representatives of the wealthier East and those of the newly settled West. The royal governors sometimes favored the East against the "leveling" demands of the West, and when such an alignment occurred the Westerners could easily be outvoted be-cause representation of their districts lagged far behind the actual growth of population.

The Rights and Liberties of Englishmen

The judicial systems of the colonies were modeled on those of England. In small matters justice was administered by local justices of the peace, as by the county courts of Virginia. More important civil and criminal cases were tried in courts presided over, as a rule, by judges appointed by the governors. In Virginia the Council served as the highest court, though the great landholders on it were not necessarily lawyers. Appeals from these courts could be taken to the Privy Council in England, but this arduous and expensive procedure was not practicable for the ordinary citizen. The English common law, which is the body of decisions in former cases used as precedents in later ones, prevailed in the American courts except where it was superseded by specific legislation, colonial or Parliamentary. English judicial process, including arrest only by war-rant, the right of accused to a writ of habeas corpus, the right to a trial by jury, and the right to present and to examine witnesses, besides the rule of assumed innocence until guilt is positively proved, also obtained in the colonies. In no sphere of government were English institutions more directly or more advantageously transplanted in America and better maintained after the Revolution. Nor was any other English action more conducive to revolution than the interference after 1763 with colonial judicial procedure.

Conflict between the colonies and the mother country was inherent in the original guarantee that Englishmen in the colonies would enjoy all the rights and liberties of Englishmen at home, on the one hand; and on the other the presence of colonial legislatures which, despite their real powers, were not autonomous but subject to the will of the home government. The colonists admitted at most that they owed obedience to the English government only in external affairs such as imperial trade regulations. They tended to avoid even this admission by claiming that their legislatures had the same power that the Glorious Revolution won for Parliament. That same Revolution, however, was cited by Englishmen as making Parliament the sole ultimate lawgiver in all matters whatsoever for the whole empire. This conflict remained insignificant so long as neither side was impelled to test its theory in practice. Such impulsions first became visible in new mercantilist regulations of the eighteenth century, and then in Parliamentary enactments that went beyond mercantilist principles and sought to make the colonies help pay for wars.

New Mercantilist Regulations

When colonial manufactures for export became possible, England forbade the·development of those colonial industries which would compete with established English industries. Thus the Woolens Act of 1699 forbade the sale of colonial woolen textiles in any market outside the colony of manufacture. This affected Ulster in Ireland much more than the American colonies. The Hat Act of 1732 forbade the colonists to make hats out of beaver fur in shops employing more than a limited number of apprentices, or to export their products. The Iron Act of 1750 encouraged the export to Britain of colonial pig and bar iron, but forbade further colonial investment in manufacture of semifinished or finished products. The obvious purpose of these laws was to protect British industries by forcing the colonists to send raw materials to the mother country and buy back the manufactured articles. Their immediate effect was not very oppressive, but for the future the colonists were discouraged from developing large-scale industries in forbidden fields. The English laws against American manufactures, like so many others, were considerably violated as illegal factories sprang up.

The Money Question

English mercantilists held one trump card: control over the coinage of money. The over-all purpose of mercantilism was to make the colonial economy a source of English wealth which could be collected in bullion,

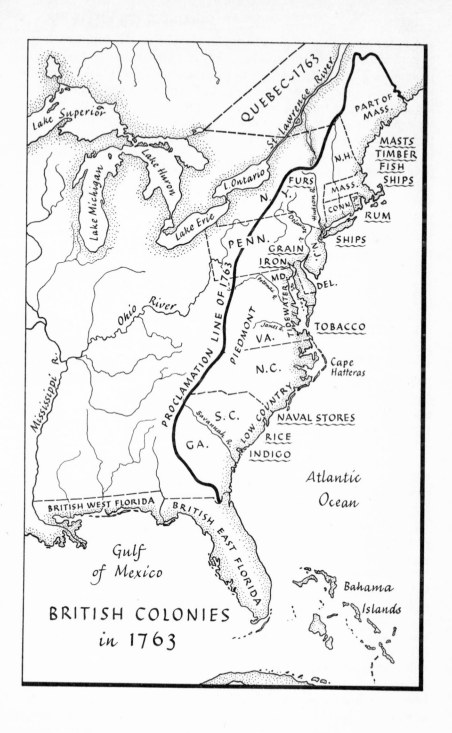

BRITISH COLONIES
in 1763

and at the same time to prevent the diminution of the Empire's supply of gold and silver. Therefore, the export of specie from the Empire was prohibited. The creation of a balance of trade with the colonies favorable to the mother country was not difficult. Even in the eighteenth century the colonies were frontier communities, producing chiefly raw materials for export; they were in great need of basic manufactures such as cloth, tools, glass, and cutlery, and were desirous of improving their standard of living by importing articles of luxury. England was the greatest European producer of the first class of goods, and the Navigation Acts effectually cut off colonial imports from her competitors except by smuggling, which went on, especially with Holland. The northern colonies produced little that was sent directly to England. How could they make up the difference between the value of the goods they exported and that of their imports? It was done by means of the favorable trade to Spain, Portugal, the Wine Islands and the West Indies in fish, lumber, foodstuffs, and slaves. The colonials were paid considerable sums in Spanish silver dollars and Portuguese gold pieces, which could then be sent to England to meet their unfavorable balances with the mother country.

But as the business of the colonial community grew, the need appeared for a domestic circulating medium—a money supply within the colonies. Lacking this, all local trade had to be carried on by barter, and the settlement of debts for services or loans was exceedingly difficult. The colonies had no supplies of precious metals, and England made no attempt to create a colonial currency. The Spanish and Portuguese coins might have supplied this need, but the continuous adverse balances with England acted as a siphon to draw them off. The colonists cast about for some way of discouraging the export of foreign coins to England. The first such effort was in Massachusetts, where foreign silver was melted down and recoined as the "pine-tree shilling" which contained less silver than the English shilling, and would therefore be undesirable for payments to England and remain in the colony. The home government attacked this as a depreciation of the currency and made it one of the charges that led to loss of the Massachusetts charter. Unable to create currencies of their own in this fashion, the colonies then had recourse to another stratagem: they overvalued foreign coins in terms of English money. Thus, while in England the Spanish dollar was valued at 4s.6d., in New York by act of the legislature it was valued at 8s., and in Pennsylvania at 7s. The theory was that this gave the Spanish dollar a greater purchasing power in the colony, and that people would therefore prefer to spend it at home rather than to send it to pay for purchases in England. This was not satisfactory to the English government, and in 1704 a royal proclamation, later embodied in an act of Parliament, officially set the rates at which foreign coins would be accepted. However, the act allowed the colonies to accept foreign coins at one-third more than the rate in Britain, and coins circulating at this rate came to be called "proclamation money." In spite of this concession colonies which had set a higher rate continued by various subterfuges to violate the law.

Financing Colonial Wars

The outbreak of the wars with the French created a new problem, that of financing colonial expeditions. There was not much free capital which might support a bond issue, and it was as impracticable in the eighteenth as in the twentieth century to equip and pay military expeditions on a pay-as-you-go basis out of current taxes. The New England colonies, which were the chief participants in the early colonial wars, therefore resorted to paper money issues which were made legal tender within the particular colony. The laws always established a definite period during which the money was to be accepted (or "current") and levied additional taxes, which should be sufficient to redeem and retire it at the end of the period of currency. The paper money, however, turned out to be not only an excellent method of financing war, but a welcome addition to the circulating medium, hence the practice was continued in peace times and imitated between 1700 and 1760 by all the colonies. The last to follow suit was Virginia, which did not resort to paper until the French and Indian War put her under a heavy burden of expense.

The colonies did not all manage their paper issues wisely. Western Europe had had very little experience with this kind of currency. In England none was issued by the government and bank notes were not legal tender. Some depreciation of colonial paper resulted when, because of inexperience, the times of redemption were extended over too long a period. The taxes were often insufficient to redeem the issues, and the money was allowed to circulate beyond its period of currency instead of being called in and destroyed. Many of the later issues were based not only upon taxes but also upon "land-banks," that is, they were issued directly to farmers on their lands as security. It was difficult to force farmers to pay either interest or principal promptly, particularly since the legislators and the sheriffs were mostly farmers themselves. New England was the worst offender in this respect.

In Massachusetts, when the earliest issue had depreciated beyond cure, it was stabilized at a fraction of its face value. A new issue was called "new tenor" as against the "old tenor." When this second issue in turn depreciated it became, by the same process, "middle tenor," and a third issue of "new tenor" was made. Thus within the same colony three kinds of paper money circulated. One can easily imagine the difficulties which this practice created in business as well as the continuous inflation which it represented. When the farmers in western Massachusetts proposed to set up a private land-bank, the eastern merchants appealed to England

and obtained a ruling that the South Sea Bubble Act of 1720, which had been directed at speculative excesses, forbade land-banks. In 1751, Parliament passed a law forbidding the New England colonies to make any further issues of legal-tender paper money.

The British government had made an earlier attempt to restrict the issues of paper money by instructing the royal governors to veto acts which did not levy adequate taxes to redeem the notes or which extended the period of currency beyond five or ten years. But the governor often found it easier to disregard his instructions than to oppose a determined legislature which could and did refuse to pay him his salary unless he approved the paper-money bills. The British merchant did not suffer from colonial monetary experiments as long as the debts due him were payable in England at sterling rates, and normally this was the case. But he encountered trouble when he had to collect his debts *in America,* through resident agents, who might be compelled to accept either specie at the overvalued rate or legal-tender paper. This was the situation in Virginia where, by the middle of the eighteenth century, English and Scottish tobacco merchants had established resident "factors" or agents. The "Virginia merchants" in London, joined by their colleagues in Liverpool and Glasgow, made representations to the Board of Trade and their protest eventually resulted in 1764 in the extension of the Act of 1751 to all the colonies. Since business in the colonies was in the doldrums after the French and Indian War, the deflationary effect of the Currency Act of 1764 was resented by merchants as well as farmers.

American farmers have usually suffered under burdens of debt—partly because of their willingness to mortgage their farms in the hope that the value of their land will rise—and schemes to inflate the currency and cheapen credit have generally appealed to them. English laws against such schemes were responsible for some of the eagerness with which the western regions embraced the Revolution in 1776. Eastern businessmen found these laws useful insofar as they protected colonial creditors, and harmful insofar as they protected English creditors. For them, the solution of the currency problem lay in the overthrow of English rule and the administration of "hard-money" policies by American authorities for the benefit of American creditors. What had been a three-cornered struggle over currency in the colonial period was reduced by the Revolution to a two-sided conflict which long persisted.

Growth of the Spirit of Independence

By the middle of the eighteenth century the businessmen of the seaports were beginning to rival their English competitors and to reach out for the trade, manufacturing, and financial independence which would permit them to take the lead in the exploitation of American resources. The rise of business activity gave employment to lawyers, who were displacing the clergy as the intellectual leaders of the middle and New England colonies and becoming effective mouthpieces of American interests in opposition to British rule. In the cities the ranks of artisans rapidly swelled. Everywhere planters, farmers, frontiersmen, businessmen, clergymen, editors, lawyers, and artisans thought of themselves as Americans, and became hypersensitive to any encroachment on their traditional liberties. They chafed at anything that implied colonial inferiority; and without quite formulating the thought, they were moving inexorably towards the creation of a new society, distinctively American in that it was freer (if slavery be overlooked) and more diverse in racial and religious composition than any Old World society. Long before the American Revolution began, as John Adams said, it occurred in the hearts of men.

COLONIAL WARS

Many settlers had come to America in order to escape the interminable wars of Europe. This was literally true of Quakers and other religious pacifists. The majority of settlers were not pacifists, but they were isolationists in the sense that they wanted to avoid embroilments in international politics and wars which did not concern them. They largely agreed with the statement of Increase Mather: "There never was a generation that did so perfectly shake off the dust of Babylon, both as to ecclesiastical and civil constitution, as the first generation of Christians that came into this land for the gospel's sake." The colonists felt themselves to be as remote from Europe spiritually as they were in fact remote from it geographically.

From the very beginning, however, Americans were willing to fight when they believed that their interests required it. Conflict with the Indians turned the mass of colonists into militiamen at a time when wars in Europe were still fought by professional soldiers. Americans also recognized their obligation to support England against European rivals. Their support was desultory during the Anglo-Dutch Wars of the seventeenth century. But during the seventy-five years beginning in 1689, England fought France in a series of four wars for world supremacy, and the interest and obligation of the colonists led them to take an increasingly important part in these. If Americans were to protect their settlements and push them into the mountains and beyond, they would have to fight France as well as the Indians.

Intermittent Imperial Wars, 1689-1748

Close ties between the English colonists and the Iroquois Confederation for a time protected the frontiers of New York and Pennsylvania, but late in the seventeenth century the Spaniards in the South and the French north of New England waged sporadic warfare against the English settlements. King William III organized the Grand Alliance of European powers to thwart the ambitions of Louis XIV and this led to warfare in Europe and America. French raiding parties attacked frontier towns in New England, pushing back the line of settlement, and French privateers attacked colonial fishermen and traders. New Englanders organized an expedition that captured Port Royal, Nova Scotia, in 1690, but another expedition under Sir William Phips attempted to take Quebec and failed. What was known in America as King William's War (1689-1697) ended in a draw. Port Royal was returned to the French, and this seeming neglect of colonial interest gave a foretaste of grievances to come.

Spain was on the French side during the next three wars. Thus the colonists were faced with a threat from both south and north. The War of the Spanish Succession (1702-1713), called Queen Anne's War in America, began in Europe when Louis XIV placed his Bourbon grandson on the throne of Spain. The French in Canada and Louisiana were now united with the Spaniards in Florida against the English settlements. South Carolina begged England for help, as did Massachusetts, but they were left to protect themselves as best they could while England spent her resources in Europe. The middle colonies, protected by the Iroquois, tried to preserve "neutrality." Spaniards attacked Charleston and South Carolinians attacked Pensacola, with Indian tribes changing sides indiscriminately, and there was no decisive result. Massachusetts was pushed back along the frontier, while her troops again captured Port Royal and another expedition against Quebec failed. The peace treaty established British authority over the Hudson Bay country, Acadia, and Newfoundland. France kept Cape Breton Island, where Louis XIV built the great fortress of Louisbourg, and this French stronghold was a gun cocked at New England. Britain's chief prize in the Treaty of Utrecht (1713) was the "*Assiento* Privilege" of selling slaves into the Spanish Empire.

During the generation of peace before the outbreak of the third war in 1744, the English colonies experienced their most rapid expansion of population and wealth. Their ability to wage war increased accordingly, and so did their desire that colonial interests should not be neglected by the mother country. England's violations of Spanish colonial trade monopoly and Spanish retaliations led in 1739 to the War of Jenkins' Ear. An expedition against Cartagena on the Gulf of Darien, Colombia, under Admiral Edward Vernon, which included among colonial volunteers Lawrence Washington, brother of George, was a disastrous failure. On the other hand, General Oglethorpe successfully defended the southern frontier against Spanish attacks. Meanwhile, France became engaged in the War of the Austrian Succession on the continent of Europe, and in 1744 she joined Spain in fresh hostilities against the British. The American phase of the conflict is known as King George's War (1745-1748). The greatest of colonial military enterprises was the Massachusetts expedition that captured Louisbourg in 1745. Governor Sir William Shirley brilliantly organized this and it was commanded by a Maine fish and lumber merchant, William Pepperell, who was knighted for his success. The amphibious expedition was remarkable chiefly for unorthodox tactics derived from Indian warfare, which confused and frightened the French. But by the Treaty of Aix-la-Chapelle in 1748 the British returned Louisbourg to France in exchange for Madras in India. That the home government should barter away New England's great victory for the sake of gains in remote India infuriated the Americans, and they were only partially conciliated by England's payment to Massachusetts of the cost of the expedition. It was a meaningful lesson of the subordination of colonial to imperial interests.

The Final Struggle with the French

Before the French and Indian War began in 1754, the expansion of the frontier produced a significant change in strategy. During the first three wars, the colonists had fought defensively on the frontier and offensively at sea. Now the strategy was reversed. As the colonies breached the Appalachian walls and looked beyond into the great valley of the Ohio, they believed that their destinies drew them westward, and both sides prepared to fight for the interior of the continent as the greatest prize in the world. France sent expeditions into the Ohio country to confirm her claims and to build a string of forts which should effectively hold the English colonists east of the mountains. Since Virginia claimed a large part of the Ohio Valley, Governor Dinwiddie took the lead in the attempt to expel the French from the rich interior. In 1753, he sent George Washington, a young surveyor who had already shown singular qualities of leadership and character, to protest to the French commander on the Ohio that he had invaded English ground. This action having no effect, the Governor gave Washington a company of militia to try other means. But the French had already built Fort Duquesne at the strategic site of modern Pittsburgh, and a militia company was no match for them. At Great Meadows, Washington fired on a French force, killing the commander and twenty men. Then he hastily threw up a log stronghold, and correctly named it Fort Necessity. Trapped by superior French forces, he was forced to surrender on July 4, 1754. But he and his company had fired the first shot of a world war which ended with the practical destruction of France as a colonial power in America.

For the English colonists the issue was between expansion beyond the mountains, with all that portended for the future of the American people, or subordination to the absolutist and Catholic French monarchy they hated. English liberty and the opportunity to create a successful new society on that foundation would not be easily surrendered by Americans. A danger signal to them was the growing success of the French in winning away from the British their traditional Iroquois allies who held the key to the defenses of the middle colonies. The Board of Trade in London ordered the Governor of New York to call a conference of commissioners from all the colonies and make a treaty with the Iroquois chiefs. The result was the Albany Congress of June 1754.

Albany Congress

This Congress of delegates elected by the colonial assemblies was the first instrument of continental union in American history. Just as the regional New England Confederation had been organized in the seventeenth century to protect those colonies against external dangers, so the Albany Congress was called to protect the thirteen colonies, and defense against foreign danger continued thereafter to be a leading motive for the creation of a central government. It was Benjamin Franklin who saw most clearly the implications of the Albany Congress. When he was elected delegate of Pennsylvania, he published in his *Gazette* a warning that the French were full of confidence because the English colonies would never "agree to any speedy and effectual measures for our common defense and security." He printed a cartoon which provided a slogan later for the Revolution: a picture of a snake cut into bits with the caption, "Join or Die." At Albany, Franklin offered his famous "Plan of Union."

This would have divided political authority between a new central body and the thirteen local governments. The central body would be composed of an executive, the president-general, appointed by the Crown; and a legislature, the Grand Council of representatives chosen by the assemblies in proportion to the taxes paid by them into the general treasury. This government would have control over relations with the Indians; power to make war and peace with them and to raise armies and navies; power to regulate new settlements; and power to levy taxes, particularly customs duties. These are roughly the chief spheres of federal authority as afterwords defined, with the addition of foreign relations. Franklin was ahead of his time. The British government objected to the Plan as giving too much control to the colonists, while the colonists held that it took too much power away from their assemblies. These refused to adopt it, though it had been approved by the Congress. The Albany Congress accomplished little beyond inconclusive attempts to win over the Iroquois to the English cause and recommendations that the colonies see to their defenses.

Fighting on the Frontier

The thirteen colonies, although they were eager to defeat France in the West, fell into petty bickering over the distribution of the burdens of war. Assemblies refused to vote taxes or raise military forces unless the governors gave in on points of authority, and only four colonies contributed their full quota of militiamen. The British sent over two regiments of regulars under General James Braddock to help the colonies, and he put George Washington on his staff. In the summer of 1755, Braddock led his forces against Fort Duquesne but, through incompetence, he allowed them to be trapped and routed and was himself mortally wounded. This left the Virginia frontier exposed. Governor Dinwiddie made Washington, aged twenty-three, commander-in-chief of the Virginia militia, and he fought a disheartening war against heavy odds—but learned the art of defensive holding operations which he used to great effect in a later war.

The New York frontier was defended chiefly by William Johnson, a great landowner of the Mohawk Valley whose beautiful Georgian house and stone fort still stand. Johnson was an expert diplomatist who was able to hold enough Indians in support of the British to fend off a French invasion at Lake George in September 1755. But the French held on to Crown Point on Lake Champlain and built a powerful new strong point at Fort Ticonderoga. All along the frontier the Indians, egged on by the French, raided settlements and massacred with great daring and savagery, while fear gripped the colonies and England. This prompted revenge on the fifteen thousand French settlers of Nova Scotia (Acadia) who were expelled and scattered throughout the English colonies. Only those who reached Louisiana were able to recreate a community life, and their descendants, the "Cajuns," have retained their own language and customs to this day.

The Seven Years' War

From these beginnings in America, the war spread in 1756 throughout the world and it lasted long enough to be called the Seven Years' War. Prussia was allied with Great Britain, and France won strong allies in Austria, Russia, and Spain. In America and elsewhere, British fortunes soon ebbed. The Earl of Loudoun was appointed military commander in America, but he proved dilatory, and the French General Montcalm advanced southward to Lake George while reinforcements from Europe strengthened his rear. The British lost Calcutta in India; Frederick the Great of Prussia was defeated by the French and Austrians; and an English army was surrendered to the French by King George's son, the

Duke of Cumberland. Then in 1757 William Pitt (the elder) became head of the British ministry in circumstances and with results not dissimilar to the assumption of power by Winston Churchill in 1940.

Pitt believed that America should be the main theater of war, that if the French could be expelled from Canada and the West, British power would henceforth be securely based on a rich and expanding North American Empire. He subsidized Frederick the Great to keep the French occupied in Europe, used the navy to control the seas and cut French communications, and concentrated the military strength of Great Britain in America. He appointed General Jeffrey Amherst commander in America, with James Wolfe brigadier general under him. In 1758, with Admiral Boscawen, they captured Louisbourg. Colonel Dudley Bradstreet and a small army of New Englanders marched westward and broke French communications at the exit of the Saint Lawrence from Lake Ontario. General Forbes and Washington captured Fort Duquesne, henceforth named Pittsburgh for the Prime Minister. Even greater successes were won that same year by Clive in India and Frederick the Great in Europe. In 1759, the first British Empire reached its zenith. Victory after victory brought Britain closer to ruling the world than any power in modern times. The greatest of these victories was the capture of Quebec, on which Pitt, true to his strategy, had concentrated Britain's main offensive effort.

Victory over the French

The plan against Quebec called for co-ordination between Wolfe's forces, moving by water up the Saint Lawrence, and Amherst's forces, moving north by lakes and land. Amherst captured Crown Point and Ticonderoga but got no farther. Nevertheless, Wolfe pressed on and, after two failures in flank attacks, deployed troops above Quebec on the Plains of Abraham and won the city with one volley. He himself was killed but he knew the victory was his before he died. Montreal surrendered the next year, and the French Empire in North America was truncated. The Indian allies of the French in the West rebelled against their fate in the Conspiracy of Pontiac (1763) to no effect.

Great Britain might have gone on to further conquests, but the new King, George III, who was jealous of Pitt, dismissed him and made peace by giving up some of the fruits of victory. For a while it was even thought that Canada might be returned to France in exchange for the sugar island of Guadeloupe in the West Indies. France was allowed to give Louisiana to Spain in payment for her support, but Britain took over the Floridas, all French claims in North America east of the Mississippi, all of India, and lesser positions elsewhere—emerging as the greatest empire since ancient Rome. During these triumphant years, industrial machines increased in England to supply textiles for her expanding markets, so that British industrial supremacy came to match political supremacy.

Americans rejoiced with the mother country in outbursts of loyalty and congratulation. Well they might, because it was English power as well as colonial effort that had won for the colonists a degree of security and scope for expansion equal to their most ambitious dreams. But the problems of victorious peace are often more difficult than those of war, and King George III, after the peace treaty, threw away even more of what Pitt had won for him than he had in the treaty itself. He lost the loyalty of his American subjects by the ineptness of his statesmanship in organizing the peace.

Part II

BEGINNINGS OF THE REPUBLIC
1763-1789

CHAPTER 8

The Colonies and the Empire
1763-1774

THE DECADE AFTER THE TREATY OF 1763 WAS MARKED by a succession of controversies between the British colonies in North America and the home government, the cumulative effect of which was to create a crisis in the Empire. Reduced to simplest terms, this continuing conflict was one between local and imperial interests. Victory over the French brought Great Britain to heights of national power and prestige never before reached by a modern European country, but it also imposed on the nation unexampled responsibilities and burdens. The efforts of British statesmen to work out the problems of empire were often bungling and shortsighted. No peace-time minister showed genius at all comparable to that of William Pitt as War Minister, and the policies of the government, instead of being based on a long-range imperial plan, were largely improvised to meet immediate needs and problems. The successive ministers were very conscious of the political and financial situation in England, but were appallingly ignorant of American sentiment and attitudes.

To Americans it seemed that the triumph over the French had removed from them the chief threat to their physical security and the major external obstacle to their future development. By the same token, they felt far less dependent on the mother country than previously. To Americans, victory implied enlarged opportunity, not increased responsibility; their spirit was one of growing self-reliance and impatience with restraint. They were undisposed to share the burden of empire, and were jealous of their own political rights and liberties. Under these circumstances some conflict of interest between the home government and the outlying provinces was to be expected. The times called for farsighted statesmanship in high places and an unusual degree of tactfulness if the vast British Empire was to be preserved.

American patriots afterwards laid on the King the major blame for dissolution of the colonial empire. They were incorrect in thinking of him as another Stuart tyrant, for that he did not try to be. King George III came to the throne in 1760 as a young man determined to play a larger part in government than his Hanoverian predecessors had done. But he worked within the framework of the system which had been developed in the years since the Stuarts had been overthrown. When he became King, the Whigs, inheritors of the Glorious Revolution and champions of Parliament against the royal prerogative, had long been supreme, but they were split into factions, rallying round individual leaders in the hope of jobs. George himself played the patronage game and gathered a following called "the King's Men," becoming a powerful political leader. With this nucleus in Parliament he maneuvered to gain a majority for ministers of his own liking, and in the end he created a new party. The term "Tory" came to be applied to this, but he and his following accepted the old Whig idea of the supremacy of Parliament. What George III sought was personal control over the ministry and Parliament. His motives were not unworthy, for he entertained elevated ideals of the public good, but he made himself largely responsible for the policies which eventually cost him part of his empire.

In 1761, the ministry of William Pitt gave way to that of Lord Bute, and in 1763 the latter was succeeded by the ministry of George Grenville, who as Chancellor of the Exchequer and leader of the Commons was directly responsible for the hated Stamp Act. Beginning in July 1765 the ministry of the Marquis of Rockingham was in office less than a year. After that the Rockingham Whigs, more nearly than any other group, constituted the party of the Opposition. They objected to the personal power of the King, which was clearly established by 1770 when Lord North became First Lord of the Treasury, but it must not be supposed that the Whigs as a group supported the American patriots in their resistance to Parliament. Men like John Adams and Thomas Jefferson called themselves Whigs, and William Pitt was like them in his emphasis on the ancient liberties of Englishmen and his belief in the restraint of government by law, but he was a lonely political figure in this period. Furthermore, he valued empire far more than the American patriots did. Edmund Burke castigated British policy on many occasions, but he avoided the theoretical issue of Parliamentary supremacy and argued in terms of expediency. A few men who were regarded as extremists, like John Wilkes and Dr. Richard Price, supported American principles of liberty whole-heartedly; but the net effect of the astuteness of the King in identifying his own cause with that of Parliament was to leave American champions of human rights and self-government with only slight support in English political circles.

THE PROCLAMATION OF 1763 AND THE WESTERN QUESTION

The ineptness of the King and his ministers played a larger part in bringing on the American Revolution than any conscious attempt to destroy the liberties of the colonists. Coupled with ineptness, however, was a failure to perceive that the colonies were rapidly maturing, that their interests and ambitions could not be safely ignored, that their growing society could not be hemmed in. The Americans believed that the expulsion of the French was their victory as much as the mother country's. The West, they felt, was their prize. The powerful impulse to expand was shared alike by the newest immigrant from the Old World who was looking for cheap land, the small farmer who wanted the chance to pull up stakes and move to new land any time he felt like it, and the members of organized land companies who were looking for new domains of profit in the vast interior. An open road to the West was perhaps the most important single ingredient of the American dream.

To policy-makers in England, viewing the problems of the empire as a whole and particularly aware of immediate British interests, it seemed, however, that there was now good reason to delay the development of the country beyond the mountains. Previously, the actual occupation of outlying regions by bona-fide settlers had strengthened the hands of the British in their conflict with the French, but the threat of French rule there was now removed. The Indians, to whom promises had been made, were restive; and the fur trade offered the prospect of great profit, which British merchants might richly share. It was to the interest of fur-traders and their backers in the home country to keep the unsettled western country as a reserve for the Indians, and some regulation of the trade with them was necessary to prevent their ruthless exploitation and demoralization. In England it seemed that, for a variety of reasons, the situation called for tighter imperial control of the American West.

At the same time the colonists, who were so eager to surge westward, were increasingly unwilling to accept limitations on individual freedom and determined to maintain the largest possible local control of matters regarded by them as domestic. Certain of the colonies, notably Virginia, had strong claims to western lands based on original charters, and wanted to extend their own jurisdiction over the interior. If it was to the interest of fur-traders to leave the Indian country a wilderness, both land companies and prospective settlers wanted it opened up. Any sort of centralized control of the Indian trade was objectionable to certain irresponsible traders, as it was in general to colonial governments. In this welter of conflicting interests it would have been exceedingly difficult

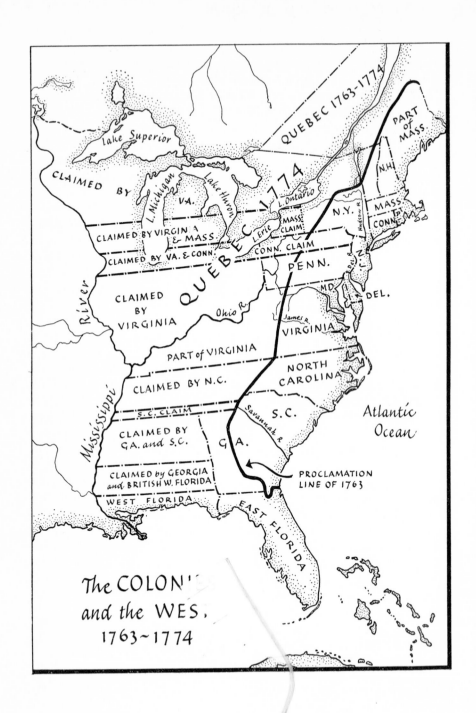

The COLON[IES]
and the WES[T]
1763~1774

under the best of circumstances to work out a generally acceptable western policy. The policy actually followed was temporizing and vacillating;
it served to alienate American opinion without bringing compensatory
benefits to the empire, the fur-traders, or the Indians.

A plan for western policy was submitted to the King in June 1763 by
the Earl of Shelburne, as President of the Board of Trade. This was
intended to be temporary and did not pretend to be comprehensive. It
drew a line along the Appalachians beyond which settlement was forbidden, but this took account of existing settlements. Before this plan was
accepted, news reached England of Pontiac's Conspiracy, which had begun
in May and clearly showed that there was a real problem of defense
against the Indians. While this dangerous revolt was still in process,
Shelburne was succeeded by the Earl of Hillsborough. His modifica-
tions of the earlier proposals were incorporated in the Proclamation of
October 7, 1763, which announced among other things the erection of
the distinct governments of Quebec, East Florida, and West Florida. This
proclamation drew a line of demarcation along the crest of the Appalachian highlands beyond which lands should not be granted; it did not allow
for existing settlements further to the westward, and it ordered the frontiersmen to withdraw. Trade with the Indians was permitted under a
license system.

The next major step in the development of British western policy was
the attempt to regulate trade with the Indians, under the Plan of 1764.
Control was placed in the hands of the Indian superintendents, Sir William
Johnson in the North and John Stuart in the South, and an elaborate
system of trading centers was set up. The complicated scheme proved
unenforceable, and it was specially resented by the governments of the
southern colonies. The policy had to be modified so as to leave trade more
under local control. Meanwhile, the land companies brought great pressure to bear on the home government and this caused the Proclamation
Line of 1763 to be moved westward, following the negotiation of treaties
with the Indians under the leadership of the superintendents. The best-
known of these was the Treaty of Fort Stanwix (1768), which left parts
of southwestern New York and northwestern Pennsylvania in Indian
hands but from Fort Pitt set the boundary at the Ohio River. This was
supplemented on the south by the Treaty of Lochaber (1770) and a survey which carried the line roughly to the Kentucky River, satisfying some
but by no means all of the ambitions of the Virginians. The period after
1768 was marked by great pressure on the home government by the
various land companies for grants or the renewal of old grants, by much
activity on their part in "buying" land from the Indians beyond treaty
lines, and by a considerable increase in settlement on the frontier. In the
colonies impinging on the West, however, it was believed that imperial
restrictions were designed to protect Indians and fur-traders and con-

stituted a hindrance to settlers. Meanwhile, there was enough vacillation in imperial policy to create a situation of uncertainty if not one of chaos.

At the end of the decade of western policy which began with the Proclamation of 1763 came the Quebec Act of 1774. Designed to reconcile the conquered French Canadians to English rule, this made concessions to them which now seem statesmanlike: religious freedom to them as Roman Catholics, and the establishment of legal and political institutions in the French tradition. But to the Protestant colonists, living under English law, these provisions smacked of "Popery" and amounted to the recognition of the rival French Catholic civilization which they had fought to hold at bay. Worse still, all the territory west of the mountains as far south as the Ohio River was annexed to Quebec. There was a clause saying that the claims of other colonies should not be prejudiced, but the Americans believed that the hated French were now privileged to expand southward into the very domain from which they had been expelled. The chief prize of victory in the war was being awarded to the losers. In the same year, 1774, new and stricter regulations for the granting of lands were announced. It was to these that Jefferson referred when he spoke in the Declaration of Independence of "raising the conditions of new appropriations of lands." By 1776, revolution seemed necessary for a number of reasons, but one of the most important of these was to regain for British Americans the fruit of the French and Indian War—the West.

The Stamp Act and the Taxation Question

The Americans, by their resistance to taxation, played a part in the defeat of the original plans of the home government for the West. The war itself had more than doubled the national debt of Great Britain, which now amounted to about £130 million; and the sudden expansion of the empire greatly increased the regular military and administrative expenses. Annual costs in America which were borne by the British government had increased several times beyond the prewar figures and stood at nearly £500,000. The American colonies were direct beneficiaries of the victory over the French. British officials and Parliament thought it was only fair that the Americans should share some of the costs, and such men as Benjamin Franklin did not object to the principle.

But Americans pointed out that they too had incurred debts connected with the war, and that their local governments were already taxing them heavily to pay these. Furthermore, American commerce paid English port duties into the British Treasury, and British businessmen profited greatly by that commerce. If the British government had cautiously avoided the appearance of seeking new sources of revenue in America, and had realized more fully on the old ones, probably nothing more than normal grumbling would have resulted. But Americans were eager to seize any opportunity to call revenue measures "unconstitutional," and when the British government gave them one, the natural dislike of taxes gave force to outcries against infringements of colonial rights.

Enforcement of the Trade Laws

George Grenville, Chancellor of the Exchequer, decided that the laws which were originally devised in the spirit of mercantilism to regulate colonial trade should be extended so as to produce revenue. The customs service in America cost more than the duties the officials collected. In mercantilist theory this was not illogical, because the purpose of the laws was to prevent foreign commodities from entering the colonies. In line with this purpose, the tax that American distillers were supposed to pay on molasses imported from non-British sources was prohibitory. Everyone knew that the law of 1733 did not actually prevent the importation of foreign molasses, great quantities of which were smuggled into the colonies. Toward the end of the French and Indian War the British government made vigorous efforts to enforce the law and provoked a controversy over writs of assistance. These were general warrants issued by courts to enforcement officers, permitting them to invade premises and make arrests without the traditional warrant specifying the premises, the persons, and the reasons. James Otis, an eloquent Boston lawyer, opposed writs of assistance so vehemently in the courts that John Adams described him as a "flame of fire." Facing the realities of colonial evasion and opposition, Grenville now concluded that if the tax were reduced from 6d. to 3d. per gallon and the efficiency of the customs service were increased at the same time, the molasses trade could be brought into legal channels and made to pay a revenue into the Treasury.

This meant that Britain would abandon the mercantilist purpose of the original tax on molasses and substitute a tax for revenue such as had never before been applied to any important item of colonial commerce. Grenville was incautious enough to admit his purpose in the Act, generally called the Sugar Act, which he put through Parliament in 1764. The preamble stated that new regulations should be established "for improving the revenue of this Kingdom." The law cut in half the duty on molasses and placed additional duties on luxuries such as sugar, wine, coffee, and silk. It was believed that the lower duty on molasses would not discourage distillers of rum from importing it, while higher duties on articles of consumption would not prevent the wealthier classes from buying foreign luxuries. The latter reasoning also lay behind a provision of the law that the drawbacks, or refunds, of duties paid on European articles re-exported from England to the colonies, should stop. The law provided new methods of enforcement to stop smuggling. Not only were customs officers required to stay at their posts, but jurisdiction over smuggling cases was given to the Admiralty Courts. The Admiralty Courts had been established to hear only cases involving maritime affairs, outside the boundaries of any particular colony. To give these courts jurisdiction over customs cases seemed to be an invasion of the colonies' traditional right to reserve local affairs to the jurisdiction of their local courts. Their own courts used juries; the Admiralty Courts did not.

Thus the Americans could find several grounds for the claim that the Revenue Act of 1764 was "unconstitutional," that is, contrary to the former practice. The most important of these was that it asserted the power of the British government to impose "taxation without representation" insofar as this was a revenue act rather than merely one in regulation of commerce. Protests were widespread, but Grenville ignored the outcry he had caused and proceeded to violate colonial rights more grievously.

Failure of the Stamp Tax

This violation was by means of the Stamp Act of 1765. The notorious measure provided that revenue stamps must be bought at prices from a half penny to a pound and affixed to all public or semipublic papers, including bonds, notes, legal documents, newspapers, pamphlets, advertisements, and so forth. This was an "internal" tax, since it drew revenue from transactions taking place entirely inside the colonies rather than transactions across their boundaries, such as trade. Cases involving violations of the Act were also placed under the jurisdiction of the Admiralty Courts, although Americans were appointed as agents to administer the law. The revenue thus raised was to be spent in the colonies to pay for their defenses. Formerly the British government had tapped "internal" sources of revenue in the colonies by laying requisitions on the colonial governments and had left to their assemblies the decision how these should be raised—or, indeed, whether they should be paid at all. Often the assemblies had failed to meet requisitions, and the Stamp Act was designed to bypass these legislative bodies and reach directly into the pockets of the colonists.

Probably no law in American history produced such violent opposition as the Stamp Act. The law bore hardest on those people who were most able to make their opposition known and felt: lawyers and journalists. Businessmen everywhere were faced with the prospect of paying a fee on every operation of theirs that involved papers. A wave of resentment united the colonists as never before. Clergymen took up the cause and sounded blasts against the law from their pulpits. Legislatures and town meetings adopted blistering resolutions. Soon action superseded words and mobs took vengeance on British officials. Merchants formed nonimportation associations committed to a boycott of British goods. Bands of "Sons of Liberty" were formed to prevent enforcement of the Stamp Act.

Patrick Henry in Virginia and Samuel Adams in Massachusetts took the lead in stirring up opposition by means of inflammatory oratory and other forms of agitation.

Trade with Great Britain fell to a fraction and the colonists refused to pay their debts to creditors in England. The Massachusetts Assembly called a congress in New York to organize opposition on a continental scale and delegates from nine colonies met in October 1765. This was the first organization initiated by the colonists themselves to unite the country. The Stamp Act Congress adopted resolutions denouncing the law as an unprecedented and unconstitutional invasion of the rights and liberties of the colonists. Some leaders proposed the more radical doctrine that their "natural rights" were violated. They saw that the ambiguous nature of the British constitution made it possible to answer their legal argument by pointing out that Parliament was itself the court of last authority on the limits of its powers, that the Stamp Act itself became a valid precedent and part of the British constitution by virtue of its enactment. The doctrine of natural rights appealed to an authority presumed to be higher than any man-made law *or* constitution, namely, the law of nature. According to philosophers such as John Locke, natural rights, including the right of self-government, were inherent and inalienable. But few colonists were ready as yet to appeal to a doctrine containing implications beyond the immediate issue. They clung to the argument that the British constitution had been violated. They were not represented in Parliament, therefore that body had no right to impose an internal tax on them.

To this, British officials answered that the colonists were *virtually* represented in Parliament. They meant that every British *interest* was represented there, even though every geographic district in England or the colonies was not. Many of the new industrial districts of England, such as Manchester and Birmingham, were not directly represented in Parliament until the Reform Act of 1832. Instead, many "rotten boroughs" with little or no population were entitled to seats, and these were controlled by single individuals or handfuls of great landowners. But the Americans had become accustomed to a system of representation based on geographic districts rather than interests, and the corrupt English system of the day seemed a poor substitute for it. They rejected the doctrine of virtual representation. At the same time, they knew that if the colonies were given seats in Parliament their few representatives would be easily outvoted. Hence they made no serious demand for representation in the English legislature, demanding instead that sole jurisdiction over internal taxation be returned to their own assemblies.

More effective than American arguments was the American boycott of English business. In a curious way the doctrine of virtual representation was shown to have some validity, because English businessmen insisted that Parliament repeal the Stamp Act before they were ruined by the colonists' boycott. William Pitt denied that Parliament had the right to take the money of the Americans "out of their pockets without their consent," but he believed that Parliament had absolute authority over colonial trade and manufactures. If, he said, the colonists violated a law against manufacturing, Britain should send men-of-war to bombard their cities. Benjamin Franklin, who was serving in England as the agent of several colonial assemblies, testified with great effectiveness before the House of Commons, urging repeal of the Stamp Act on grounds of common sense, and his published testimony attracted wide attention.

The Grenville ministry was dismissed in July 1765, though not because of American affairs. A ministry under Lord Rockingham, which Pitt refused to join, succeeded; and this remained in office until June 1766. In March of that year Parliament passed the Declaratory Act, in which it asserted its authority over the colonies "in all cases whatsoever," and then repealed the Stamp Act, which was manifestly unenforceable and to which British merchants had strongly objected. The Declaratory Act passed the Commons without a division and the Lords with virtually no opposition, showing that opinion in regard to the *right* to tax was practically unanimous in Parliament. On the other hand, the repeal of the Stamp Act, on grounds of expediency, was debated bitterly. The phrase "in all cases whatsoever," in the Declaratory Act, was a pointed repetition of the terms of the Act of 1719 in which Parliament had made Ireland totally subservient to it, but most Americans ignored the ominous language. They celebrated the repeal of the Stamp Act with balls, toasts, and fireworks. Gratitude inspired protests of loyalty to King and Parliament, "the Guardians of the English Nation." The Virginia House of Burgesses carefully entered in its journal a statement of colonial rights in flat contradiction of the Declaratory Act, and then allowed matters to "remain in status quo."

THE TOWNSHEND ACTS

Matters might have remained there but for several circumstances. The problem of raising revenue remained. The Stamp Act had only caused further drain on the British Treasury to pay for the unused stamps and useless administrative expenses. King George turned to William Pitt, called the "Great Commoner" but now raised in rank to Earl of Chatham, to head a government which should unite the King's Men and the old Whigs. Chatham was more sympathetic to the American defense of ancient English liberties than any other Parliamentary leader, but he was ill and anxious to avoid responsibility. The showy new Chancellor of the Exchequer, Charles Townshend, assumed the effective leadership. He was no friend of American rights. He devised a scheme to reduce the taxes on English landowners, reduce the costs of military defenses in the colonies, and raise new revenues from colonial trade. These measures, he hoped, would end the deficit.

The scheme was clever. Townshend had no respect for the argument that internal taxes were unconstitutional, but he tried to get around that issue by laying import duties on the colonists' purchases of English paint, lead, paper, and tea. Such duties might masquerade as "external taxes," but when the colonists admitted Parliament's right to impose external taxes they meant taxes to regulate trade rather than to raise revenue. John Dickinson of Pennsylvania pointed out this important distinction in his influential *Letters of a Pennsylvania Farmer* (1768). The Townshend duties, he declared, were of the revenue sort and beyond the power of Parliament. Townshend's scheme also aimed to reduce the power of the colonial legislatures by paying the salaries of governors, administrative officials, and judges out of the money collected under the new import duties. Writs of assistance were provided for, and new Vice-Admiralty Courts were set up to help enforce payment of the duties. These measures were regarded in the colonies as encroachments on American rights and liberties, and as a clear sign that the home government was determined to subordinate these to imperial control.

The Townshend Acts threw the colonies again into turmoil. The English government suspended the New York Assembly when it refused to comply with all the requirements of a law which quartered English soldiers in the homes of colonists when public quarters were not available. The General Court of Massachusetts sent a letter to the other legislatures protesting against the Townshend Acts. When it refused to withdraw the letter it was dissolved, as were the Virginia and New York legislatures for receiving the letter. These high-handed actions by the English government showed that the narrow issue of taxation involved the much greater issue of colonial self-government.

Merchants once more turned to a boycott of English imports. It became a patriotic thing to establish colonial manufactures of textiles and paper, and tea drinking was foresworn. Customs officers were mobbed, and when disorder reached a certain stage in Boston, two regiments of red-coated British regulars were quartered on the town. The citizenry resented their presence and on the night of March 5, 1770, bloodshed resulted. Bystanders watching a detachment of troops passing through the streets tossed a few snowballs, along with insults, and the troops, who were getting tired of abuse, were ordered to fire and killed four citizens. This was the "Boston Massacre." It was seized upon by agitators like Samuel Adams who raised a fearful clamor and indulged in vast exaggeration. The trial of the soldiers, at which John Adams bravely appeared for the defense, resulted in the acquittal of all except two, who were branded on the hand, but the regiments were removed to Castle William in Boston harbor to prevent further trouble.. Lesser incidents occurred in other colonial towns. The opposition to the Townshend Acts, however, was not as widespread as opposition to the Stamp Act, and it made much less impression on British merchants.

The Chatham ministry gave way to that of the Duke of Grafton (1768-1770), and then Lord North became head of the government in 1770. He yielded to colonial opposition because he believed that duties on English imports into the colonies only defeated the imperial interest in building up such trade. He repealed all the Townshend duties except the one on tea. The tax of 3d. per pound on tea was retained in order to maintain the principle of Parliament's authority to legislate for the colonies "in all cases whatsoever." Once more the government conceded the substance of colonial demands while denying the principle on which they rested. Conservative-minded Americans were inclined to accept Lord North's concessions as a victory and ignore the theoretical issue. A few years of quiet followed. Customs duties were collected efficiently and smuggling virtually stopped. In spite of this, prosperity increased. Men like Benjamin Franklin were satisfied.

A more radical group of American leaders were unwilling to accept peace on these terms. To them the vital issues were the preservation of the historic rights, privileges, and immunities of Englishmen which had been promised them in their first charters, and the maintenance of at least the degree of political self-government they had already attained. As Thomas Jefferson, one of the younger patriots, saw it, an admission by the Americans that they held their political existence at the will of Parliament would be a surrender of common sense. He and other bold thinkers were approaching a position which was irreconcilable with views of the British constitution generally held in England. Lord North said the language of America was this: "We are subjects of the King; with Parliament we have nothing to do." Even as a Tory he could accept no such doctrine, and the Whigs as a group could not, because of their historic emphasis on the authority of Parliament even over the King. Many Americans were willing to dodge the question of ultimate authority, but to more radical leaders it seemed a betrayal of liberty to accept substantial concessions from Parliament and ignore what they regarded as violations of principle. They saw grave danger of the eventual loss of personal freedom and self-government if the colonists were lulled to complacency.

Committees of Correspondence

Such radicals as Samuel Adams and Dr. Joseph Warren of Boston and Patrick Henry of Virginia worked hard to overcome the complacency of Americans during the three years of calm that followed Lord North's concessions. In this period was created a form of organization which later became a prime instrument of revolution in America, France, and elsewhere. The "committees of correspondence," were more or less clandestine bodies which met regularly and organized propaganda and other activities. Unity of mind, swiftness of communication, and consistent work to arouse and lead the populace were their objectives. Town committees were started in Massachusetts, and provincial committees were afterward set up in Virginia and elsewhere. By 1773, the leaders had created a continental organization with local branches in all the colonies. Governors could not destroy these by dissolving the colonial legislatures.

The committees would not allow Americans to forget their grievances. Documents setting forth colonial claims were widely circulated, and evidence of British designs for the future was exaggerated into condemnations of the present course of British officials. For example, private letters from Governor Hutchinson of Massachusetts to friends in England were obtained by Benjamin Franklin and made public by the committees. In one of these Hutchinson had written that English liberties must be diminished in Massachusetts if the Empire was to be preserved. For this, the General Court voted Hutchinson's impeachment. Franklin, although he had not supported the American radicals, was publicly excoriated in the House of Commons for his part in the affair and was called "a Skunk, or American Pole Cat." It is said that the wise and witty Doctor did not again put on the suit of clothes he wore on that day until the day in 1782 when he signed the treaty in which Great Britain acknowledged American independence. Even religious groups, especially the Congregationalists and Presbyterians, were organizing committees of correspondence to unite the colonists against the Church of England and the proposed creation of an American bishopric. The Americans had become highly sensitive to even the smallest threats to their liberties. The English themselves were noted the world over for their stiff-necked jealousy of their rights. In this respect the colonists had now become more English than the English.

THE BOSTON TEA PARTY

The East India Company held the monopoly of English trade with the Orient, and the officials of the company acted as Crown agents to govern India. By and large they were a corrupt and brutal group who plundered the people of India and the company alike. In 1773, the company was close to bankruptcy, while mismanagement had left millions of pounds of tea and other goods to spoil in its warehouses. A disaster to it would injure its English shareholders and the Bank of England, cause a loss of revenues to the English Treasury, and endanger Britain's rule in India. The company's directors feared that the government would seize the occasion to strip it of its authority in India. The American colonists

were themselves partly to blame for the company's plight because they
had cut down their consumption of taxed tea, but they felt that the
validity of their own charters would be injured if the company's charter
were violated, therefore they supported it against the government. Lord
North made no attempt to violate its charter, but his program of aid resulted in an affront to the Americans more severe than if he had wiped
out the company. He thought the Americans could be bribed into drinking the tea of the East India Company if its price were lowered more
than enough to compensate for the duty of 3*d.* per pound. He was warned
that Americans treasured principle more than they liked cheap tea, but
he would not believe it.

The Tea Act of 1773 was therefore intended to bail the East India
Company out of some of its difficulties. The company was granted permission to sell tea directly to American consumers without regard for
the old Navigation Act which had required it to be sold to English
dealers, who had sold it in turn to American merchants. The company
was given a monopoly over the tea trade in America. No American
merchant was allowed to deal in the article and no American tea-drinker
could buy it from any other source. The savings which the company
could effect by eliminating the profits of middlemen allowed it to offer
its tea to consumers at a lower price, even after the duty was paid, than
that of any smuggled tea. It was a neat scheme to make Americans swal-
low their principles with their drink.

The granting of monopoly rights to private interests in one part of
the Empire over consumers in another part was not unprecedented, but
such a monopoly had never been given to a single person or company
by the English government, although this was the common practice
of the French and Spanish governments. The English were now trying
to play economic favorites in the Continental style. It seemed to Americans that if their wants as consumers could be exploited by Britain
in favor of a monopolistic system, their position as freemen would be
deeply undermined. The Tea Act of 1773 directly affected both smugglers
and legitimate merchants and threw them both on the side of the radicals
and the committees of correspondence. In Boston smuggling was prevented by the presence of a naval squadron, but the ports of New York
and Philadelphia were still fairly open. The first outcries against the Tea
Act were raised in the latter two cities, led by the smugglers. But merchants in all lines quickly followed suit as they saw the menace of
monopoly to all trade.

Company tea was shipped into the colonies in huge quantities. Those
willing to taste it found that the leaves were rotten from storage. The
East India Company was accused of planning to take over monopolistic
control of all American business and make itself ruler of the land. But,
"Thank God," John Dickinson said, "we are not sepoys, nor Marattas,

but British subjects." He urged night watchmen to call out, as they made their rounds, "Beware of the East India Company!" Everywhere drinkers of tea were warned that it would ruin their health, destroy American prosperity, and wipe out American liberty. One warning stated: "Do not suffer yourself to sip the accursed, dutied stuff. For if you do, the devil will immediately enter into you, and you will instantly become a traitor to your country."

The colonists feared that feminine love of tea would make Lord North's diabolical scheme a success. Englishmen congratulated themselves that they had found in the colonial women a weakness easy to exploit. It was said that even the New Englanders could not boycott the tea because, for all their noise against Britain, they were a henpecked lot at home. But American women gave up the brew, turning to coffee and unpalatable but untaxed substitutes. To make sure that the boycott would be effective, the Sons of Liberty busied themselves tracing every sale of tea and rallying public pressure against the purchasers. The boycott was soon so complete that in most of the colonies agents of the company resigned their jobs, the governors refused to support the company, and ships loaded with tea returned to England. But in Boston the situation was exceptional in several respects. The Sons of Liberty were strong and well-organized, while Governor Hutchinson was determined to stand fast against the opponents of the Act. The agents of the company refused to resign and received the protection of the Governor in Castle William. Three tea ships lay in the harbor under the protection of British war-ships. Citizens met at Faneuil Hall and petitioned the Governor to allow these to return to England. Later, on that same night of December 16, 1773, three bands of fifty men each, disguised as "Mohawks," went aboard the ships and dumped the tea into the harbor.

The identity of the men was kept secret, although evidence suggests that Samuel Adams and John Hancock were among them, and the rank and file were doubtless recruited from among the Sons of Liberty. The Boston Tea Party gave the signal for similar parties in other ports during the following year. Nothing could be done to prevent this violence be-cause the populace was too strongly in favor of it. The disappearance of tea from the American market was complete. It did not reappear until after the Revolution, and by that time Americans had developed a taste for coffee as their favorite beverage which they have never lost. The radicals justified the violence, under the "great law of nature and reason" that every society has a right to defend itself from ruin and tyranny with-out regard to statutes.

The British view was different. All England was excited. It was evi-dent that the colonial governors had lost control of the situation, and legal action against participants in "tea parties" seemed futile because American juries would be composed of patriots. "Hypocritical bandits" was one of the kinder descriptions of the colonials in the English press. Lord North was confused. Who could have foreseen that the Americans would oppose so violently the sale of tea at cheap prices? Even the Earl of Chatham said the Boston Tea Party was "certainly criminal." Sentiment was general that, since individuals could not be punished, the colonies as a whole must be. Lord North said that the quarrel was no longer about taxation; the question was whether the mother country had any authority whatever over the "haughty American republicans." He did not give in to demands that Boston, that nest of "puritanical rebels," should be taught a lesson by the hanging of a hundred of its inhabitants, but he decided on a policy of punishment that had precisely the opposite effects from those he intended.

King George III supported Lord North, saying they must "master" the Americans. Thus by 1774 the British attempt to reorganize the Empire developed into a contest of wills between the colonists and the home government. No responsible Americans yet spoke of independence as a desirable outcome of this struggle. But they had seen in specific issues a threat to all their liberties and the British government had made claims, chiefly in the Declaratory Act, which were subversive of colonial liberty in all spheres. The colonists had opposed particular acts of the British government with a violence which seemed to Englishmen excessive, but which was in fact proportionate to the sweeping claim of the British government to authority over the colonies "in all cases whatsoever."

CHAPTER 9

Towards American Independence, 1774-1776

GOVERNMENTS ARE OFTEN CONFRONTED BY THE NECESSITY of choosing between dread alternatives: they must either press their official authority to an ultimate test, thereby risking failure, or compromise theoretical authority for the sake of immediate peace and order, thereby risking ultimate loss of authority. Between 1763 and 1773, the British government wavered between the two poles of the dilemma. It compromised on immediate issues by repealing the Stamp Act and most of the duties imposed by the Townshend Acts. On the other hand, it made broad and provocative assertions of theoretical authority and refused to yield on the specific issues of writs of assistance and the tax on tea. After the Boston Tea Party, the government turned to the policy of making an ultimate test of its claims to authority over the colonies. This fateful decision made impossible the solution of the problem of imperial control by adjustment, mutual accommodation, and compromise. It gave the Americans no third choice between subordination and independence.

THE COERCIVE ACTS

Lord North's decision to punish Boston for the sins of the "Mohawks" was based on a fatal misjudgment. He thought that by singling out Boston he could divide the colonies. He believed that if Boston was forbidden to function as the trade center of New England, merchants of other ports, eagerly snatching the opportunity to steal her markets, would refuse to support the little city in her struggle with the home government. Ignorance of the temper of the patriots from Maine to Georgia, and cynicism regarding their motives and their ability to see beyond immediate interests, could not have been more complete. Instead of giving accurate information, the governors and other royal officials appear to have told the British authorities what they wanted to hear.

Lord North introduced in Parliament in March 1774 the Boston Port Bill. It required the city to pay the East India Company for the tea that the "Indians" had destroyed, and also the customs duty on it. Until the citizens paid these costs British men-of-war would close the port to all shipping. The bill passed Parliament without difficulty, the members evidently accepting North's assurances that Boston would be isolated and quickly repent.

News of the Port Act, which was to go into effect June 1, reached Boston early in May, and the Committee of Correspondence went into prompt action. In preparation for such an emergency, a system of rapid communication with committees in other towns had been established. Paul Revere rode express to New York and Philadelphia with appeals for aid, and other riders fanned out into the interior and down along the seaboard. The gist of the appeal was that Boston must be supported by all the colonies, else the British government, successful in this place, would bring to heel one by one the other ports that had offended the East India Company, and soon the liberties of all could be destroyed with ease.

The argument was convincing to patriots everywhere. George Washington asked whether Americans should "supinely sit and see one province after another fall prey to despotism?" Sympathy for Boston was specially pronounced in Virginia. Late in May the House of Burgesses passed resolutions, "cooked up" by a little group of fervid patriots that included Patrick Henry and Thomas Jefferson. These called for a day of fasting and prayer on the day that the Port Bill was to become effective. The royal Governor, Lord Dunmore, dissolved the House of Burgesses as a result, but on June 1 a group of the "late" burgesses, including Washington, marched solemnly to Bruton Church in Williamsburg and heard a proper sermon. Elsewhere in the colonies on that day shops were closed by merchants, flags were hung at half-mast, and copies of the law were burned. Far from increasing divisions among the colonies, the strong exercise of British authority encouraged them to forget former suspicions of Puritan cant and city mobs and to regard the Bostonians as martyrs on the altar of liberty. The Virginia resolutions spoke of "our sister colony of Massachusetts Bay."

Among the patriots, however, there were differences of opinion about the precise steps to be taken in the effort to secure a redress of grievances. Samuel Adams and the Boston Committee, representing chiefly the artisan class rather than merchants, asked that an absolute boycott be imposed against all British trade (exports as well as imports) by all the colonies. Merchants elsewhere, especially in Philadelphia and New York, feared that such an extreme measure would ruin them; and in the South, there was doubt about the wisdom of forbidding exports—on which the prosperity of the planters depended and which were the only means whereby they could pay their honest English debts. Hence the suggestion, made in several quarters, that a general congress of colonial representatives be called for purposes of consultation and joint action met the favor of conservatives and came to be accepted by patriots everywhere. The Bostonians pointed out that such a body might obtain repeal of the Port Act too late to save them from starvation. The other colonists thereupon donated food in such quantity that the residents of the blockaded city were reported to be "as sleek and round as robins." During the summer plans went forward for a congress, which at the suggestion of Massachusetts was to be held in Philadelphia. Meanwhile, the British government by further extreme action played into the hands of the radicals.

Lord North made another error of judgment. He decided that he could divide the radicals of Boston from the conservatives by further coercion. He would do this by reorganizing the government of the province so as to place power in the hands of "respectable characters" who, he felt sure, would rally loyally to the support of Great Britain. He put three laws through Parliament in May 1774. The Massachusetts Government Act provided that members of the upper branch of the legislature should no longer be elected by the lower house but be appointed by the king; that the royal governor should appoint and could remove all judges of the lower courts; and that town meetings could be called only at the pleasure of the governor. The Administration of Justice Act provided that soldiers and officials accused of abuses could be tried in England or other colonies rather than in Massachusetts. The Quartering Act provided that troops should be quartered in the homes of citizens whenever public order required their presence in a particular area. These laws, together with the Boston Port Act, were what the colonists called the "Coercive" or "Intolerable" Acts.

The Massachusetts Government Act was resented most bitterly of all because it showed that the British government was willing to take legislative authority away from the people and place it in the hands of the king. Far from weakening the radicals, the new laws strengthened them. Many conservatives who had belittled charges directed against British intentions now concluded that the government would not hesitate to destroy American liberty utterly. Strongly supported by public sentiment, the Boston Committee of Correspondence took over the leadership of the populace. Outside Boston, British authority ceased to exist and committees of correspondence and town meetings ruled Massachusetts. Mobs of farmers outdid the Boston Sons of Liberty in violence against Crown officials. The latter found it best to give up exercise of their offices and flee to the protection of the troops in Boston. In all the colonies, the worst predictions of the radicals seemed about to come true and the ranks of the patriots swelled as fear and loathing of British tyranny mounted.

The Quebec Act, to which we have already referred in connection with the land question, was not a punitive measure inspired by the Boston Tea Party, but it was tossed into the colonial caldron in June. It was regarded as proof of a plan to raise up forces of French Popery against English Protestantism and to turn over the continent to them. The favors offered to the French Canadians in that law contrasted ominously with the injuries visited on the English colonists and infuriated the latter. In fact an argument used in England in favor of the Quebec Act was precisely that it would check the "fierce fanatic spirits in the Protestant colonies." This threat against all thirteen of the colonies roused frontiersmen and farmers to support the radicals of the seaport towns and cities. The laws of May and June 1774, which became known before the Continental Congress assembled in the autumn, greatly increased the likelihood that that body would be captured by the advocates of resistance, not conciliation.

THE FIRST CONTINENTAL CONGRESS

The body of somewhat more than fifty men, representing all the continental colonies except remote Georgia, who met in Carpenters' Hall, Philadelphia, during the months of September and October 1774, is remembered as the first American Congress in a long and continuing series. It was a convention of patriots which assumed the right to speak for the colonies as a whole. Occasionally, in later months, a former member of this historic body slipped over the line into the group designated as Tories or Loyalists; but, if John Adams can be believed, Tories were despised by this gathering "like spiders, toads, and snakes." The delegates had been chosen by the legislatures in some instances, and by revolutionary or at least extralegal bodies in others—but in nearly all cases the processes of selection were orderly. In Virginia, for example, the delegates were elected by a provincial convention, which had been called by former members of the dissolved assembly and amounted to another House of Burgesses. There was less regularity in some other places, notably in New York where sentiment was specially confused, but as a rule the patriots gained control of existing political machinery where they could, and when blocked by royal officials they created new machinery of the sort they were accustomed to. Meanwhile, committees of correspondence operated with great effectiveness behind if not on the scene. The colonists were realizing on their long training in self-government.

The Earl of Chatham called this Congress "the most honorable Assembly of statesmen since those of the ancient Greeks and Romans." Various shades of opinion were represented among the members—the term "radical" being commonly applied by writers to those who most strongly favored resistance, and "conservative" to those most hopeful of conciliation. From the heated scene of Boston came Samuel Adams, who was unsurpassed in "popular intrigue" but whose single-minded devotion to the cause of colonial rights was unmarred by considerations of personal gain or glory. From the same colony came his distant kinsman John Adams, a stocky and forthright man who was such a pillar of strength in the next few years that he was described as "Atlas" and "Colossus." He himself thought the delegates from Virginia the most spirited and consistent of any that were present. Those who had most to say in public were Patrick Henry and Richard Henry Lee, sometimes described as the American Demosthenes and Cicero, both of whom were radical. Peyton Randolph, a large and genial man from their province, presided over this body with dignity and firmness, as he did over the House of Burgesses at home. Although modest George Washington was no speechmaker, he gained everybody's confidence, and if he was not one to favor reckless measures, few men perceived the essence of this conflict so clearly.

Though Christopher Gadsden, an aristocrat of South Carolina, had a record of opposition to British policy that was not unworthy of comparison to Samuel Adams's, the attitude of the other Southern delegations was less certain than that of Virginia. The rest of the New Englanders were expected to support Massachusetts, while the deputies from the Middle Colonies comprised the most doubtful group of all. John Jay of New York, a bright young lawyer and an excellent speaker, was a man of conservative temper, and it was in his province that opinion was most divided. Benjamin Franklin had not yet returned from Europe to Pennsylvania, and John Dickinson from that colony was regarded as a moderate, while Joseph Galloway, speaker of the Pennsylvania House of Representatives, was probably the outstanding conservative in the Congress. Charles Thomson, reputed to be "the Sam Adams of Philadelphia," was elected secretary, much to Galloway's chagrin, and became the permanent holder of that office. Some of the differences of opinion among these leaders persisted, but in 1774, facing a common external danger, they succeeded in maintaining a high degree of unity, which was a notable achievement in itself. The Massachusetts men worked quietly in private while Southerners took the lead in public. The early actions of the Continental Congress followed the logic of events that were skillfully exploited, and a policy of resistance was agreed to before the more conciliatory members could effectively object.

Resistance but Not Rebellion

The delegates had little more than opened their sessions and decided that each colony should have an equal vote, when they were disturbed by reports that British General Gage was bombarding and burning Boston. These rumors were proved false but they created great sympathy, along with fear and indignation. Meanwhile, the proscribed town meetings of Massachusetts had organized the Suffolk County Convention, and the strong "Resolves" of this extralegal but representative body were brought speedily to Philadelphia by Paul Revere. These called for the making of military plans against possible British forays from Boston, and for the imprisonment of every official of "the present tyrannical and unconstitutional government" if any patriot leader should be seized. More to the point, however, were the resolution that the Coercive Acts should not be obeyed, the proposal that trade relations with Great Britain should be severed, and the announced determination to act only on the defensive.

Less than two weeks after the Congress held its first session, the delegates adopted by unanimous vote a resolution approving the action of their countrymen of the Massachusetts-Bay, and they published this along with the Suffolk Resolves. John Adams described the day of that vote (September 17) as the happiest of his life, and he was now convinced that America would support Massachusetts or perish with her. The die was cast for resistance to British policy, and Boston was assured that she would not stand alone so long as her conduct remained defensive. Also, Congress soon went on record as favoring the suspension of commercial intercourse. The agreement not to import or consume British goods was unanimous, and nonexportation was approved in principle before the end of the month, though there was sharp conflict on this latter question and it was not finally settled until the famous "Association" was adopted toward the close of the session (October 20, 1774).

In the meantime, while committees were busily at work on statements of colonial rights and the infringement of them, conservative Joseph Galloway introduced (September 28) a "Plan of Union" between Great Britain and the colonies which would have patched things up much too tightly for the radicals. This called for a President General to be appointed by the King, and a Grand Council to be chosen by the various colonial legislatures, which, as an inferior and distinct branch of the British legislature, was to govern the colonies in conjunction with the latter. The assent of both this continental colonial body and Parliament would be necessary to give validity to laws. According to the Plan, local and internal affairs would be left to the existing colonial governments, but it sounded like a scheme of consolidation, not a guarantee of ancient liberties. Furthermore, an important purpose of Galloway was that the Congress, after adopting his Plan of Union, should avoid provocation of the mother country while negotiating with her about it. That is, he would decline to share in resistance to the Coercive Acts.

Galloway himself believed that his Plan was favored by all the most loyal and the wealthiest Americans, and that it was opposed by "Congregational and Presbyterian republicans," bankrupts, and hopeless debtors to British merchants. He connected the radicalism of the New Englanders and the Scotch-Irish frontiersmen with their religious doctrines, and attributed that of the Southern planters to their debts. Like most simple ascriptions of motive, this represented a distorted view. Yet Galloway was not far from wrong about the groups that were most opposed to his proposals, and it is to his credit that he himself recognized the need for unity and allowed debate of his Plan to be postponed. Actually it failed little of adoption when it came up later, but ultimately the radicals caused it to be repudiated wholly and expunged from the records.

Thus the control that the advocates of resistance had gained at the beginning was reasserted and maintained. Moderate counsels prevailed, however, when Congress came to a statement of aims and grievances. It seemed wise strategy to object only to British actions since 1763 and to urge a return to the relatively mild system of mercantilism that was in operation before that date. By this time some outstanding patriots— including James Wilson of Pennsylvania, Thomas Jefferson, and John Adams—had taken the position in their writings that Parliament had no authority whatever over the colonies and that the tie with the mother country was only in the person of the King. While admitting that the colonists had acquiesced in the control of commercial matters by Parliament, they denied both the historical justification and practical need for it. The status they sought was closely akin to that of a member of the (British) Commonwealth of Nations today, but such a solution of the imperial problem would have been opposed in England by those who feared the growing personal power of the King. The Congress did not take this position regarding the nature of the Empire for important practical reasons. The Earl of Chatham had warned the Americans that they could expect no support from Whigs if they did not admit the authority of Parliament to regulate imperial affairs, including external commerce. So long as the patriots continued to hope for redress of grievances, it was the part of wisdom to maintain harmony with the English political leaders who might influence the government to repeal offensive measures.

In the dignified Declaration they adopted on October 14, the delegates acknowledged the practical necessity of Parliamentary acts in regulation of external commerce and announced their "cheerful consent" to the operation of these. At the same time they solemnly asserted their rights—based on "the immutable laws of nature, the principles of the English constitution, and the several charters or compacts"—and specified the infringments on these in acts of Parliament since 1763. They could not submit to these acts, they said, and, pending a revision of them and a restoration of the former state of happiness and prosperity, they were resolved to enter into a nonimportation, nonconsumption, and nonexportation agreement. This they did in the "Continental Association," which they adopted the following week. The agreement with respect to exports was not to become effective for almost a year, and a concession had to be made in the case of rice, but this was a long step toward an absolute boycott of British trade and the establishment of colonial union. The mood of self-sacrifice found further expression in the resolution to discourage horse racing, gambling, cockfighting, shows, and all forms of expensive entertainment. Enforcement of the measures was not left to merchants, but to local committees authorized by the Congress. As events soon showed, these were dominated by radicals and were exceedingly effective. Congress had forged a strong weapon of defense and retaliation.

It did not close the door to conciliation, however, for this body also addressed a petition to the King. In this the delegates assured their "Most Gracious Sovereign" of the loyalty of the colonists, blamed "designing and dangerous men" in the British government for colonial oppression, and begged him to check those men and thus restore harmony in the Empire. The adoption of the petition to the King was a victory for the moderate and conservative patriots, and it gave George III an excellent opportunity to draw them away from the radicals by concessions. But the stubborn monarch had already decided on a policy of rule or ruin. In September he had said that "the colonies must either submit or triumph," that "there must always be one tax to keep up the right," and that as such he approved of the tea duty. By November he had declared that the New England governments were now in a state of rebellion, and that blows must decide whether they were subject to England or independent. If the radicals consented to petition the King solely as a tactical maneuver to demonstrate that reconciliation was impossible, nothing could have suited their purpose better than the King's decision to concede nothing and decide the issue by arms. King George III himself made American independence the only alternative to complete submission.

Critics and opponents of the ministry in Parliament would not support the patriots' contention that the Declaratory Act was unconstitutional, but Lord Chatham proposed that the British troops be removed and that the government should return to the old system of obtaining revenues for imperial expenses by requisitioning the colonies and leaving it to their legislatures to decide how the money should be raised. Edmund Burke went further. He asked for repeal of the Coercive Acts and denial of the jurisdiction of the Admiralty Courts over "internal" cases. These proposals were supported by only a minority in Parliament, but Lord North decided that before the government could safely adopt the King's policy of testing the issue by arms, a last effort should be made to satisfy the opposition and unify the country by making a conciliatory offer of his own. He also hoped that such an offer might win over New York and break the unity of the colonies. Therefore the Prime Minister, early in 1775, introduced in Parliament a "Conciliatory Resolve." It did not repudiate the principle of the Declaratory Act but promised that Parliament would refrain from exercising its authority to tax any colony that taxed itself sufficiently to fulfill requisitions made by Parliament. This would only change the method of collecting internal taxes, and no mention was made of the other grievances of the colonies beyond tax matters. Slight as the concession was, it was bitterly opposed in Parliament by the King's Men. On a plea for unity, the House of Commons passed the measure. This gesture would have seemed meaningless to the patriots in any case, and, actually, news of it reached America one day after the King's policy of force had resulted in the battles of Lexington and Concord on April 19, 1775.

LEXINGTON AND CONCORD

Recourse to arms had been decided upon by the Continental Congress only as a defensive measure. But the patriots had their own definition of what would constitute defense, namely, resistance to any attempt by the British troops in Boston to check the quasi-revolutionary activities of the patriots. The Continental Association, as administered by the radicals in Massachusetts and elsewhere, had taken on some of the character of a revolutionary government. Agents of the Association enforced the boycott with great energy, inspecting the affairs of businessmen and the customs offices, going into offices and kitchens to enforce the rules, and supervising their communities in order to impose a Spartan regime in private and public life. Loyalists cried in alarm that the authority of the legislatures was usurped and the mild rule of Parliament replaced by the tyranny of mobs. Names of violators of the Association were published in the press; and when publicity did not bring obedience, tar and feathers were used in some localities. Rarely if ever have Americans submitted to a stricter regulation of their daily lives.

The aim of the Association was to force by economic measures a peaceful capitulation by the British government. This policy may be regarded as a primitive example of what the twentieth century calls "economic sanctions." But powerful governments, such as that of Great Britain then, are indisposed to yield to economic pressure so long as they see—or think they see—a possibility of easy victory in shooting war. The situation in Boston was ready-made for an appeal to arms. The population offered no resistance when regiments occupied the town, but they made life as difficult for the soldiers as they could, refusing to provide quarters for them or to sell supplies to them. The troops on their part heightened the tension by licentious behavior, robbery, and violence—their offenses being multiplied and exaggerated in the propaganda of the Committee of

Correspondence. Clergymen hurled anathemas against Lord North and handed out arms to their congregations. Massachusetts patriots urged the other New Englanders to join them in raising an army of 18,000 men. Though companies of "minutemen" were organized and military stores were collected, the leaders still clung to the policy of purely defensive action.

The position of the British troops in Boston became humiliating. They were virtually under siege, and their chief function seemed to be the protection of refugee British officials and American Loyalists. Taunts were thrown at General Gage and Major Pitcairn that if they dared venture into the countryside, the minutemen would hustle them back with musket bullets. Pitcairn, in March 1775, nevertheless led a contingent to Salem without incident. British regulars were contemptuous of the New England militiamen. They lacked all the obvious military qualifications except one which European military theory of the time held in low esteem: the ability of the individual musketman to take aim at a particular target and hit it.

As the spring of 1775 advanced, the patriot cause was suffering. Congress had been torn by demands to exempt the staples of certain colonies from the rules against exportation, and the New York Assembly refused to approve the Association, although local committees enforced its provisions. Loyalists took heart and conservative patriots urged the provincial assemblies to send more petitions to the King. Those of Georgia and New York did so. Lord North was hopeful that his Conciliatory Resolve would divide the colonies, and General Gage decided that a march into the countryside was all that was needed to discourage and scatter the overblown rebels. It was his duty to enforce the Coercive Acts. He received orders to arrest Hancock and Sam Adams, who were in the neighborhood of Lexington, and spies informed him that the minutemen were collecting powder at Concord. The General decided to make a careful demonstration of authority by marching to Lexington and Concord.

British "aggression" outside Boston, the arrest of patriot leaders who were guilty only of supporting their rights as freeborn Englishmen, and the confiscation of means of defense which the militia system entitled citizens to possess—these were precisely what the radicals hoped would rouse Americans to their danger. The Boston Sons of Liberty and Committee of Correspondence had established close co-operation with patriots of the countryside. Their spies and watchers foiled Gage's plan for Major Pitcairn to slip from Boston secretly with a detachment of troops. The moment Pitcairn set out, Paul Revere saw the signal-light in the tower of Old North Church and rode express to Concord, giving warning to the patriot leaders at Lexington and rousing the farmers as he went. His cry in the night was not extemporized; it sounded the determined plan of the patriots to fight defensively if the British gave cause.

When Pitcairn and his company of infantry marched into Lexington in the dawn of April 19, 1775, a company of minutemen faced them across the village green. Who fired first is to this day uncertain, although patriot propaganda left no doubt that the redcoats did. The point is of no importance because the British sally was the sort of "aggression" to which Congress had authorized resistance, and the minutemen had mobilized in order to resist it. Eight of the embattled farmers were killed on the Lexington green, then the minutemen scattered. American farmer-soldiers were not accustomed to volleys fired from the hip by neat ranks of disciplined professionals. But they were trained in hunting and Indian fighting, and while the redcoats marched on to Concord the minutemen took up the positions of sharpshooters, behind stone walls along the road and under any cover that offered.

At Concord a company of minutemen made a stand at the bridge and the British detachment turned to march back. Pitcairn failed to find either Hancock or Adams and destroyed only part of the military stores. On the return march, the troops received the aimed fire from cover of farmers who had rallied from miles around. The British, who would not break ranks, lost more than 200 men in killed and wounded. The minutemen closed in behind the column and took up positions around Boston, holding it under seige against another sally. Before he heard the clash of resounding arms, Patrick Henry in Old Saint John's Church, Richmond, had already pronounced his most famous words: "Give me liberty, or give me death!" Events had now proved that Americans would fight for their liberties against the Coercive Acts, though their attitude toward a struggle for full independence remained a question.

The story of "the shot heard round the world," accumulated lurid details in the telling. Major Pitcairn's soldiers were said to have butchered men, women, and children and devastated the countryside. The British and Loyalists also invented atrocities on the part of the minutemen, accusing them of scalping, cutting off noses and ears, and gouging out eyes like Indians or devils. The patriots had the better of the contest of propaganda because their superior communications enabled them to get their story to the public first, and also because, atrocities aside, none could deny that the British had provoked the fight and that American "peasants" had put the British regulars to flight. The latter fact was especially important in both its immediate and long-range effects: it buoyed the hopes of the patriots and encouraged them to rely too much on undisciplined militia.

Conservative talk of conciliation was drowned out. New York, the weakest link in the patriot chain, became stronger when it went over to the radicals. Association committees ruled the colony. They confiscated

British supplies intended for the troops in Boston, took over the customs-house, and frightened the British garrison of New York City into going aboard warships in the harbor. Loyalists were silenced. Everywhere in the colonies, militia companies began to prepare for war. Guns and equipment in the King's arsenals were seized. Even Quaker Philadelphia turned warlike and mustered military escorts for the delegates of the Second Continental Congress. This body held its first session early in May while the echoes of the shots fired at Lexington and Concord still lingered.

THE SECOND CONTINENTAL CONGRESS

The Second Congress met in the State House in Philadelphia (later Independence Hall) rather than in Carpenters' Hall. In effect it was a continuation of the first and had much the same membership. Peyton Randolph presided over it until he was called home, and his successor in the chair was a new member, John Hancock of Massachusetts. His successor as a delegate from Virginia did not arrive until after the Congress had been about six weeks in session. This was Thomas Jefferson, a tall, sandy-haired young planter, already noted for his zealous patriotism and his "happy talent for composition." If he was to become the most famous penman of this body, Dr. Benjamin Franklin was its most renowned elder statesman. Just returned from England, where he had served as a colonial agent until he despaired of conciliation, the most famous of living Americans contributed his immense prestige to the cause of the patriots and his intimate knowledge of English and European politics to their councils.

If an appeal to arms and the God of Hosts was all that was now left to the defenders of colonial rights, as Patrick Henry had said, the first task of the Congress was to deal with military matters, and the odds against the colonists necessitated the maintenance of unity. The provisions for a Continental Army and the selection of a commander-in-chief were the most important early actions. John Adams of Massachusetts, where the seat of the trouble was, showed political wisdom in recommending George Washington of Virginia for the supreme command. Colonel Washington, who had resigned his commission in considerable dissatisfaction toward the end of the French and Indian War, and had devoted himself assiduously to his extensive private affairs until the controversy with the mother country aroused him, had never wavered in his support of colonial rights from the time of the Stamp Act onward. His determination to resist tyranny by force, if need be, was suggested by his appearance at the sessions of Congress in uniform. About this time he wrote: "Unhappy it is . . . that the once-happy and peaceful plains of America are either to be drenched with blood or inhabited by slaves. Sad alternative! But can a virtuous man hesitate in his choice?" He was a fine figure of a man at the age of forty-three, and he inspired the confidence of all by his good sense, balanced judgment, and irreproachable character. Later events were to show that the choice of him was little less than providential, and men hoped from the beginning that the unanimity of it was prophetic.

French secret agents were present in Philadelphia and held out the prospects of aid from England's historic enemy, but acceptance of it would have amounted to a denial of the avowed purposes of the present conflict. From being a struggle for the restoration of rights it would have become a movement for national independence. At this time Congress summed things up in a "Declaration of the Causes and Necessity of Taking up Arms" (July 6, 1775), to which Jefferson made important contributions though it was chiefly the work of John Dickinson. The potentialities of the situation were set forth in a rather boastful passage:

> Our cause is just. Our union is perfect. Our internal resources are great, and, if necessary, foreign assistance is undoubtedly attainable. . . .

Independence, itself, was mentioned as a threat in a passage which perhaps protested too much:

> We mean not to dissolve that union which has so long and so happily subsisted between us. Necessity has *not yet* driven us into that desperate measure. . . . We have not raised armies with ambitious designs of separating from Great Britain, and establishing independent states. . . .

Why, then, did Congress raise an army? The answer rang clear:

> For the preservation of our liberties, being with one mind resolved to die free men rather than live slaves.

The logic of its position forced Congress to assume some of the legislative and executive powers of a revolutionary government. To meet the expenses of the Continental Army, for example, it printed paper money, violating thereby one of the central prohibitions of the old Empire. Benjamin Franklin saw clearly the implications of the situation and eagerly embraced them by drawing up "Articles of Confederation and Perpetual Union—" in effect, the constitution of an American republic. But, strictly speaking, Congress was nothing more than a body of delegates—each of whom could act only on instructions from his colonial assembly or the extralegal body that had supplanted it. Thirteen revolutions were required before the delegates to Congress could be instructed to cap the movement with a national Declaration of Independence. In each colony a struggle occurred between militants and conservatives for control of local affairs. Antagonisms between West and East, and between merchants on one side and radical artisans and small farmers on the other, came to the fore in many of these local struggles. Economic lines were less sharply drawn in the South than in the North. In general, however, conservatives saw that not only English rule, but also their own position in society was endangered, and they hesitated. While the issue of these conflicts remained in doubt, Congress was disposed to evade the full revolutionary implications of its own actions.

Franklin's plan of union was not debated by Congress except privately, and John Dickinson obtained approval of a petition to the King. No answer to the petition of the First Congress had been received, and there was no chance whatever that Britain would accept anything less than submission to the Declaratory Act, but the militant radicals themselves admitted that it was wiser to move slowly towards independence so that it might be achieved in unity. Dickinson's petition was duly sent, but stirring new events had intervened and the King really had to answer the patriots who fought at Bunker Hill.

Civil War in the Empire, 1775

That fight (June 17, 1775) was technically a defeat for the raw militiamen, but they won a victory in terms of the damage they did the redcoats. After Lexington and Concord, motley American forces rapidly gained numbers around Boston. In June they occupied the Charlestown peninsula, entrenching themselves on Breed's Hill and the more elevated Bunker Hill behind it. From these positions cannon could command the city and harbor of Boston. Instead of cutting the Americans off by utilizing their sea force and seizing the narrow neck of land behind them, the British foolishly made a succession of direct attacks. Eventually they took both positions, amid scenes of carnage that were not exceeded in the entire Revolution. Among the American losses was General Joseph Warren, and among the British was Major Pitcairn. The redcoats marched up the slope in long close-order lines, the front rank stopping every few feet to fire a volley. The Americans held their fire against the enemy until they could "see the whites of their eyes," and at this highly effective range their muskets took terrific toll, but the next British line filled the gaps and moved forward. The Americans finally withdrew only when they ran out of ammunition. The British losses were so heavy that the victory had no savor. General Gage wrote to his government that the spirit and conduct of the Americans were far superior to what they had shown in former years when fighting for the king. The ministry decided that the war must be prosecuted to victory, and that conciliation would now be regarded as an admission of defeat.

General Washington heard reports of Bunker Hill while en route to his new command. He incorporated the New England troops in the Continental Army, set up his headquarters in Cambridge, and embarked on the long and disheartening task of welding short-term recruits and raw militia into an effective force. That a Virginian should be accepted as commander of New Englanders was itself an important demonstration of unity. Washington's personal qualities of absolute integrity, firmness, administrative skill, and infinite patience overcame the Yankees' suspicion of the gentleman planter; and from this time forward the colonial cause centered on him.

The organization of the Continental Army under Washington was final proof to the British that they faced not merely the armed "peasants" of New England, but the united thirteen colonies. In May 1775, Ethan Allen and the Green Mountain Boys had surprised and captured the forts at Crown Point and Ticonderoga. These positions were strategic keys to Canada and to unity between New England and the other colonies. Ethan Allen's feat, and the decision of Congress to retain the forts, signified the continental aims of the Americans. Thus when Dickinson's "olive-branch" petition arrived in England, it was accompanied by news that civil war on a continental scale had started in the Empire. The King refused to receive the petition. Instead, on August 23, 1775, he issued a "Proclamation of Rebellion" declaring all the colonies to be in a state of revolt. Thirty thousand British troops and three major generals were sent to put down this rebellion and mercenaries were hired from German princes.

By the time that news of the Proclamation reached Philadelphia in November, Congress had authorized the invasion of Canada. Congress had addressed friendly invitations to the Canadians to join the thirteen colonies to no effect. Canadians had been satisfied by the Quebec Act of 1774 and they were suspicious of the Protestant English colonists who had so recently inveighed against their religion and their laws. After capturing Montreal, brave General Richard Montgomery joined his forces with those of the valiant General Benedict Arnold before Quebec, but there the combined bodies of raw militiamen were defeated, Montgomery being killed. To the British the futile invasion seemed an overt aggression.

Meanwhile, Congress had answered the Proclamation of Rebellion by opening negotiations with France for aid. It appointed Benjamin Franklin, John Adams, and three others to a "Secret Committee of Correspondence." Within six months, King Louis XVI and his ministers had decided to encourage the rebels by supplying munitions from the royal arsenals and all kinds of stores. The fictitious Hortalez et Compagnie was the channel through which aid flowed to the Americans while France was maintaining technical neutrality. During the next few years, all but a small fraction of Washington's munitions came from France, and without them the American cause could not have been sustained. The French government did not render this aid because it loved liberty or Americans. Many Frenchmen—including powerful personages, leading writers, and the philosophers of the Enlightenment—idealized the American cause almost beyond recognition. But this did not influence officials like the

Comte de Vergennes, the Foreign Minister, who reasoned that France could regain her rightful place as the leading power in Europe by helping to destroy British sources of wealth in America.

Congress, in December 1775, authorized a Continental Navy and issued letters of marque and reprisal to American shipowners. A large share of the American merchant fleet was converted into armed vessels entitled under international law to prey on British commerce. The privateers did their work well, and the prizes, which were divided among owners and crew, were so rich that they laid the foundations of new fortunes and attracted recruits to man the vessels to the detriment of the Continental Army. The French government allowed American privateers to use French ports so that they could waylay British ships within sight of English shores.

By the end of 1775, Congress had shown that it was willing to accept the King's definition of its actions as rebellion, and that it would prosecute war aggressively, assuming all the powers necessary for the tasks at hand. Nevertheless, the delegates hesitated even to debate the question of independence. Positions taken in the war of propaganda were partly responsible. The Americans had claimed that they were resisting only the unjust measures of a corrupt and tyrannical Parliament and that their loyalty to the King was unimpaired. The radicals found they had done too good a job of distinguishing between the King and his government. British accusations bore heavily on the theme that they were plotting independence, and denials by Americans made it awkward for them to perform an about-face. During the winter of 1775-1776, therefore, the patriots stood in a political no-man's-land: they were breaking their ties with the mother country and yet were unready to advance towards independence.

THE DECLARATION OF INDEPENDENCE

The radicals had relied time and again on events to force the more reluctant patriots to take forward steps, and they were rarely disappointed. In December 1775, Parliament forbade all trade and contact between British subjects and the American colonists. This was called by the Americans the "Act of Independency," and they asked why Americans should maintain a connection the British government had broken.

Paine and Common Sense

In January 1776, a powerful assault on that connection was launched by Thomas Paine, who was not afraid of the word "independence." His pamphlet, *Common Sense,* turned American eyes to a strange new destiny outside the British Empire. Paine was an Englishman of ardent libertarian principles. As an excise officer, he had tried to organize his fellow officials so as to gain an increase in salary. Expelled from the service, he came to America as the land of promise in 1774. Throwing himself into the radical movement, he became its most extreme and skillful propagandist. He believed that the war required a supreme effort which the people would not make so long as they were told that "Good King George" would protect their liberties against Parliament inside the Empire. The Americans needed, Paine believed, a stirring "war aim," and an end to delusions that a middle way could be found between independence and slavery.

In *Common Sense*, Paine attacked the King in unheard of terms. The "Royal Brute," he wrote, was a "hardened, sullen-tempered Pharaoh" who by corruption had gained control of Parliament and the ministry. From attacking George III, Paine went on to attack the institution of monarchy as an absurd form of government. One honest man was worth "all the crowned ruffians that ever lived." Monarchs derived their power from the crimes of robber barons. Paine appealed to a law superior to the British constitution, the law of nature, to discredit all government as "a badge of lost innocence," and monarchy as the most unnatural form of government. Furthermore, it was unnatural that an island should govern a continent. Such a connection exposed Americans to economic exploitation and costly involvements in European politics and wars. This philosophy of natural rights was the "common sense" of Paine's title and it seemed to Americans very good sense. In ringing words he called for a declaration of independence in order that Americans might set up their own government according to the laws of nature.

Modern political science has rejected the notion of natural-rights philosophers that primitive society was, in Paine's words, a "bower of paradise" which the institution of government had destroyed. But the doctrine seemed very plausible to Americans who had been advancing for generations on the frontier and whose individual liberties had been interfered with by autocratic British power. Eighteenth-century philosophy encouraged Americans to glorify the simplicity of American life and to regard the influence of decadent Europe as the serpent in their earthly paradise. Paine's amazing eloquence made the ideas of philosophers, which were already current in enlightened circles, understandable and convincing to the mass of Americans. At a critical moment of indecision in the struggle against Great Britain, he reminded them of their opportunity to create an ideal society and summoned them to seize it.

> O! ye that love mankind! Ye that dare oppose not only the tyranny but the tyrant, stand forth! Every spot of the old world is overrun with oppression. Freedom hath been hunted around the Globe. Asia and Africa have long expelled her. Europe regards her as a stranger and England hath given her warning to depart. O! receive the fugitive and prepare in time an asylum for mankind.

Loyalists answered *Common Sense* by pointing to Paine's exaggerated indictment of the British constitution, but he had carried the debate beyond the point where the virtues of the British constitution mattered. The authority of the "rotten old state" of England over American freemen must be destroyed. Freedom had been snuffed out in one European country after another: in Corsica at the hands of the French; in Sweden, where despotism succeeded constitutional rule; in Poland, which was being divided among neighboring tyrants. Americans must act in time, as John Dickinson now said, against this "damn'd conspiracy of Kings and Ministers." Paine's pamphlet was read and talked about everywhere. It served to abolish hesitation and confusion, brought over many converts to the patriot cause, and emboldened the radicals to make independence their public goal.

Growth and Triumph of the Spirit of Independence

Defense against British encroachments on American liberty gave way during the spring of 1776 to positive assertion of what Americans could hope for if the British tie should be destroyed. Paine's vision of an asylum of freedom was made specific in the writings and speeches of the radicals. American trade might be expelled from the protected British market, but under American laws of free trade merchants could invade the markets of the world. Relieved of obedience to the Quebec Act of 1774, pioneers could invade the vast trans-Allegheny country and create a rich and powerful empire for liberty. Independence would give Americans control over their foreign relations and, as Benjamin Franklin said, prevent Englishmen from dragging them into "all the plundering wars, which their desperate circumstances, injustices, and rapacity, may prompt them to undertake." Furthermore, independence would open the highest positions in society to merit. Thus not only political liberty, but economic and social freedom and opportunity in a rich and powerful republic would follow in its train.

In these terms, the issue of independence was debated publicly for the first time in Congress in January 1776. The issue split the delegates into two camps, and on the first trial vote the radicals lost. A mistaken rumor concerning royal instructions to General Sir William Howe and Admiral Sir Richard Howe, when they took command over the British forces, strengthened the conservatives in Congress. The two Howes had refused to accept the command unless the King would also authorize them to enter into peace negotiations. George agreed, and rumors of this made American conservatives argue that conciliation was still possible and that the question of independence should meanwhile be shelved. But once more the folly of George III came to the aid of the radicals: he had instructed the Howes to make no peace with the rebels on terms of American liberty within the empire. Only surrender and submission would be acceptable, and the King's wish that the Americans should be chastised before they were offered even these peace terms was also embodied in the commanders' instructions.

While the conservatives in Congress imposed delay, the individual colonies proceeded to establish independent governments. In the Carolinas the patriot cause was weakened by suspicions of the frontiersmen that the seaboard Whigs would use their power against Western interests. In North Carolina bitter memories survived from the "Regulators' War" of 1770. But in March 1776 the North Carolina legislature instructed its delegates in Congress to vote for independence, and the erstwhile Regulators of the western counties turned to the support of the patriot cause. In Pennsylvania the Scotch-Irish frontiersmen joined city artisans in favor of independence. Germans were on the whole indifferent to the issue, while the dominant group of wealthy Quakers was pacifist and conservative. Frontiersmen and artisans overthrew the proprietary government and, under the leadership of Franklin and Paine, set up the most radical of all the new state governments. The Pennsylvania delegates were then instructed to vote for independence. In most colonies radicals seized the opportunity of leading the struggle against Britain in order to install more democratic local governments. Conservatives were constrained to go along rather than yield control of the revolutionary movement completely to them. Loyalists were proscribed and their property in many states was confiscated. When General Gage evacuated Boston he carried more than a thousand of them into exile, and Loyalists elsewhere were forced to seek the protection of British warships.

While the radicals in Congress waited for instructions in favor of independence to accumulate, they pointed the way to it by several important actions. In March, the Secret Committee of Correspondence sent Silas Deane as diplomatic agent to Vergennes. In April, Congress opened American ports to trade with all nations except Great Britain, thus overthrowing the mercantile system. In May, Congress advised the colonies to suppress every vestige of British authority within their borders and to establish governments whose authority would be derived solely from the people.

Then, on June 7, 1776, Richard Henry Lee of Virginia, following instructions from his province, moved: "That these United Colonies are, and of right ought to be, Free and Independent States." The phrasing of the motion shows that the radicals presented independence as an accomplished fact which Congress should merely ratify. Nevertheless, the debate was bitter when the question at length came up for decision. The final action concealed evidence of opposition, since the rule of procedure was that the vote of each colony was cast in accordance with the position of the majority of its delegates. The sentiment of individuals was not unanimous. The New York delegation was uninstructed and abstained from voting, though they afterwards acceded. After considerable maneuvering all the other colonies supported Lee's motion on July 2, 1776. This was the day that John Adams expected to be commemorated by succeeding generations as the day of deliverance, but the formal adoption of the entire document which we call the Declaration, including Lee's resolution, occurred on July 4, and that has always been regarded as the birthday of the American Republic.

The document had already been drafted by a committee consisting of Thomas Jefferson, John Adams, Benjamin Franklin, Roger Sherman, and Robert Livingston, of whom the three first were the active members. They set forth the causes which impelled Congress to this "mighty resolution." The youngest member of the committee except Livingston and its most eloquent writer, Thomas Jefferson, actually made the draft and it was not subjected to enough changes to invalidate his acknowledged claim to the authorship of the most famous American state paper.

The Meaning of the Declaration

The Declaration of Independence is one of the great generative documents of modern world history. It inspired emulation in every subsequent democratic movement from the French Revolution of 1789 to the recent upsurges of the Hindus and Moslems of India and the peoples of the former Dutch East Indies. This is because Jefferson, correctly reflecting dominant patriot opinion in 1776, did not rest the case for independence on the specific grievances of the colonists but on general philosophic principles. These principles were the common heritage of English and French thinkers of the seventeenth and eighteenth centuries and they had already been incorporated in the Virginia Declaration of Rights, but Jefferson gave them their classical expression:

> We hold these truths to be self-evident, that all men are created equal, that they are endowed by their Creator with certain unalienable Rights, that among these are Life, Liberty and the pursuit of Happiness. That to secure these rights, Governments are instituted among Men, deriving their just powers from the consent of the governed, That whenever any Form of Government becomes destructive of these ends, it is the Right of the People to alter or to abolish it, and to institute new Government, laying its foundation on such principles and organizing its powers in such form, as to them shall seem most likely to effect their Safety and Happiness.

These phrases are immortal because they make the people, and the people's will, the sovereign determinant of public polity. Probably nothing in the political literature of the world has been fought over more than the words: *all men are created equal.* Men of conservative persuasion, even Americans, have time and again dismissed these words along with other expressions in the Declaration as "glittering generalities," since human beings are obviously endowed with unequal abilities. But other Americans have appealed—successfully on the whole—to this principle of the Declaration on the ground that men are endowed with equal legal and political rights, regardless of their personal inequalities. It is in this sense that Jefferson's famous dictum has been given force by subsequent American development. When he announced it, glaring contradictions existed in the society about him, most obviously in the matter of chattel slavery. He had placed in his original draft an indictment against King George for furthering the slave trade. Southern and New England delegates had struck it out, but, like Jefferson, most of the patriots, Southern as well as Northern, regarded slavery as an evil which would presently be abolished. The Declaration lighted a beacon that searched out the darker corners of American society and led reformers to wage war against whatever could not bear the light. The question whether its "truths" were indisputable "facts" is of little importance compared with the influence of the Declaration itself in converting its principles into realities.

Jefferson altered the standard trinity of rights, derived from John Locke—"life, liberty, and property"—into the seemingly less materialistic "life, liberty, and the pursuit of happiness." The last phrase, however, was assumed by him and everybody else to include the right to own property, and the full establishment of this was a recognized motive, as it was one of the important fruits, of the Revolution.

Equality before the law and the right to life, liberty, and property were not very startling conceptions in 1776. Jefferson's assertion of the right of revolution was more notable. John Locke had formulated it *after* the Glorious Revolution as a rationalization of what Parliament had done, but Parliament itself had never admitted that it acted other than conservatively to protect the English constitution from royal "rebels." For a government to assert the right of revolution seemed to invite anarchy. Here, however, the invitation was to establish self-government, and the American patriots were determined to make their new governments genuinely responsive to the popular will and therefore secure against popular rebellion. Their success in this respect was so great that no aspect of the American political system has been more striking than its durability. Yet citizens of the United States have generally been sympathetic with political revolts against tyrannical rule elsewhere—such as those against the Spanish and Portuguese governments, leading to the establishment of the independent Latin-American republics.

Highly significant among the principles of the Declaration was the idea of government by compact. Here there could be no dispute about the correspondence of practice to theory: the organization of a government by free association of the governed and the formulation of a contract between them and their political authorities which the latter must obey even more strictly than the people. This was no more than a repetition on the national level of what had been said and done by Americans for a century and a half on the local levels. It was the long and successful experience of Americans in organizing government by compact that made this central theme of the Declaration the most "self-evident" of all the principles.

Jefferson placed specific grievances in a subordinate position in the Declaration, and offered them in deference to the proposition that, although the right of revolution against tyranny was inherent, prudence dictated that "governments long established should not be changed for light and transient causes." He recited a long and rather tendentious "train of abuses and usurpations . . . all having in direct object the establishment of an absolute Tyranny over these States." Leading the list were instances of interference with colonial legislatures and the judicial process. "Imposing taxes on us without our Consent" was one of the counts in the indictment, but mercantilist laws were not mentioned. The Quebec Act of 1774 was condemned as a scheme to introduce absolute rule into the colonies. Chiefly the grievances related to direct attacks on American liberty and self-government. King George III was blamed for them all, and Parliament was referred to only by implication.

> He [the King] has combined with others to subject us to a [Parliamentary] jurisdiction foreign to our constitution, and unacknowledged by our laws; giving his assent to their pretended acts of legislation.

This was not an accurate description of the relations between the colonies and Parliament during the years prior to 1763; and those once-amicable relations were now forgotten while the full-blown radical theses were advanced that Parliament held no rightful authority over the colonies, and that the King had forfeited his authority by abusing it.

Beyond all considerations of advantage in propaganda, the sweeping assertion of absolute popular sovereignty in the Declaration of Independence caused the document to mark a watershed in human history. It was flung into a era dominated by absolute monarchs, and it has by no means lost its point in a twentieth-century world which totalitarian governments threaten to dominate. It was primarily an act of faith by the immortal signers that if peoples were free to create their own governments, they would create governments that would guarantee freedom, and subsequent history has largely justified this faith.

Most Americans greeted the Declaration of Independence with joyous enthusiasm. Copies of it were sped to every city and village for public reading and celebration. The "Liberty Bell" in the Pennsylvania State House rang out, and it was echoed in belfries across the land. The Phrygian cap worn by liberated Greek slaves, the liberty pole, the American eagle, and a great variety of designs for an American flag replaced the old royal symbols. Conservative patriots joined the radicals in hailing independence, but with certain reservations. Some hoped it might merely be used as a bargaining point to win reconciliation with Britain. Some were firmly opposed to any movement to carry into practice the advanced principles of the Declaration. Like John Dickinson, who enlisted as a private in Washington's army after losing the fight in Congress against independence, many conservatives would defend American liberty against Britain, but they would also oppose in varying degree the growth of popular rule in America.

During the long war that followed, conservatives often feared that the Loyalists were right in their contention that British rule was the only alternative to mob rule. Some radicals made no secret of their purpose to make the revolution a fight against planter and merchant aristocracies as well as against Great Britain. It was an uneasy alliance between divergent groups that fought for American independence, and their contentions foreshadowed a large part of subsequent American history: on the one side to carry out the "principles of 1776"; on the other to embalm these in a document of purely antiquarian interest. The central idea in this revolt was the attainment of self-government, and the almost-deified leader of it was George Washington, an aristocratic planter and relatively conservative in his social ideas, who yet recognized the necessary sovereignty of the people and aimed at justice to all human beings. Men supported him irrespective of classes. Its spiritual prophet was Thomas Jefferson, and through the years the democratization of society has proceeded—too slow for some and too fast for others—in the spirit of the great Declaration.

CHAPTER 10

The American Revolution

REVOLUTION HAS BECOME ALMOST A CHARACTERISTIC institution of modern civilization. In modern times, revolutions have not been confined to *coups d'état* or palace revolutions, which affect little more than the personnel of governments. Forms of government have been overthrown and new forms substituted, in what may be called political revolutions. Occasionally whole classes of a population have lost their economic, social, and political positions and society has assumed new class configurations. Such social revolutions are typified by the French Revolution of 1789 and the Russian Revolution of 1917.

No economic or social class was dispossessed by the American Revolution. The wealthiest classes produced the most conspicuous Loyalists and many individual Loyalist merchants and landowners were proscribed, but they suffered for their opinions and actions, not for their class affiliations. Patriot merchants and landowners were often strengthened in their economic positions. The American Revolution did level downwards the social and political status of the wealthier classes at the same time that it raised the poorer classes to something approaching equality with the rich in everything but riches, and it widened opportunity for any man to achieve wealth and other forms of distinction. Therefore, it may well be called a *democratic* revolution insofar as it accelerated that process of equalizing rights and access to privileges which marked the American adventure from the beginning and continues to mark it. Social revolutions have often eventuated in abiding political tyranny, and this above all differentiates them from the American Revolution, which did nothing of the sort. This was predominantly a political revolution. As such, it had a double aspect: a colonial people overthrew the rule of their mother country; and the subjects of a king overthrew the institution of monarchy and made themselves citizens of a federated republic which they erected in its place.

The various aspects of the American Revolution may be subsumed under the single word, freedom: freedom of the whole people to advance their individual social, economic, political, and cultural ambitions; freedom of a colonial people to govern themselves; freedom from hereditary monarchs and nobles in a republic; freedom even for local self-government within a federal frame. Pre-eminently a *liberating* movement, it is distinctive if not unique among the major revolutions of world history. It produced no guillotine, no program of "revolutionary justice" carried to the point of tragic bloodshed. The respect for individual rights which was an impelling motive with the patriots at the outset was not violated by immoderate reprisals against even the enemies of the revolution. There were numerous confiscations and many Loyalists left the country, but perhaps no revolution of comparable scope ever abided by its first principles more faithfully. This was partly because it had high-minded leaders, partly because the Americans until very recently had enjoyed a large degree of freedom and self-government in a land of unexampled opportunity. After they had cut the tie with the mother country their main task was to maintain or develop their institutions, and there was relatively little that they wanted to destroy.

THE WAR: CHARACTER AND GENERAL CONDITIONS

The indubitable fact of American moderation in revolutionary action has led to the growth of a legend that the War of Independence was an Arcadian affair consisting of gentlemanly jousts in picturesque costumes, shadowed only by the sufferings of Washington's Army at Valley Forge. Actually it was a grim conflict and long drawn out. Both sides began the war with the thought that victory would be quick and easy, and both sides were slowly disabused. The Americans depended for victory chiefly on geography. They controlled the huge territory from Canada to Florida and from the mountains to the ocean. British troops might install themselves at one point or another but they could not control more territory than they actually occupied, and Britain simply could not support an army large enough to occupy any considerable portion of the American domain.

American geographic reasoning was basically sound and Washington's strategy was dominated by it. Nevertheless, enthusiastic patriots underestimated the time and positive military effort that would have to be spent before the stubborn government of King George would admit the impossibility of conquering America. After the first few months Washington himself did not make that mistake. He struggled manfully to convince Congress and the states that positive effort and planning for a long war were necessary.

The optimism of the early days was shown by the fact that the first Continental soldiers were enlisted for terms of only a few months. This optimism was modified but it persisted in dangerous degree. State governments refused to conscript soldiers or to order their militia to co-operate with Washington's troops except when danger inside their own boundaries threatened. Americans preferred militia service: a few days or weeks of fighting on home grounds in good weather, with wives and mothers handy to cook good meals, and then back to the farm for the harvest. The Continental Army was made up largely of the more ardent patriots and it also had a good share of homeless adventurers. Even so, the turnover was enormous. After 1776, the total number of Continental soldiers was usually less than 5000, yet several hundred thousand men (and a few women) served at one time or another.

To make a disciplined and skilled army of maneuver out of these materials was a task requiring supreme talents, and the patriot cause miraculously found these in George Washington. If too much is not made of Washington's occasional and usually justifiable bursts of tremendous rage, and of a sensitiveness to criticism which he generally transmuted into patience, no weakness can be found in the man. In the darkest days the Army, and the Revolution itself, had little else to sustain them besides his character, but that turned out to be enough. Congress failed to provide even the minimum of support in money, equipment, or direction. At times it seemed ready to give Washington sole authority in the government as it gave him sole responsibility. The marvel is that his republicanism was proof against the temptation to follow the easy pattern of many another revolutionary military leader in similar circumstances, and make himself dictator. Several times in his life Washington had "Napoleonic" opportunities; but there is no evidence that he even saw them as such, much less that he considered grasping them. Conservative though he was in social philosophy, his faith in the people was simple and complete.

It is notable that Washington never blamed his soldiers for their shortcomings—their lack of discipline, their desertions and quasi-mutinies. He blamed Congress while deferring to it, and, even more fundamentally, he blamed the lack of centralized constitutional authority in the government. But even while he saw the long-term need for a strong government and wrote endless begging letters to Congress and local authorities pointing out the desperate needs of the moment, Washington made no apologies but compelled himself and his ragged, hungry followers to endure all in the solid faith that if the Continental Army, no matter how much it retreated or how small it shrank, could somehow remain an army "in being," victory one day was sure.

Fortunately for the United States, Britain found no leader, political or military, for her war in America of a stature remotely comparable to George Washington. Indeed, her noblest political leaders, as British historians proudly affirm, were in opposition to the King's American policy, and many an outstanding army officer resigned his commission rather than fight against American liberty. Nor did the British population as a whole respond to the war. Enlistments in the army were at low ebb and the King was forced to hire German mercenaries. Many American Loyalists joined the British Army and they fought more avidly than the English or German troops. The Loyal Greens, Tory Rangers, and other regular and irregular regiments perpetrated the worst atrocities of the war, including the Wyoming Massacre in Pennsylvania. There is some truth in the statement that the American Revolution was a civil war in which the King's party at home and in America faced the opponents of royal power in both countries. The American Loyalists, even with British support, were nowhere able to control territory in America unless a major British force was present. But the Opposition in Britain was strong enough to force a change in government after six years of war of attrition that had brought nothing but useless local victories and the defeat of two British armies.

The worst disadvantage of the British was the distance at which this war of extensive conquest had to be fought. Troops and supplies had to be transported across 3000 miles of ocean. Such an operation strained the capacity of the slow ships of the period, and American privateers multiplied the difficulty. Added to this was the fact that the three most important maritime powers besides Britain—France, Spain, and The Netherlands—entered the war against her while the other European powers joined a hostile "League of Armed Neutrality" and faced her by 1780 with a world-wide conflict in which she had no allies. Heavily opposed at home, attempting to conquer a distant enemy-controlled continent and hold off all Europe, King George III finally gave up. There is poetic if not literal truth in the story that it was the American hornet's nest that drove him insane.

The War: First Phase, 1776-1778

Time and again Washington avoided the ultimate test of arms by tactics of retreat, and he was wise in so doing, but he knew that retreat never won a war. Bunker Hill had been lost in June 1775, but Washington seized an equally good vantage point on Dorchester Heights and set up cannon capable of bombarding the British troops in Boston. As a result, General Sir William Howe ordered Boston evacuated on March 17, 1776. Washington marched to New York the portion of his soldiers who were willing to go. Howe waited at Halifax for his brother, the Admiral, to arrive with reinforcements. In July, the combined British forces entered New York harbor and full-fledged war was imminent, though the Howes asked first to parley. Congress designated Benjamin Franklin to meet them at Staten Island. Since he was instructed to negotiate on no basis except American independence, and the Howes had nothing to offer except clemency to the rebels if they surrendered, there was no negotiation. Washington's untrained troops were outnumbered almost two to one, but he decided to fight, partly because a demonstration would support the New York patriots in their struggle with Loyalists.

Long Island to Valley Forge

The American regiments on Long Island, outflanked as a result of faulty intelligence, were dangerously defeated there on August 27, 1776, but retreated skillfully to Manhattan after a disappointing performance in the field. General Howe landed on the southern tip of the island, occupied New York, and forced Washington to retreat to Harlem Heights, where he won a minor victory in September before retreating further. It was about this time that Nathan Hale was hanged by the British as a spy after uttering words that were cherished by American patriots ever afterward: "I only regret that I have but one life to lose for my country." If this was not the darkest hour of the Revolution, as it has been called, it was probably the most confused period of Washington's leadership; he seemed to be groping in a fog. After an engagement at White Plains, which was a defeat though costly to the enemy, he retreated into New Jersey. The American forces were dangerously dispersed. Fort Washington on the Hudson, which was not evacuated in time, was taken by direct British assault, and Fort Lee across the river was abandoned with the loss of precious stores. These events fitted nicely into the British strategic plan, which was to sever the colonies by effecting a meeting between troops under Sir Guy Carleton moving down the waterways from Canada, and the Howes in New York. This might have succeeded at this time had not Benedict Arnold, who had retreated after the failure of the Canadian expedition, fought a masterful naval action against Carleton on Lake Champlain in October, so that the latter gave up for that year (1776) and returned north.

The British pursued Washington across New Jersey. His forces had already dwindled alarmingly because of desertions and the expirations of enlistments. The terms of so many others were to run out by the end of the year that it looked as though he would soon be without an army. Congress forsook Philadelphia for Baltimore. In the middle of December, Major General Charles Lee, who was extremely critical of Washington and had delayed bringing up his forces to join the commander-in-chief, was captured by a British patrol through his own imprudence. The game appeared to be nearly up when Washington executed a brilliant counterstroke. From his encampment in Pennsylvania on the west side of the Delaware, he took his troops in small boats back across the river—now floating with ice—and captured nearly a thousand surprised Hessians at Trenton the day after Christmas. Washington himself said, "this is a glorious day for our country." General

Lord Cornwallis was immediately dispatched with what seemed an overwhelming force to capture the "Old Fox," but the Americans evaded the main body, handily defeated a detachment at Princeton in January, and then retired to the hills at Morristown to make winter quarters. The men who had been induced to stay a little beyond their term soon departed, and the British could hardly have known how weak Washington was. As a result of his brilliant campaign they abandoned most of New Jersey, and before summer fresh enlistments had swelled his little army.

The British plan for the year 1777 was still to effect a union between the forces in Canada, which were to be led by Burgoyne in this invasion, and those in New York. But first General Howe was to move on Philadelphia. Luckily for the Americans, the co-ordination of the widely separated British land and sea forces was imperfect. There was no good way to prevent Howe from attaining his immediate objective. Early in the summer, availing himself of sea power and considerably mystifying his foes, he took most of his forces toward Philadelphia by way of the Chesapeake Bay and head of the Elk River, thus avoiding the forts on the Delaware. Washington placed his army in Howe's path at Brandywine Creek southwest of Philadelphia, but, partly because of the failure of his intelligence, suffered a defeat (September 11, 1777). The British occupied Philadelphia and Congress fled to York, Pennsylvania. Noting that the forces of the enemy were divided, Washington tried desperately in October to match the stroke he had made at Trenton, but his operations at Germantown were too complicated, a fog handicapped his movements, and a near-victory was turned into a defeat. He was unable to retrieve his fortunes before he made winter quarters at Valley Forge, some twenty miles from Philadelphia. He had maintained his army, which was the most important thing, and it was there that he really trained it, but his prestige was dimmed at just the time that other military leaders were gaining bright laurels.

Burgoyne's Surrender

In the North, a decisive and almost incredible victory was won at Saratoga. "Gentleman Johnny" Burgoyne led upwards of 7000 troops south from Canada in leisurely fashion and took Ticonderoga on July 6, 1777. The loss of the cannon and ammunition there was serious for the Americans but Burgoyne was already oversupplied with both. He and his officers, including Baron Riedesel, the genial commander of the German mercenaries, would not sacrifice their comfort for the sake of speed, and the ponderous invading army proceeded through the forests at a snail-like pace. They ran out of supplies and the farmers of New England and New York were given time to rally. Militiamen harried Burgoyne's troops, built roadblocks, destroyed bridges and cornfields,

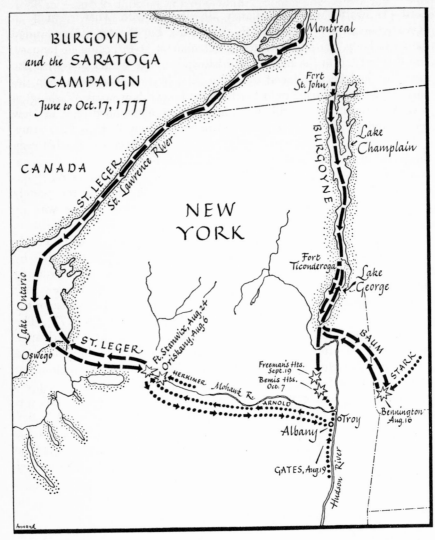

BURGOYNE
and the SARATOGA
CAMPAIGN
June to Oct. 17, 1777

and drove away cattle. The British at length reached Fort Edward, but Burgoyne hesitated to cross the Hudson at Saratoga and push on to Albany without sufficient supplies. He sent a motley detachment of British, Indian, Tory, and German troops under Colonel Baum, who spoke no English, to capture supplies in Bennington, Vermont.

The stroke was intended to win by surprise, but the German and British troops wore cumbersome and dazzling European uniforms. Unable to hide, they made excellent targets for militiamen as they crashed through the forests. The Green Mountain Boys rallied near Bennington, and General John Stark took command. "Wherever the King's forces point," Burgoyne complained, "militia, to the amount of three or four thousand assemble in twenty-four hours." Burgoyne had the support of the Six Nations of the Iroquois Confederation to offset the rebel militia; but he was appalled by the savagery they directed against Loyalists as well as patriots, and he lost their support when he insisted on civilized restraints. Meanwhile, their atrocities had excited the Americans to fever pitch. The wily Yankees played upon the British conviction that Loyalists would rally in force wherever British troops appeared. On his march to Bennington, Colonel Baum handed out arms freely to Green Mountain Boys who asked for them. When a large party asked for admission into his lines as Loyalists, he instructed his outposts to welcome them. Once inside, the Yankees opened fire, rushing up to the mouths of cannon to pick off artillerymen. In a mountain pass west of Bennington, Baum's forces were practically destroyed (August 16, 1777) and he himself was mortally wounded.

Part of the British plan was for Colonel St. Leger to proceed eastward from Fort Oswego on Lake Ontario, whither he had come from Canada by water, and to join Burgoyne, but he was held up by the stubborn defense of Ft. Stanwix, to which he was forced to lay siege. General Herkimer and his militia were ambushed when they sought to relieve the fort and forced to retire after heroic fighting. But when Benedict Arnold led troops into the Mohawk Valley against St. Leger, the latter, deserted by his Indian allies, gave up the siege of Fort Stanwix (August 24) and retreated. Both of Burgoyne's flanks were exposed by these American successes at Bennington and Stanwix. His Indian allies deserted him, and the Canadians, losing interest in fighting Britain's battles, took off for home. Burgoyne had no reason to expect aid from Howe, who had to contend with Washington's army, and that British general had turned southward to Philadelphia when things seemed to be going well in the North. Meanwhile, the mutual suspicions of Yorkers and New Englanders, on which the British had depended to weaken patriot opposition, were dissipated when Congress gave command in the North to General Horatio Gates. The New Englanders regarded General Philip Schuyler as a "damned Dutch aristocrat," and they were unjust to his real achievements, but they rallied with enthusiasm to Gates. New Englanders swarmed in from the east, American forces from the Mohawk Valley moved into positions on Burgoyne's west flank, and General Washington spared a few Continental troops who came up from the South. General Clinton, left in New York with a small body of troops, attempted to come to Burgoyne's relief, but he was too late.

Incapable of imagining defeat, General Burgoyne courageously moved across the Hudson and attempted to break out of the American ring near Saratoga. The Americans held firm. In the fighting at Freeman's Farm and Bemis Heights, Benedict Arnold particularly distinguished

himself. Sharpshooters picked off officers in the British camp; food supplies ran low; and champagne parties for the officers' ladies gave way to
hospital duties for them. The Americans repelled assaults on their lines
and poured ceaseless fire into the British camp. In October, Burgoyne,
who now had bullet holes in his gorgeous uniform, asked for surrender
terms. Then the onlookers witnessed the extraordinary spectacle of British
troops stacking their arms in front of American rebels while the band
played "Yankee Doodle," and this was duly reported to the incredulous
world. A goodly number of British aristocrats and a dozen members of
Parliament were bagged. Burgoyne at dinner with Gates proposed a
toast to George Washington. Released on parole to return to England, the
defeated General did his utmost to dispel the myth that Americans would
not fight. Although Englishmen were loath to believe that Burgoyne's
conduct of the campaign had not been at fault, the French accepted Saratoga as proof that the American cause was worth backing to the limit.
For this reason, the victory is rightly called the turning point in the War
for Independence.

THE FRENCH ALLIANCE

Prior to Saratoga, French aid to the American cause was tendered cautiously under cover of neutrality and in fear that a victorious Britain
would turn on France. Silas Deane, agent of Congress in France since
the spring of 1776, was privately welcomed by officials there and was
allowed to fit out American privateers in French ports. King Louis XVI
himself had little interest in the American cause, but his foreign minister,
Vergennes, worked with such enthusiasts as the playwright Caron de
Beaumarchais to send aid to America. In September 1776, Congress sent
Arthur Lee and Benjamin Franklin to join Deane as commissioners, hoping to obtain public recognition of American independence. Franklin
was now seventy years old and famous in Europe as a scientist and
philosopher, but his greatest achievements still lay ahead. In France he
was lionized by the sophisticated as the apotheosis of the "natural man"
—simple and wise, virtuous and witty. The New World sage carefully
cultivated his popularity for its value to his country. Throwing away his
powdered wig, he wore a frontiersman's fur cap—and the French ladies
promptly imitated his romantic headgear with a hair-do à la Franklin.
His portrait appeared everywhere, the worlds of fashion and learning
vied for his company, and crowds followed him wherever he went.
Franklin's head was not turned, but he clothed his extraordinary diplomatic skill in the modest benevolence of the true "friend of man."

More than diplomatic skill was needed to bring the French monarchy
to a public alliance with the American enemies of monarchy. The treasury
was approaching that depleted state which precepitated the Revolution of

1789. Recognition of American independence would inevitably bring war with Great Britain. French officials fearsomely studied the chances and refused to go beyond secret aid until they got news of Burgoyne's surrender. Then Franklin made a master stroke. The events at Saratoga caused the government of Lord North to consider making concessions in order to end the American rebellion. His offer amounted to that complete self-government within the empire which patriots had asked for prior to 1776, but now it was too late. Congress had firmly instructed Franklin to accept no terms short of British recognition of American independence. Nevertheless, he entered into negotiations with a British agent and carefully implanted the idea among French officials that their great opportunity to disrupt the British Empire would be lost if they did not hurry to offer attractive terms.

Thus Franklin devised the diplomatic strategy which was to be used by the American government in many later situtaions. This was to exploit the disunity and rivalries of the European powers by threatening to throw America's weight onto one side or another, as circumstances dictated, in order to obtain advantage for the United States. It seemed to Vergennes that a reunion of Britain and her former colonies would result in an assault on France which would strip her of the remnants of her empire in the West Indies. If, on the other hand, France combined with the United States against Great Britain, success in establishing American independence seemed quite likely. American trade would be diverted from England to France, the United States would become a strong economic and political support of France, and that country could reassert its supremacy on the continent of Europe. These were the arguments that Vergennes urged on his King, and the young and weak-willed Louis XVI succumbed to them. His Finance Minister, Turgot, warned him that war with Britain would ruin his government, but the King dismissed Turgot and plunged ahead. It was a decision that was vital for the American cause and suicidal for the French monarchy.

France was bound in the Bourbon Family Compact of 1761 to make war only in company with Spain, and she needed the help of the Spanish Navy if her own fleet was to avoid quick defeat by that of the British. But the Spanish government of Charles III was fearful that a successful American republic would seize possessions of Spain in the New World and give encouragement to rebels in her colonies. Vergennes offered Gibraltar and the Floridas to Spain, and did not hesitate to bait the hook with promised territory between the Appalachians and the Mississippi River—thus indicating the dangers to the United States which accompanied its entry into the game of European power politics. Still Charles III hesitated to embrace the cause of rebellion against monarchy, so Vergennes went ahead without Spain.

He wanted a binding commitment from the United States to be

France's permanent ally in return for recognition and large-scale military aid. Congress hesitated to make a permanent alliance in order to win the independence which was intended to sever America from European leading strings, but the practical necessities of the moment prevailed, and instructions were sent to the commissioners to give Vergennes what he wanted. At its inception, American foreign policy was geared to participation in European politics to whatever extent might be necessary to secure American interest, without regard for isolationist preferences.

The Treaties of 1778

Accordingly, on February 6, 1778, Franklin, Deane, and Lee signed two treaties with the government of Louis XVI. The first was a treaty of recognition, amity, and commerce. In it France recognized the independence of the United States of America and agreed with this new sovereign power on terms of commercial co-operation and international law. Each government accorded to the other "most-favored-nation" status, that is, granted to its shipping and trade the most favorable terms accorded to any other power. Liberal rules of international law were adopted in conformity with the "Plan of 1776" which Congress had drawn up for incorporation in all American treaties. These rules were adapted to the situation of governments having small navies but large merchant marines. They affirmed that in wartime neutral-owned ships might carry belligerent-owned cargoes of noncontraband and be immune from capture by any enemy ("free ships make free goods"); and that contraband be defined narrowly to exclude naval stores, food, clothing, and money, leaving little but arms and ammunition subject to capture when carried on a neutral ship. In the current situation the French and the Americans wanted neutrals like the Dutch to carry supplies for them, and the Franco-American rules contradicted those favorable to a big-navy power which Britain followed. The American Plan of 1776 contained the seeds of a world-wide alliance of maritime powers against Great Britain, and the French treaty was its first fruit.

The other treaty was one of permanent military and political alliance, the only treaty of the sort that the United States signed until after the Second World War. Both governments agreed to wage war against Great Britain until American independence was assured; to conclude no separate truce or peace with Great Britain; and to guarantee each other's possessions in America "forever against all other powers." In the territorial provisions, France showed that it was not recovery of her empire in North America that she sought: if Canada were wrested from Great Britain, it should become part of the United States, and France could acquire only such West Indian Islands as might be taken from the enemy. Thus the risk of the return of French power to the northern and western frontiers of the United States was guarded against. Vergennes believed that the erection of an independent republic in North America was enough to strengthen France by weakening Britain.

The terms of the French treaties were amazingly favorable to the young and struggling republic. Only the clause making the alliance *permanent* could be construed as disadvantageous, because it might lead the United States into some future war on the French side when American interests would demand neutrality or opposition. But the makers of American foreign policy in 1778 considered this risk preferable to that of defeat in the current war. In January, Lord North had introduced in Parliament his bills granting self-government within the Empire to the Americans, and these were passed early in March. Franklin had incited the two greatest powers in the world to compete for American friendship. Their offers raced across the Atlantic, and the patriots in and out of Congress did not hesitate. In 1775, they might have accepted "dominion status" but now they chose independence. Carping voices were raised that the French Alliance would bring absolute monarchy and popery to crush American freedom, and there was plentiful irony in the spectacle of Louis XVI embracing American radicals as his "very dear great friends and allies." But the patriots rejoiced over the Alliance as a brilliant American diplomatic victory.

After signing the treaties, the American commissioners were publicly received by Louis XVI in a brilliant court ceremony, and the king sent Conrad Gérard as his minister plenipotentiary to the United States. Congress, mightily impressed, tried to receive him with fitting ceremony. It also attempted as a body to carry on negotiations with him, but the impracticality of a legislature's assuming the functions of a foreign office soon led to the creation of an executive Committee for Foreign Affairs to conduct day-to-day business under the supervision of Congress. The actions of Gérard and of his successor, La Luzerne, showed that the French government intended to make the United States a satellite serving French interests. They did their best to take control of American foreign relations away from Congress and turn it over to Vergennes, and succeeded to the extent that Congress instructed its commissioners in France to subordinate themselves to the French Foreign Office. Fortunately, Franklin and his colleagues did not obey these instructions.

The aid France now sent to America was extremely generous. Direct loans provided almost the only hard money Congress had to bolster up issues of Continental paper. Many French officers with the connivance of their government had already volunteered for service in America. While most of them only sought high rank and pay, a few, notably the gallant and idealistic if vainglorious young Marquis de Lafayette, were genuinely devoted to the patriot cause. Now the French government ordered its military and naval forces to join the war. In March 1778, while France was still at peace with Britain, the French fleet under command of the Count d'Estaing and carrying 4000 soldiers sailed out of the Mediterranean and across the Atlantic to deliver a blow against the British naval and land forces at Philadelphia. France and Britain formally declared war in June 1778.

Isolation of the British

The Spanish government resented the French violation of the Family Compact. Charles III decided that it would be wise to prolong the war and thereby weaken the Americans, and that Spain might, without joining them, go to war against Britain in order to win Gibraltar and other positions. Spain made a few secret loans to the United States under cover of personal favors to American agents, but would not hear of recognizing American independence. She extorted from France extraordinary terms which were incorporated in the secret Convention of Aranjuez in April, 1779. The most important provision was that France would continue fighting until Britain gave up Gibraltar to Spain. Since the United States was committed to France to make no separate peace, this meant that the Americans, without knowing it, were now committed to fight until Spain won the rock of Gibraltar.

All Europe seemed ready to seize the opportunity of Britain's embarrassment in America to settle old scores with the mistress of the seas. The Dutch built up a booming trade with the United States by way of their Caribbean island of St. Eustatius. Under protection of their neutral flag, and of a special Anglo-Dutch agreement on the principle "free ships make free goods," the Dutch carried an enormous quantity of supplies of all kinds to the little island, where they were transferred to ships which ran them into American ports. The British government decided that war with the Dutch was preferable to toleration of this trade, and therefore declared war in December 1780. The Dutch government was only slightly more sympathetic with the American cause than the Spanish government, but Dutch bankers made loans to the United States which kept the American government afloat when French loans gave out. In October 1782, when peace was at hand, the Dutch government entered into a treaty with the United States which recognized the independence of the latter and contained liberal trade provisions, the second such treaty in American history.

Meanwhile, no less an autocrat than Catherine the Great of Russia turned to harry Britain and thus to aid the American rebels. In 1780, she organized the "League of Armed Neutrality," comprising all the remaining maritime powers of Europe. This League threatened to use force to protect neutral shipping against the British fleet. It adopted the principles of the American Plan of 1776 and faced Britain with the possibility of war with all Europe unless she permitted neutrals freely to carry cargoes owned by Americans or other enemies. Vergennes saw the League as an instrument conducive to the recovery of French power in Europe and encouraged it accordingly, just as he had incited the Dutch to offend Britain to the point of war.

Thus the American Revolution was utilized by the European Powers to further their own ends. They aided the American cause in varying degree in order to pull Great Britain down from the world supremacy she had won in 1763. The American War became almost a sideshow in the struggle of Europe to re-establish the balance of power. The scheme of Vergennes to displace Britain on the continent of Europe was remarkably successful. By 1780, Britain was fighting with her back to the wall. The necessity to protect shipping and possessions in the seven seas overextended the British Navy, and it lost control of the English Channel for the first time in a century. The raids on the English coasts by the intrepid John Paul Jones were an evidence of this.

It was scarcely possible for Americans to win the war without the direct and indirect aid of the European Powers. The gamble of rebellion had been premised on calculations of such aid, and American diplomacy was exerted to widen the breach between Britain and her rivals. The Republic in its infancy was entangled in the politics of the Old World, and accepted all the attendant risks in order to attain the great goal of freedom.

YEARS OF TRIAL, 1778-1779

The surrender of Burgoyne at Saratoga was of little help to General Washington during the winter of 1777-1778. General Howe established his forces pleasantly in Philadelphia, where a good share of the people of wealth and fashion welcomed them. The officers were feted in a gay round of dinners, balls, and theatricals. Farmers of the surrounding countryside eagerly carried provisions into the city in exchange for hard money. General Howe had hit upon the comfortable strategy of waiting for starvation and disaffection to defeat Washington's Army.

Ordeal in the East

The strategy was not at all unreasonable. Washington fixed on Valley Forge as winter quarters because it was within striking distance of Philadelphia, and he hoped to maintain a menacing attitude towards Howe's Army, but the condition of his troops became so pitiful that he could do no more than hold a remnant together. The soldiers had literally worn out their clothing in the summer campaign; some huddled naked in dugouts, while others stood guard or gathered firewood in the snow without shoes or shirts. Officers of high rank used scraps of blankets for clothing. Farmers scorned Continental paper money and refused to bring food into the camp. Some of the troops starved, many more died of disease, and hundreds deserted.

What had happened to the patriot cause that its champions were subjected to such horrors? The ineffectiveness of Congress and the agencies it had created, and its inability to coerce the states to meet requisitions, were part of the answer. Equally or more important was the unwillingness of civilians to sacrifice opportunities for private gain in a time of low public credit and skyrocketing prices. While the Army starved and froze, food and clothing sought more promising markets.

The troops at Valley Forge felt themselves neglected by Congress and abandoned by the people at large. One soldier wrote: "Poor food— hard lodging—Cold Weather—fatigue—Nasty Cloaths—nasty Cookery— Vomit half my time—smoak'd out of my senses—the Devil's in it—I can't Endure it—Why are we sent here to starve and freeze?" Vermin invaded the camp. General Anthony Wayne forced himself to visit every hut of his troops once a week, and often wished he had neither sight nor hearing. An impetuous fighter, "Mad Anthony" Wayne preferred a hopeless attack on the British to inaction. But the troops lacked arms as well as shoes, and they could not even attack enemy foraging parties. The miracle of Valley Forge was that a remnant of the soldiers remained loyal and justified Washington's iron determination to hold out, to maintain an army at all costs.

The soldiers did more than hold out. Tried and toughened, they became the nucleus of a new army. General von Steuben, a Prussian volunteer, was appointed adjutant general and whipped this ragged remnant into a disciplined fighting force. He applied Prussian drill techniques, which he wisely accommodated to the temper of the Americans. He said that in the Prussian army a soldier obeyed orders without question. But in the American army he was obliged to say to a soldier, "This is the reason why you ought to do that," and then the soldier did it. Steuben was a remarkable combination of slave driver and democrat, and the men learned from him the arts of drill, tactics, and maneuver. Seldom before or since have American soldiers risen more nobly to the challenge sounded by Tom Paine in the first of his *American Crisis* pamphlets:

> These are the times that try men's souls. The summer soldier and the sunshine patriot will, in this crisis, shrink from the service of their country; but he that stands it *now*, deserves the love and thanks of man and woman. Tyranny, like hell, is not easily conquered; yet we have this consolation with us, that the harder the conflict, the more glorious the triumph.

Washington himself came through the winter strengthened by adversity. The "Conway Cabal" attempted to displace him as commander-in-

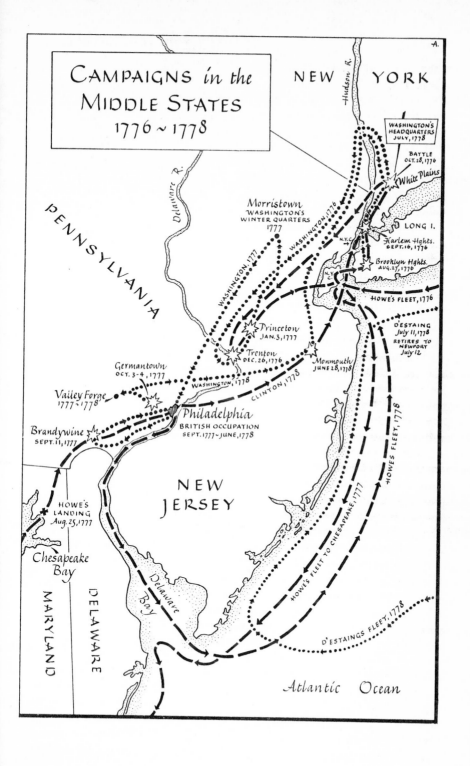

CAMPAIGNS in the
MIDDLE STATES
1776 ~ 1778

A.

NEW YORK

PENNSYLVANIA

Delaware R.

Hudson R.

WASHINGTON 1776

WASHINGTON 1777

Morristown
WASHINGTON'S
WINTER QUARTERS
1777

WASHINGTON'S
HEADQUARTERS
JULY, 1778

BATTLE
OCT. 28, 1776

White Plains

LONG I.

N.Y.C.

Harlem Hghts.
SEPT. 16, 1776

Brooklyn Hghts.
AUG. 27, 1776

N.Y.C.

HOWE'S FLEET, 1776

D'ESTAING
July 11, 1778
RETIRES TO
NEWPORT
July 12

Princeton
JAN. 3, 1777

Trenton
DEC. 26, 1776

Monmouth
JUNE 28, 1778

Germantown
OCT. 3-4, 1777

WASHINGTON, 1778

CLINTON, 1778

Valley Forge
1777~1778

Brandywine
SEPT. 11, 1777

Philadelphia
BRITISH OCCUPATION
SEPT. 1777~JUNE, 1778

HOWE'S FLEET, 1778

NEW
JERSEY

HOWE'S
LANDING
Aug. 25, 1777

HOWE'S FLEET TO CHESAPEAKE, 1777

Chesapeake
Bay

MARYLAND

DELAWARE

Delaware
Bay

D'ESTAINGS FLEET, 1778

Atlantic Ocean

chief with General Gates, the hero of Saratoga. Congress appointed Gates President of the Board of War, an embryo War Department, and the intrigue was carried on in his behalf, whether or not he had a direct part in it. Washington's defeats could be compared unfavorably with his glorious victory, and some Congressional leaders were unduly fearful that the Commander-in-Chief would turn into a military dictator. Thomas Conway, a former French officer of Irish birth whose promotion to major general had been opposed by Washington but was voted by Congress anyway, made insolent references to the latter in a letter to Gates which seems to have been destroyed. Conway was reported to have said: "Heaven has determined to save your country or a weak general and bad counselors would have ruined it." Gates's bungling efforts to disentangle himself—first by saying that the letter from Conway had been stolen and then that it was forged—and Washington's vigorous letters to him and Congress discredited him. Towards spring, when rumors of the "plot" became widespread, there was a sharp reaction in Washington's favor. The people and Congress rallied to him and Gates was soon removed to a subordinate command. The selfless patriotism of the Commander-in-Chief was all but universally appreciated, and his critics were helpless in the face of his enormous prestige and popularity. Conway's loose talk was not wholly quieted until summer. Then he was dangerously wounded in a duel with General John Cadwalader, one of the many staunch supporters of Washington, and he soon begged the latter's forgiveness. "You are in my eyes the great and good man," he said. By now Washington had become to nearly all Americans the greatest hero of all time, and this view of him persisted. Doctrinaires were reluctant to believe that a republic has need of heroes; but it was the good fortune of the American Republic to find one who, far from exploiting the adulation that was accorded him, made it a source of strength to the cause he served.

One day in the spring of 1778, Washington's Army was mustered into ranks to hear the news of the French Alliance, and broke into hoarse cheers. The British authorities relieved the gouty General Howe at his own request and gave his command to Sir Henry Clinton, who assumed it in May with orders to evacuate Philadelphia. This he did in June, setting out for New York by land with a long baggage train. Washington ordered an attack on the slow-moving British at Monmouth Courthouse in New Jersey. He entrusted the advance corps to General Charles Lee, who had recently entered into ambiguous relations with the enemy while a prisoner of war. Almost before the action began, that officer ordered a retreat. Then occurred perhaps the most famous instance of Washington's loss of temper. A French officer said later: "I saw for the first time what fury was, because anything more appallingly terrible than the face of General Washington when he appeared on the scene and galloped toward

Lee, I have never seen, nor has any one else. It was like the God of Battles intent to kill or destroy." Washington called Lee a coward, thundered a volley of oaths at him, and set about reorganizing the lines. They held, but during the night the British went on toward New York and the attack could not be renewed. A court-martial found Lee guilty on several counts, including disobedience to orders. At Monmouth Court-house Washington saved the newly trained American Army from disaster, and he claimed a victory, but the losses were about even.

Clinton was in New York when a French fleet under d'Estaing approached. The latter, hesitating to force his way into the harbor against Lord Howe's warships, turned instead to Rhode Island. Washington was thus disappointed, as he was several times thereafter, in his hope of cooperating by land with the French in an attack on Clinton. In Newport, the British had developed a strong naval base. New England militiamen under General John Sullivan flocked to attack this by land in support of d'Estaing, but delays that were caused by the difficulties of co-ordination gave time for Lord Howe, whose fleet had been reinforced, to sail from New York to Newport. Before the French could give battle, a storm separated the two fleets and d'Estaing then took his ships to Boston. "Heroes of Flight" was what Sullivan's disgusted troops called them. In the fall, the French fleet went to the West Indies. It damaged the British there, but the first results of Franco-American military co-operation were slight indeed. The New Englanders gave up the attack on Newport, and Washington ended the year (1778) in camp at White Plains, New York—where he had been two years before, when the British were in Manhattan. After all his maneuvering he was back where he had started.

The War in the West

A notable success in the West was achieved in 1778-1779 by Lieutenant-Colonel George Rogers Clark and a body of Virginia frontier militia. They floated down the Ohio past the mouth of the Tennessee, marched overland to the Mississippi, and captured the fort of Kaskaskia in July 1778. Clark then took possession of Cahokia, farther up the river, and extended his authority to Vincennes on the Wabash—the whole region being organized as the county of Illinois, State of Virginia. But Lieutenant Governor Henry Hamilton of Detroit, notorious on the frontier as the "hair-buyer," recaptured Vincennes, and Clark performed his greatest exploit when he and his little band marched heroically across the drowned lands in the dead of winter and took it back in February 1779. They also took Hamilton, who was sent as a prisoner to Williamsburg. Thus Americans fought for and won territory which had been forbidden them by the British legislation of 1774. There is no record, however, that the victories of Clark and his men were used by the commissioners in the final peace negotiations as arguments for American possession of the West. Nor did Clark himself accomplish his full purpose—to destroy the Indian menace at its source by capturing the British posts, whence the Indians were incited. He was never able to take Detroit, the main enemy post.

At about this time the British were making a special effort to enlist Indian allies. This was not in the spirit of the Howe brothers but it was in that of Lord George Germain, who was directing military affairs in England, and of the commissioners who bore Lord North's conciliatory proposal to America in June 1778, and were infuriated when Congress would neither receive nor discuss it. Lord Carlisle, the head of the commission, urged his government to wage a war of extermination against the rebels; and he issued a proclamation threatening the Americans with burning and pillaging—in modern terminology, with total war. Whigs in Parliament expressed horror when scalping knives appeared on the lists of army supplies, but the ministry asserted that if it did not hire the savages, the Americans would. Generally speaking, the Indians fought on the British side because the rewards were greater. In 1778 and 1779, the frontier was terrorized by Indian raiding parties in which Loyalists strongly participated. Colonel John Butler, a Tory, was the leader in the Wyoming Massacre in Pennsylvania in the summer of 1778; and his son Walter joined hands with the Mohawk chief Joseph Brant in the Cherry Valley Massacre in New York State in the fall. An expedition led by General John Sullivan in 1779 wreaked terrible vegeance on scores of Indian villages in New York, but it did not fully accomplish its purpose since it never reached Fort Niagara, the real seat of the trouble, and Brant continued to harass the frontier.

❊   ❊   ❊

So far as the main forces were concerned, the war in 1779 degenerated into raiding. Washington strengthened his defenses on the Hudson, particularly at West Point, guarding against the old British plan of dividing the rest of the states from New England. Fortifications were started by him at Stony Point and constructed at Verplanck's Point. Clinton seized both of these points in a sudden rally, but did not succeed in drawing the "Old Fox" from his lair. Washington's plan was to take them back, and this was admirably executed by General Anthony Wayne with troops drawn from the new Light Infantry who were well trained in bayonet fighting. More prophetic were the British raids to the south, in which use could be made of sea power. Such a raid toward the end of 1778 led to the capture of the port of Savannah. An ill-co-ordinated Franco-American attempt to recapture the city failed in the following autumn. Washington continued to hope that his Army and the French Navy could engage in a successful joint operation against Clinton in New York, but for the time being he had to content himself with watchful waiting.

LAST PHASES OF THE WAR, 1780-1781

Meanwhile, in England, Lord North became disgusted with the whole enterprise of the war and begged his King to relieve him of office, but George III saw the triumph of the Whigs as the only alternative to North's ministry and forced him to carry on. The King now tortured himself with fears that England faced ruin and the loss of all her colonies —which would be followed by invasion by the French and Spanish and defeat in the home islands. These nightmares steeled him to continue the struggle in the face of rising opposition. As if to give support to his fears, the Irish, feeling themselves even worse victims of British tyranny than the Americans, raised claims and an army ominously like those of the American patriots. The North ministry quickly made concessions to them, including some relaxation of restraints against Irish industry and Roman Catholicism, but this liberalism only resulted in riots in England itself by Protestants who raised the cry: "No Popery!" One mob forced the members of Parliament to barricade themselves and maltreated members of the ministry.

These "Lord George Gordon Riots," so named after their Scottish leader, exposed rotten features of the English society of the era. The bitter poverty of London slum dwellers led them to turn political demonstrations into wild uprisings for bread and plunder, and fires were set all over London. After the rioters with great difficulty had been put down, the Americans were blamed: it was said that Dr. Franklin's agents were the instigators. Franklin had indeed hoped for a liberal reform or revolutionary development in England, but the riots actually put an end to attempts by responsible Whigs to reform the government, and fear of mob rule strengthened the King's hand. He was able to win the elections of 1780 for his supporters in time-honored fashion by paying out huge sums of money and dealing out plums on the civil list.

King George came through the crisis of 1780 strengthened in his determination to win the war. During that year and the early part of the next, American fortunes declined to their lowest point since the weeks before Trenton. Clinton followed up the allied failure at Savannah by taking the garrison from Rhode Island and sailing with a strong force to South Carolina. In May, he took Charleston and all the American forces with it. He returned to New York with part of his Army, leaving Lord Cornwallis in charge. There were many Loyalists in the Carolinas, but there were also patriot bands under such leaders as Sumter and Marion. These harassed the British regulars and waged bitter civil war against the Loyalists.

Treason and Mutiny

This was the year of Benedict Arnold's treason. Offended because Congress failed to take him at his own high estimate, Arnold, as military governor of Philadelphia after Howe's departure, turned to luxurious living, spurred on by his extravagant young wife, Peggy Shippen, and was eager to cut a wide social swath among the Loyalists of the Quaker City. Desperate for money, and resentful because of a reprimand which was recommended by a court-martial as a result of his irregularities, he turned to the British. He had been giving military information to them for some time when, in order to increase his value, he had himself appointed commander of West Point so that he could sell this key fortification to the British along with his own honor.

Clinton was wary and demanded first-hand evidence from Arnold that he would indeed betray West Point. He sent his aide, Major André, up the Hudson to meet Arnold behind the American lines. André's ship was forced by American fire to return without him and, unluckily for the gay and witty Major, he was carrying incriminating papers and wearing a disguise instead of his uniform. Attempting to return by land, he was captured and executed as a spy. Arnold heard of his capture in the nick of time and escaped to New York. The British did not like him and paid him less than he wanted, but he got a brigadier general's commission and more than £6000 altogether. The Americans had prided themselves on the purity and faithfulness of their leaders, and Arnold's treason was a severe blow to their morale, but fortunately he had no confederates. The patriots burned him in effigy and it was commonly said that no man since Judas Iscariot had earned such black hatred.

Mutiny broke out in the Continental Army a few months after Arnold's treason, though the events were not connected. The underlying reason for the revolt was that the soldiers, largely because of the ineptitude and impotence of Congress, were ill-clad and badly fed and had been long unpaid in a time of spiraling inflation and apparent civilian plenty. The immediate occasion for the mutiny of the Pennsylvania Line, which began on New Year's Day, 1781, and was followed by that of the New Jersey Line, was a dispute over the terms of their enlistment. The regulars claimed that they had signed for only three years, not for the duration, and that they were being held too long. They defied their officers and shed some blood. Clinton sent spies among them and they demonstrated their patriotism by delivering these over for execution. A committee of Congress patched things up with the Pennsylvanians, and the mutiny of the Jerseymen collapsed after a couple of the leaders faced a firing squad. Congress blamed the states for the trouble, but both Congress and the states now bestirred themselves. Conditions were distinctly improved by summer, thus facilitating Washington's Yorktown campaign.

From Camden to Yorktown

Meanwhile, there had been major disaster and minor success in the South, where the war was especially exhausting and destructive. Congress gave General Gates command of the Southern Department, and he had an army composed chiefly of militia to employ against the ruthless Cornwallis. In August 1780, Gates's forces were disastrously defeated at Camden, South Carolina, and the fame of the victor of Saratoga was sadly dimmed. On Washington's recommendation, he was replaced by General Nathanael Greene, who organized a new army and waged a damaging campaign. Employing guerilla tactics, the Americans won minor victories at King's Mountain (October 6, 1780) and Cowpens (January 17, 1781). Cornwallis moved on into North Carolina, nevertheless, and appeared to have maneuvered Greene out of the state when the latter turned and made a stand in March at Guilford Courthouse. He is said to have made a bargain with his militiamen, who were the butt of jokes and complaints at this stage, that they should fire two volleys before they ran away. Cornwallis made Greene retreat but the British casualties were so great that the victory was worthless. Cutting in behind the Earl, Greene set out to reconquer the Carolinas, which he did with considerable success, while Cornwallis plunged into Virginia, creating consternation as he went.

Washington's own state, to which he never showed any favors, was now governed by Thomas Jefferson, who had more than his share of troubles as a war governor. Virginia had been largely denuded of troops in order to reinforce Gates, who had been defeated, and Greene, who for reasons that seemed sufficient had turned the other way. The state was drained of supplies and its treasury was empty. It was practically defenseless, and in a condition bordering on exhaustion. Clinton had already dispatched Arnold to this region which was so accessible by sea, and the latter had conducted a slashing raid before retiring to the coast. He had afterwards been reinforced by General William Phillips, who had surrendered with Burgoyne but had been exchanged. Cornwallis set out to link his forces with theirs and, after devastating the countryside, to proceed to a seaport whence, as he thought, the transporation of his troops to New York would be easy. Besides militiamen, only small forces under Lafayette and Steuben opposed him. He inflicted damage chiefly by means of raids, the most famous of which was that of Tarleton. This dashing horseman sought to capture the state legislators, who were in Charlottesville since Richmond was untenable, and Governor Jefferson at nearby Monticello. He did not have the satisfaction of catching them,

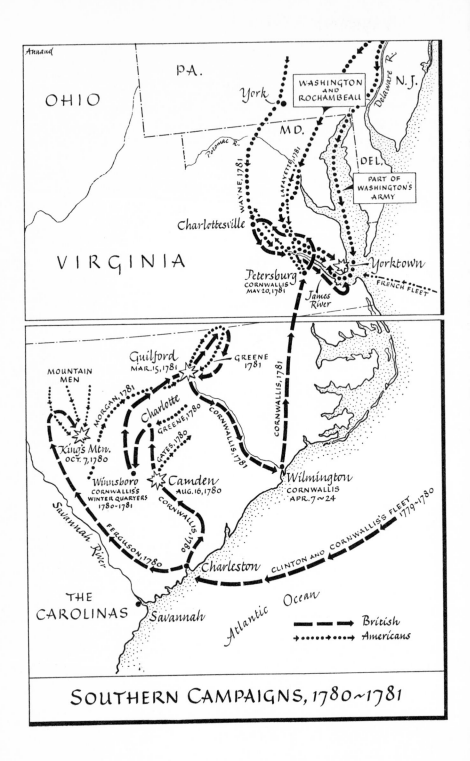

SOUTHERN CAMPAIGNS, 1780~1781

but the successive British invasions caused the government of a proud commonwealth practically to collapse. Meanwhile, Lafayette eluded the stronger enemy forces and, with General Anthony Wayne, whom Washington had ordered to join him, harassed Cornwallis until at length the Earl arrived at Yorktown, a small port on a deep river near the coast and a safe enough place while the British ruled the sea.

For months Washington had been hoping and planning for a major operation in conjunction with his allies, and French military aid was now available. On a trip to France, from which he returned in the spring of 1780, Lafayette had convinced Vergennes, who had begun to lose interest in this interminable American war, that France must give substantial military and naval aid if the Allies were ever to win it; and in the following summer the Comte de Rochambeau had arrived in Newport with more than 5000 troops. But the French fleet that brought this army was soon bottled up in Newport by the British. One element necessary to victory was lacking—French naval superiority. This was supplied a year later by De Grasse for a brief period that proved long enough, but the aid did not come at the place that Washington had expected. The operation he had in mind was against Clinton in New York, and until the last minute that General expected a move against him. The thought was natural enough, since the forces of Washington and Rochambeau were joined above New York in the summer of 1781. But Cornwallis had got himself into a position which was untenable without naval support, and Washington learned that De Grasse was making for the Chesapeake. Therefore, he quickly and skillfully adjusted his long-cherished plans to a new situation. Instructing Lafayette to keep Cornwallis on the peninsula, deceiving Clinton to the last, and keeping his own troops in ignorance of their destination, he set them moving southward late in August, while Rochambeau's regulars closely followed.

The operations of the Allies were conducted with clocklike precision, while the enemy were confused and baffled. About the time that the ragged Continentals and the white-coated French left Philadelphia, after a review before Congress which gratified the members of that body, the British Admiral Graves sighted De Grasse's ships in the Chesapeake. He engaged them indecisively, and then, discovering that the arrival of the French fleet from Newport had further increased the odds against him, he sailed back to New York. De Grasse, now in full command of the situation, transported most of the Allied troops down Chesapeake Bay, and on September 28 they began the siege of Yorktown. With a large body of Virginia militia that had recently been assembled, the American forces somewhat outnumbered the French, and together they outnumbered the forces of Cornwallis two to one. Clinton organized a relief expedition but it did not actually put to sea until October 19, the day that the unfortunate Earl surrendered.

For the second time an army of British regulars laid down its arms in America. On this momentous occasion the redcoats marched between the French regulars, resplendent in the white dress uniform of the Bourbons, and the Continental Army, which could muster only enough uniforms for the front rank, while the rear ranks stood in rags. Many of the British pretended that they surrendered only to the French, but their own bands played "The World Turned Upside Down" and the French played the rebel "Yankee Doodle."

The news of the surrender at Yorktown came like a stroke of lightning in England. Lord North staggered as if he had been hit. Yet in a military sense the Franco-American victory need not have ended the war. Britain could have looked upon it as a defeat in one campaign and proceeded to mount another. George III, Lord North, and many a Tory leader found it impossible to believe that Britain had lost a war, but the events at Yorktown convinced many others of the correctness of the opposition's view that this war had been a mistake from the beginning. Yorktown turned out to be the last battle primarily because it produced a revulsion in British public opinion that brought another political group to power. A secondary reason was the European situation, which American diplomats skilfully exploited.

Peace and Independence

During the winter of 1781-1782, the King and his ministry gradually lost control of Parliament. The landed gentry who had hoped to make Americans pay for the Seven Years' War were disgusted by the redoubling of the national debt; Gibraltar was under siege by the Spaniards; the British Navy had lost control of the West Indies; and even in India, British rule was threatened. It seemed the part of wisdom to make peace in order to avoid complete loss of the British Empire. In February 1782, the Opposition won a majority in Parliament for a motion to make no further effort to reduce the Americans to obedience. Burke, Charles James Fox (who liked to compare the King to Satan), and others now worked to make Yorktown a lever to push the King's Men out of power. George III was forced to allow Lord North to resign in March, and then the Whig Rockingham formed a new government. Later in the year, after Rockingham's death, Shelburne, a follower of the late Earl of Chatham, became head of the ministry. It was his government that made the peace.

In the month of April 1782, Admiral Rodney showed that Britain was far from beaten in the war. He returned to the West Indies and in the Battle of Saints' Passage completely defeated De Grasse. In India also, Britain by the close of the year had put an end to the French threat and the siege of Gibraltar was raised by a relief expedition. In America, strong British forces still controlled New York and Charleston, while

there was serious discontent in Washington's unpaid army. In these circumstances, Britain would accept no dictated peace. The new British
government set about making peace with the Americans as a positive
strategy to divorce the United States from France and re-establish political and economic ties with the former colonies. The Whigs had a normal
English fear for the safety of their country in the face of a Europe united
against it.

It mattered little to them whether they treated with France or with
the United States. In the spring of 1782, they approached the two governments separately, offering peace to each at the price of breaking with
the other. Vergennes refused to treat for the United States, but he encouraged Franklin to negotiate separately with the British, on the understanding that no final terms would be agreed upon without French
consent.

The Negotiations

The peace commissioners appointed by Congress were Franklin, John
Adams, John Jay, Jefferson (who did not serve) and John Laurens
(who served very briefly). Instructions from Congress, dated June 1781,
had too trustfully imposed on them subservience to the French government regarding terms of settlement. The Americans did not hesitate to
disregard their instructions. The canny Franklin saw an interesting
opportunity in the situation: by holding out to Britain the possibility of
a postwar alliance he might obtain excellent territorial and other terms.
He even proposed that Canada be given to the United States as proof
of "sweet reconciliation," a gesture which would help the American
people forget the cruelties of Great Britain. Beyond that, Franklin
dreamed of a pact between Britain, the United States, and France which
should substitute arbitration of disputes for wars and give the world a
new era of peace.

About the time that Shelburne emerged as chief minister, John Jay
returned to Paris from a fruitless mission to Spain, where he had conceived a profound distrust of Vergennes. Jay had some inkling of the
French Minister's actual plan to favor Spain in a peace settlement and
prevent the United States from gaining sufficient territory to grow powerful and free herself from French leading strings. Jay learned that the
French planned to draw the western boundary of the United States at
the Alleghenies, thus depriving the Republic of one of its chief goals in
the struggle with Great Britain. Vergennes would turn over the West
to Spain to compensate for her disappointments elsewhere. Jay, who was
equally suspicious of Great Britain, disrupted the delicate machinery
of Franklin's plans, and insisted that Britain recognize the independence
of the United States before any discussions began—because Vergennes

tolerated British references to the United States as "colonies," if for no other reason. Then Jay learned of a secret French mission to London and decided that his country was about to be betrayed by its ally. He gained the support of John Adams against what they considered the complacency of Dr. Franklin with respect to the French.

Vergennes certainly betrayed the spirit of the alliance by telling Shelburne that France would consent to unfavorable British terms for the United States. Jay insisted that he be allowed to deal directly and secretly with the British in order to avert disaster, and Franklin consented. Jay forced the British to recognize American independence prior to negotiations. Shelburne squirmed, hoping to retrieve some sort of Anglo-American federation from the ruins of empire. Still he saw an opportunity to drive a wedge between the French and the Americans, and he agreed, therefore, to extremely generous terms. The Americans signed "Preliminary Articles of Peace" with Great Britain on November 30, 1782. These were virtually unchanged in the final treaty. When Vergennes protested at the failure of the Americans to consult him, Franklin pointed out that they had not made a separate peace and hinted that the British hoped to divide the allies, wherefore he prayed Vergennes to keep their "little misunderstanding" secret. Franklin had already asked for another French loan—and got it. Vergennes, after all, was eager to bring pressure on Spain to make peace without Gibraltar, and the action of the Americans gave him a convenient argument. The diplomacy of Franklin, Jay, and Adams was brilliantly successful in exploiting the rivalries of the European Powers for American advantage. The final treaty was signed with the full approval of France on September 3, 1783, the same day on which that country, Spain, and The Netherlands signed peace treaties with Great Britain.

The Settlement

The United States was the only winner in this settlement of a world war. Besides formally recognizing the independence of the new Republic, the British agreed to magnificent boundaries: the Mississippi River in the West, the Spanish Floridas in the South, and roughly the present boundary in the North. The United States had by no means established its right to the great western territory by force of arms. Britain, France, and Spain all came to regret the territorial terms of the treaty, and time and again they tried to prevent the United States from filling up its giant-sized boots. But they were no better united afterward than in 1783.

Other articles of the peace treaty by their very generosity also gave trouble in the future. Britain recognized the "liberty" of Americans to fish in Canadian waters and they were also to be allowed to dry and cure their fish on certain shores. Debts owed by Americans to British merchants when the Revolution began were made collectible, inasmuch as the treaty promised that the creditors should "meet with no lawful impediment" to their collection. The British also felt that they must do something for the American Loyalists, almost 100,000 of whom had been exiled, otherwise British subjects would hesitate to support the Crown elsewhere in the Empire. After bitter quarrels, the Americans agreed that persecutions should stop and that Congress should "earnestly recommend" to the states that they restore confiscated property of Loyalists who had not borne arms. Both the articles on debts and Loyalists were compromises: Congress could not force the states to act, and the British knew it.

In only one respect did the treaty fail seriously to satisfy American hopes. No commercial arrangements were incorporated in it. Therefore, the young nation was shut out of its formerly protected British market and carrying trade. Americans soon realized that the imperial mercantile system had given their commerce many advantages. The closing of the British West Indies to American shipping was the most serious blow.

France, Spain, and The Netherlands in their treaties with Great Britain obtained practically nothing tangible in return for their war efforts. The French government was content to win greater prestige in the councils of Europe, although the cost of the American adventure was so great that it led to bankruptcy and a revolution which drew some of its inspiration from the American example. The Spanish government regarded this Republic with the utmost suspicion and set out to protect its colonies from the bad example and the expansionist hunger of the North Americans. Yet the suspicion of the Spanish brought them no more safety than French infatuation brought them. The Dutch were not afraid of republics, and they loaned the new government money at excellent rates of interest. But eventually—in the mid-twentieth century—the peoples of Indonesia demanded independence from The Netherlands on the American model.

Many Englishmen regarded the Treaty of Paris of 1783 as the death warrant of their country's greatness. The British negotiators had given away an empire without obtaining any guaranteed compensations such as Franklin had held out in his plan for "sweet reconciliation." The Franco-American Alliance was still in force. Americans, on the other hand, were astonished at the liberality of the boundary terms and objected only to the promises on behalf of Loyalists and debtors. Congress contentedly overlooked the commissioners' disregard of its instructions and ratified the treaty. Rightly, Americans regarded it as the birth certificate of a new nation pledged to principles of liberty and self-government more advanced than any in the world.

Rejoicing over victory and peace did not last long, however. Washington fondly believed, when he resigned his commission as Commander-in-Chief and said his moving words of farewell to his brother officers, that he and every citizen could now return to the simple enjoyment of the fruits of freedom and peace. But soon the condition of the country made it seem exceedingly doubtful that the great experiment could long endure. The main difficulty was that Americans had modified their society in various democratic ways without as yet establishing a government capable of protecting it against chaos at home and enemies abroad.

CHAPTER 11

The Internal Revolution
1776-1786

INDEPENDENCE FROM THE MOTHER COUNTRY WAS THE chief objective and main result of the American Revolution. But many peoples in the world's long history after achieving political independence have lost it by lapsing into anarchy; or, by submitting to dictatorship, they have lost their freedom as individuals. No sooner did the Americans decide to throw off external rule than they were faced with the crucial internal question: Independence for what? Whose notion of the good society should prevail in the new nation? Closely associated with the radicalism which won the vote for independence in the first place was a thoroughgoing plan for the reconstruction of American society on decentralized and democratic lines. Carried far enough, this program contained dangers of anarchy. At the other extreme, certain ·conservatives, while going along with the radicals in favor of independence after July 4, 1776, cried out against their domestic program and worked to install in America a replica of British society on centralized and aristocratic lines. Carried far enough, this program contained dangers of new tyranny.

The special character of American history derives from the remarkable answer it gave to the radical-conservative conundrum. During the Revolution, democratic features of the radical program were installed, but social anarchy was avoided; conservatism afterward came to power but dictatorship was avoided, and the constructive features of the federal system were permanently established. The Republic is not the creation of any one segment of the American people nor of any one political faction or philosophy. It is a joint result of the labors and dreams of individuals, groups, classes, and parties that were often bitterly opposed to one another in their own times. The Founding Fathers pointed the way to fruitful reconciliation by joining popular rights to nationalism, freedom to security, liberty to order.

State Constitutions and Bills of Rights

The radicals of 1776 stood for independence, popular rights, and state rights. They opposed compromise with Great Britain, aristocracy, and centralized power. Their program was supported by small farmers and frontiersmen of the outlying regions in the various states, by a number of liberal southern planters, by artisans and occasional merchants of the northern cities, and by a fraction of the educated professional classes everywhere—especially lawyers and dissenting clergymen. The radicals demanded independence in order to secure popular American rights; the British had centralized authority in order to suppress those rights; therefore, logic seemed to require the radicals to oppose centralization of government and to place all power in local governments even after British rule was abolished. Furthermore, this logic coincided with the current view of the philosophers of the Enlightenment that government was evil in proportion as it was distant from the people themselves; therefore, local government was less to be feared as the potential enemy of the people than central government.

Fortified by experience, logic, and philosophy, the radicals strengthened local government and jealously fought off "encroachments" of the Revolutionary central government, which actually was feeble. In the state governments they distinguished between the executive and judicial powers, which were in their view engines of tyranny, and the legislative power, which was in closest contact with the people and therefore most trustworthy. Even within the legislature they drew a distinction between the upper house, traditionally a more aristocratic body close to the executive and sharing some of its functions, and the lower house, the voice of the people. In the thirteen new state governments and the independent republic of Vermont, the courts were hedged about with restrictions and narrow jurisdictions fixed by the constitutions and legislatures; practically everywhere the governor was deprived of veto power over legislation; the upper houses of the legislatures were either abolished as in Pennsylvania or were made subordinate and given little more than advisory functions, while the true seat of power was lodged in the lower houses. These generally held the sole authority to initiate legislation; they held the purse strings in tight rein; they dominated the governors and in many respects the courts. They appointed, instructed, and removed the delegates of the states to the central Congress.

Government by the legislature was no more efficient in the Revolutionary states than in the Confederation; and step by step in later years the states modified their constitutions, distributing legislative authority between two houses and governmental authority among an independent legislature, independent executive, and independent judiciary. In the states as in the federal government, the dilemma between inefficiency on the one hand and potential tyranny on the other was eventually resolved by "separation of powers" among the three branches, and "checks and balances" in the relations of each to the other two. This gradual development within the states was not a defeat for the radicals. Rather, it resulted from their own recognition that a popularly elected executive was as trustworthy as a popular legislature in guarding the people's liberties, and sometimes more so. Furthermore, an independent judiciary could safeguard individuals when legislature and executive faltered. Thus each of the states eventually worked out its own marriage between popular rights and effectiveness in government.

The original state constitutions contained Bills of Rights which, along with the Declaration of Independence, were the charters of modern democracy in America. The Virginia Declaration of Rights (June 12, 1776) is the most famous of these, because it served as a model for many of the others and was typical of all of them. It was largely the work of George Mason, an aristocratic planter of liberal philosophic leanings who asserted the equal freedom of men and stated their inherent rights in much the same way that Jefferson did in the Declaration of Independence. In the Virginia document, magistrates were described as the servants of the people in whom all power is vested, and hereditary privilege was explicitly denied. The right of suffrage was claimed for "all men having sufficient evidence of permanent interest with and attachment to the community." These words were not interpreted in Virginia as requiring the lowering of the property qualifications for voters, but actually these were not high, and in the country generally the tendency was to reduce them. The Virginia Declaration of Rights circumscribed the judicial process with guarantees which became standard for state and federal courts: the right of the accused man to be confronted by accusers and witnesses; speedy trial before an impartial jury; moderate bail; no cruel and unusual punishments; no general warrants for search or arrest. It also called for freedom of the press, subordination of military to civil authority, and freedom of religion.

The Bills of Rights of other states added to the Virginia list freedom of speech, assembly, and petition; the right to a writ of habeas corpus, so that an accused person could not be held in prison without trial; prohibition of ex-post-facto laws (laws which are retroactive with respect to liability for punishment); narrow definitions of treason so that it could not be charged against a peaceable critic of government or its officials; prohibition of uncompensated governmental seizure of private property; and various other refinements of individual liberties and governmental restrictions. Vermont was unique in granting the suffrage to all adult males without property qualifications. The thirteen states generally made property qualifications for officeholders higher than those for voters. Most states also required religious tests for office holding which were acceptable only to Protestant Christians. The original constitutions were not fully democratic in the modern sense, but their tendency was unmistakably in the direction of political democracy. They provided foundations of fuller liberty and broader democracy than any in the world, foundations on which future generations could readily build.

Contrary to later American practice, the very first state constitutions were not framed by conventions that had been elected for that express purpose, though the desirability of this procedure, in order that the constitutions should be based indisputably on the popular will, had been recognized by Thomas Jefferson and others. The idea was expressed effectively by the citizens of the little town of Concord, Massachusetts; and the procedure they recommended was actually followed in their state, thus setting an American pattern. The legislature of Massachusetts asked the people to give it authority to draw up a new constitution, but the people of Concord in town meeting took the position that a legislature which should itself be the servant of the constitution was not a proper body to frame it, since the power to create implied the power to destroy. Therefore, they demanded that the people of the state should elect representatives to a special constitutional convention, and that the product of this convention should be submitted to the people themselves for ratification. Thus the sovereign people would become the direct source of supreme law. In its essentials this procedure was followed not only by Massachusetts, but afterwards by other states, by the federal government, and by many other governments in the world. This plan displayed the genius of the American people in devising practical solutions for theoretical problems. Besides providing means whereby the people could enforce their claim of government by compact, it showed how the right of revolution should be channeled into peaceful processes of change. At any time that the people, in Abraham Lincoln's words, "shall grow tired of their form of government," they can either amend it or demand a new constitutional convention. If one considers that the American people have now for almost two centuries been creating, amending, and re-creating their state and central governments, one can appreciate the stupendous value of the constitutional procedure which assumed characteristic form toward the end of the American Revolution.

The original state constitutions were the first in world history to put fully into practice the important distinction between fundamental law and statute law. This is the distinction that is referred to when it is said that the Americans were the first people to live under comprehensive *written* constitutions. The British "unwritten constitution" consists of a complex of traditions and Parliamentary statutes. Traditions may be undermined and Parliament may repeal its own statutes. Control of Parliament gives the British people indirect control over their constitution, but the American people, more suspicious of officeholders, have preferred to write out the charters of fundamental law and place them beyond reach of anyone but themselves. The statutes enacted by legislatures and the actions of officials must conform to the mandates and prohibitions of the fundamental law or they are null and void. "Judicial review," that is, the power of courts to compare the acts of citizens and governments, including statute laws, with the terms of constitutions, was incorporated in some of the original constitutions and implied in others. Judicial review was an American adaptation of the British practice of "disallowance" of colonial statutes, and this power of the courts has given rise to abuses and objections. But the people, first and last, are sovereign, and the governments which they have erected under written constitutions are their servants.

EXTENSIONS OF INDIVIDUAL FREEDOM

Religion

A considerable number of special privileges, hitherto legalized and enjoyed by particular groups, were destroyed by the revolutionary generation as being incompatible with the principles of the Bills of Rights. Among major objects of attack were the established churches. The Anglican Church held a privileged position in Georgia, South Carolina, North Carolina, Virginia, Maryland, and part of New York. The Congregational Church was established in Massachusetts, Connecticut, and New Hampshire. In all these states, the favored church was supported by public taxes, while Presbyterians, Baptists, Quakers, and other dissenting sects were discriminated against in various ways. The view of Roger Williams, that absolute separation of Church and State and equal freedom for all religions were required by the dignity of the individual's conscience, made little headway until revolutionary agitation against British rule turned men's minds against the Anglican Church as its handmaiden.

Until this time the ideal of complete religious freedom had been most nearly realized in Rhode Island and in the middle colonies and states, especially Pennsylvania, where diversity had long been tolerated. President John Witherspoon of the Presbyterian College of New Jersey at Princeton, a signer of the Declaration of Independence, was an ardent advocate of the Roger Williams doctrine, and he turned out many a graduate like James Madison who carried his views into a state legislature.

The successful but often difficult fight for the disestablishment of the Anglican Church can be illustrated by developments in Virginia, where Madison in the next decade carried on the work that was so conspicuously begun by Thomas Jefferson in this one. During the Revolution the General Assembly relieved dissenters from taxes in support of the Established Church, but it left unsettled the question whether the various Christian sects should be supported by a general assessment of the people or by wholly voluntary contributions. At this time Jefferson drafted his Bill for Establishing Religious Freedom, which was finally passed in 1785 through the efforts of Madison, while the author himself was serving as American Minister in France. The chief significance of this famous Bill, which Jefferson ranked next to the Declaration of Independence among his memorable achievements, was that it made the separation between Church and State complete and religious freedom absolute. It asserted unequivocally the principle which became orthodox American doctrine, that the State should neither support nor oppose any religious group, and that freedom of religious profession and practice should extend, not merely to Protestant sects and Christian groups, but to all forms of religion whatsoever. As a declaration of the religious and intellectual freedom of the individual this is an ineffaceable landmark in the history of human liberty. Not until a number of years after its adoption, however, did the last vestiges of the Anglican establishment disappear in Virginia. Questions regarding church properties long persisted, and so did the memories of this bitter conflict.

In other states the Anglican Church was disestablished with less difficulty before the end of the war, and most observers agreed that the new dispensation was beneficial to it in the long run. Reorganized as the Protestant Episcopal Church, it acquired an independent hierarchy of bishops which had been denied it while it was subordinated to the diocese of London. Deprived of tithes and dependent upon the voluntary support of their communicants, the Episcopalian clergy showed marked improvement as moral and intellectual leaders over the easy-going parsons of old. Furthermore, the Episcopalians adopted a constitution which reflected the democratic tendencies of the period by according to the laity much more authority within the Church than the Anglican laity enjoyed. This church gained independence and a higher degree of religious leadership by losing its special privileges and becoming truly American.

The Roman Catholic Church also benefitted from the Revolution. In Maryland, where it was strongest, its clergy and communicants helped gain religious freedom for all churches. The Carrolls, the most eminent Catholic family in America, produced a signer of the Declaration of Independence, Charles Carroll of Carrollton, and the first American Roman Catholic Bishop, John Carroll, whose diocese of Baltimore included the whole United States. The American Church had been subordinate to the vicar apostolic of London prior to 1776, and French Catholics attempted to take over the London vicar's function; but on petition of the Maryland clergy, Pope Pius VI created an independent hierarchy for the United States. The notable part played by American

Catholics, especially those of Irish origin, in the Revolution, and their numerical weakness, early established among them a tradition of loyalty to the free institutions of the new Republic as their best safeguard in a predominantly Protestant society.

The Congregational establishments in New England were not particularly affected by the Revolution. Their clergy were in the forefront of patriotic action and could not easily be attacked as enemies of liberty. But an entering wedge had opened a small crack between Church and State in Massachusetts. Dissenters were forced to pay a tax to support religion, but their money was paid over to dissenting clergymen. During the next two generations, orthodox Calvinism steadily lost its hold on the minds of even the Congregational clergy and the numerical strength of dissenting groups steadily increased until, in 1833, the last link between Church and State in America was severed in Massachusetts.

The drive for religious freedom resulted not only in the separation of Church and State and the independence of American churches from European national churches but also in a splintering of religious bodies which has been equally characteristic of the American religious scene. Freedom for any self-organized group to obtain recognition as a church encouraged a luxuriant growth of sectarianism. The very multiplication of sects is evidence that freedom of conscience was really achieved. Rationalist faiths such as Deism flourished among Americans educated in the science of Newton and the philosophy of the Enlightenment. Freemasonry claimed a large percentage of the Founding Fathers. Indeed, some conservatives interpreted the American Revolution as a plot hatched in the secret councils of foreign and American Masons. Many of the New England intelligentsia began to turn to unorthodox varieties of religion such as Universalism and Unitarianism. Among the frontiersmen and isolated settlers of the West, revivalism soon fastened fundamentalist doctrines on the minds and emotions of perhaps a majority of Americans. But an uncountable number simply ignored religion, while a few professed positive atheism. It seemed to many observers that the American Revolution harvested its worst fruits in infidelity and the mutiplication of sects; they were certain that political anarchy must follow upon such a breakdown of religious controls. But Americans as a whole reveled in religious pluralism and regarded the individual freedom it signified as a reason for loyalty to their government, the protector of the inviolate human conscience. Nothing in the young Republic was more striking than the successful demonstration in practice of the paradox of political unity through religious freedom and diversity.

Freedom of Enterprise

Just as the citadels of religious privilege were undermined by the Revolutionary generation, so certain forms of economic privilege were weakened or destroyed. The right to acquire and possess wealth was not under attack. On the contrary, this right was demanded in 1776 by the American revolutionaries as against monopolistic, feudal, and monarchical economic privileges of the old regime. As a result of the American Revolution, freedom of enterprise, that is, the equal opportunity of any individual to engage in any economic activity he chooses in order to amass wealth, and to hold onto his wealth or dispose of it as he pleases, became a living reality in America to a greater degree than before. Mercantilist restrictions were destroyed. The King's prerogative in Crown lands and in such matters as his claim to the best timber anywhere for the uses of the Royal Navy was abolished.

Yet overthrow of British rule was not sufficient to establish economic liberty within the states. Vestiges of feudal privilege survived in several of them, and these were immediately under attack. Most archaic, although not actually very important, were primogeniture and entail, which Jefferson opposed strongly. Under the Virginia law of primogeniture, the whole estate of a landowner who died intestate was inherited by his eldest son. Laws of entail in Virginia and elsewhere permitted a propertied person to forbid the alienation or division of his estate for many generations after his death, and often were an embarrassment to living owners. The tendency of both primogeniture and entail was to "freeze" property in the hands of a hereditary aristocracy. Economic mobility was furthered by their abolition, and the attainment of wealth made easier for the many.

Quitrents were a common lien on land titles, especially in the proprietary colonies, and they too were abolished. Land titles in "fee simple," that is, absolute ownership in return for the original purchase price, became the rule in all the states as had been the case in most of New England from the beginning. In the Hudson Valley remnants of manorial privileges over tenants were retained by the descendants of the patroons until well into the nineteenth century, but this was exceptional. In the Old World and in Spanish America, land was prized not only because it produced wealth but because it bestowed family distinction and privileges upon the owners. This idea was present in the southern states and persisted to some extent, but the American land system increasingly tended to take on a capitalistic rather than feudal character. Land became one more commodity available for speculation, with easy transfer of ownership and quick improvement or loss of fortune by persons to whom land ownership had formerly been denied.

The confiscation of Loyalist estates by the state governments had an important influence upon economic opportunity. Many of these were sold for the benefit of state treasuries without regard to social policy, but legislatures often broke them up into small parcels for sale at public auction or for gifts to veteran soldiers, thus strengthening the bias of the American land system towards small-scale and widespread land ownership. Furthermore, the state governments were liberal in handing out Crown lands and other wild lands to settlers. Easy access to land caused property qualifications for voting in an overwhelmingly agrarian country to be relatively insignificant as restrictions on democratic suffrage. Only after industrialism had created a large propertyless class of laborers did property qualifications assume a strongly undemocratic character, and then they were all abolished in the states.

The Antislavery Movement and Humanitarianism

Slavery was an institution that contradicted the liberal aspirations of the American Revolution, as the English were particularly fond of pointing out. But the British government had been the first obstacle to American efforts to check the development of the institution. Colonial laws against the slave trade had often been disallowed by the Privy Council because they would destroy the business of the British-owned Royal African Company. Sentiment against this traffic was specially strong in Virginia, and the most conspicuous patriot leaders there—including Washington, Jefferson, and Patrick Henry—deplored the institution. The radicals met their toughest domestic opposition when they attacked the labor system which seemed essential to staple production on large plantations. But few supporters of slavery advanced any argument except expediency, and it was generally assumed that the institution would presently be abolished everywhere. Meanwhile, the Revolutionary generation took action which was considerably responsible for the later fact that slavery became a minority interest in the Union.

The first attack was made against the most vicious branch of the commerce in human beings, the slave trade with Africa. The Continental Congress banned this in the course of its economic warfare against the mother country. But when Congress threw open American ports to world trade, Yankee shipowners seized the opportunity to gather in the profits of the slave trade as one more blessing of the new order. Some planters, especially those of South Carolina and Georgia, were eager to purchase fresh supplies of laborers, and it was this combination of shipping and planting interests that prevented condemnation of the trade in the Declaration of Independence, as was desired by Jefferson. Reformers thereupon turned to the states for action. Most of the states, including Virginia, prohibited the trade outright, but in the far South taxes or temporary prohibitions represented the maximum of attainment in this period and even these measures were circumvented.

Jefferson hoped that gradual emancipation could be started in Virginia, with the aid of the young men "who had sucked in the principles of liberty as it were with their mother's milk." But it was easier to reconcile practice with libertarian ideals in the North, where slaves were few because of economic conditions. Vermont, not yet a state, had already abolished slavery outright in its constitution (1777); and Pennsylvania, where the earliest antislavery society had been organized, chiefly by Quakers, provided for gradual emancipation before victory over the British had been won. In Massachusetts, where slavery had existed merely as usage without express enactment in law, it came to an end in 1783 as the result of a judicial decision which now seems extraordinarily symbolic. In the case of Quock Walker, the Supreme Judicial Court declared a slave free because the constitution of Massachusetts stated that all men are free and equal and that every subject is entitled to liberty. In Virginia, liberal George Wythe had similar ideas, but he was confronted with the fact that in his state the slaves constituted approximately 40 per cent of the population. Other northern states in which the proportion of slaves was higher than in Massachusetts while far lower than in the South, adopted schemes of gradual emancipation, though in New York and New Jersey there was delay in putting these into operation. In general, the difficulties in overcoming this obstacle to the triumph of the revolutionary principle of freedom were in proportion to the size of the problem, that is, to the number of slaves.

In the South, where the vast majority of the bondsmen were, there was reluctance to face the heavy financial loss, the probable disruption of the labor system, and the problem of future social relations that were involved in emancipation. Hence the reformers were checked in all the states below Pennsylvania. Nevertheless, gains were made in the liberalization of slave codes and in legalizing voluntary manumission. It seemed to many leaders that slavery was becoming unprofitable on worn-out tobacco lands, and they looked for the ultimate extinction of slavery by the operation of economic forces such as had caused its decline in the North. Planters like George Washington and Thomas Jefferson searched for new crops, and were hopeful that Southern agriculture would develop along the lines of the diversified-crop and family-farm economy of the North, as it showed signs of doing in this period. Washington willed that his slaves be freed after his wife's death. Other slaveowners made similar provision and more would have done so but for the fact that, under existing laws and customs, the status of freedmen was uncertain and often unhappy. A large number of planters, especially in Virginia, were infused with the humane spirit of the eighteenth-century Enlightenment. It was the invention of the cotton gin and the unexpectedly profitable employment of slave labor in cotton culture that defeated their hopes of the extinction of human bondage in all parts of America through the operation of economic forces. Baffled though Jefferson was throughout his public life in his efforts to reach a solution of this problem which would be acceptable to the electorate, he struck some long-range blows against the extension of slavery in this period. A provision which he drew in 1784 anticipated the prohibition of slavery in the territory north-west of the Ohio in the Ordinance of 1787. Also, his efforts at this time and later in behalf of small farmers were an indirect blow at slavery, since it did not thrive among them.

If the reformers of the Revolutionary decade achieved only limited success in the movement against slavery, they won other victories. A bar-barous relic of the past was the penal code under which death was meted out for many minor crimes which today receive short prison sentences or the attentions of social workers and psychiatrists. The legislatures gener-ally mitigated the severity of the penal code. This was particularly true in the matter of capital punishment, which was ultimately restricted by most of the states to the two crimes of murder and treason. The "crime" of failing to pay a debt remained punishable by imprisonment until well into the nineteenth century.

The American Revolution gave impetus to humanitarianism in many spheres. Private societies by the dozens were organized to improve the condition of the poor and extend a helping hand to the sick, the insane, the lame, and the blind. Individualism bore a double fruit in creating respect for the unfortunate as human beings and the determination of more fortunate people to organize themselves for the amelioration of social evils. Such voluntary organizations became characteristic of the American scene. Charity as imposed by religious injunction and directed towards good works was gradually supplemented by secular humani-tarianism imposed by the natural-rights doctrine and directed towards reform of social institutions as the best method of regenerating humanity.

THE CULTURAL REVOLUTION

Education

The passion for improvement also touched cultural life in the young Republic. The war temporarily eclipsed higher education, but peace brought an upsurge of interest and rapid progress. The name of King's College in New York City was changed to Columbia College and it re-opened in 1784 under the philosopher-president, William Samuel Johnson. The removal of the Virginia capital from Williamsburg to Richmond (1780) was a blow to the old College of William and Mary, but generally the prewar institutions flourished. The churches energetically established new colleges, such as the Presbyterians' Hampden-Sydney (1782) in Vir-ginia, significantly named for seventeenth-century English champions of principles for which Americans had been fighting, and Dickinson College at Carlisle, Pennsylvania (1783); the Episcopalians' St. John's of Annap-olis, Maryland, and the College of Charleston in South Carolina; and the

Roman Catholics' (Jesuit) Georgetown College in 1789. Such church colleges were not new in principle, for they were in the tradition of Harvard, William and Mary, Yale, and Princeton. Within a generation they were to be balanced by nonsectarian and tax-supported state universities, which were anticipated by some in this era. After the Revolution the classics continued to form the core of college curricula, but some republicans regarded classical education as an aristocratic relic which should give way to utilitarian subject matter. Others believed that the old curricula produced enlightened minds as well as gentlemen. They fought a bitter rear-guard battle against the utilitarians, and won an uneasy compromise in the "liberal arts" curriculum which persisted for generations.

In education as in so many spheres of American life, the new order of things encouraged experimentation; and the result was a rich variety of institutions—private and public, religious and nonsectarian—reflecting the diverse philosophies of a free people and meriting for American society the significant adjective, "pluralist." The local and state governments, churches and schools, businesses and clubs, humanitarian and propaganda societies in all their bewildering variety—all of them organized by the people themselves and devoted to the destruction of old evils and the creation of a better day for somebody or everybody— clearly show that a major consequence of the American Revolution was the unprecedented release of the energies and creative imagination of a people.

Literature

As individualists, Americans believed that the ultimate test of a society was the quality of the human beings it produced. In public life they could point to the simple greatness of George Washington, Benjamin Franklin, and other heroes of the era of Independence. But they also thirsted for heroes of art and science. Noah Webster sounded the call in 1783: "America must be as independent in literature as she is in politics, as famous for arts as she is for arms." But periods of public crisis are not the best times for cultivation of the quiet artistic ideals, and American society had to outgrow colonialism and frontier conditions before it could produce an important culture. Noah Webster himself admitted that homely spadework was necessary before his call would be answered by the appearance of American genius: his masterpiece was his famous spelling book and school reader for the grounding of millions of American children in literature.

American poets of the Revolutionary generation made manful efforts to answer Webster's call, but their verse, while it dealt with American subjects, followed the models of Augustan English poetry. Still it is a fact that the imagery of the American Revolution, like much of its doctrine, was derived from classical sources. Therefore it was not meaningless when Francis Hopkinson wrote an elaborate classical allegory, *The Temple of Minerva*, as a tribute to George Washington in 1781. Hopkinson tried to "Americanize" allegory in his later ballad celebrating the adoption of the federal Constitution, called "The New Roof: A Song for Federal Mechanics":

> Come muster, my lads, your mechanical tools,
> Your saws and your axes, your hammers and rules;
> Bring your mallets and planes, your level and line,
> And plenty of pins of American pine:
> For our roof we will raise, and our song still shall be,
> Our government firm, and our citizens free.

In general, classical models were followed by those writers who were conservatives in politics and fearful that the American Republic would become the playground of the mob. Thus the first American school of writers, the "Hartford Wits," loved to pillory democracy in such "Roman" satires as *The Anarchiad* (1786). Political radicals, on the other hand, found among the Indians models of natural virtue unalloyed by European aristocratic decadence. The meaning of the conflict is apparent in the names of veterans' organizations: the Society of the Cincinnati was founded for ex-officers and their eldest sons; but veterans in New York and other cities who had been common soldiers, and feared the Cincinnati as an entering wedge of hereditary aristocracy, named their organization the Sons of Saint Tammany in honor of a legendary Indian Chief.

Philip Freneau, "the Poet of the American Revolution," was the most talented exponent of political radicalism in the literature of the period. As a student at Princeton he distinguished himself in poetry, and his fiery love of liberty drew him into political writing during the Revolution. His capture and imprisonment in a notorious British prison ship embittered him against England. Next to Paine's his pen was the most effective one on the patriot side. After the war he devoted himself to writing realistic and humorous poems descriptive of American life and saturated with love of the common man. He echoed Noah Webster's demand for cultural independence from England:

> Can we ever be thought to have learning or grace,
> Unless it be sent from that damnable place?

Domestic conservatism was another target of Freneau's flaming hatred. He declared literary war against the Hartford Wits and afterward became the most effective early newspaper polemicist of the Jeffersonian party.

It was not a time conducive to poetry. The greatest literary achievement of the period occurred on the lower level of political prose. In this field the electric style of Thomas Paine has perhaps never been surpassed. Political pamphlets and newspapers offered by far the liveliest reading matter available to the public. But American drama was born shortly after the Revolution and was to some extent an answer to the demand for a native literature. Puritan objections to the theater as a glamorizer of sin were disappearing. Productions of English and European comedies and tragedies, usually by English touring companies, became frequent in the leading seaports during the later eighteenth century. The first play by an American to be acted publicly was Thomas Godfrey's *The Prince of Parthia,* produced in Philadelphia in 1767. This was a tragedy imitative of the Elizabethan English model. The issues of the Revolution were dramatized by no less a person than General Burgoyne, whose farce *The Blockade* lampooned the Boston patriots, and by an anonymous American who defended the patriots and lampooned the British in *The Blockheads.* The English dramatist Sheridan provided the model for the first American comedies.

Nevertheless, Royall Tyler's *The Contrast,* first produced in New York in 1787, contained fresh and rollicking characterizations of American types. This famous comedy dramatized the contrast between decadent English foppery and pure, plain Americanism. It created the immortal stock character, Jonathan, ancestor of Brother Jonathan and Uncle Sam. Tyler's Jonathan is a sturdy New England rustic, canny as well as naïve, honest and self-reliant. He learns through absurd experience not to ape English manners and morals; "If this is the way with your city ladies," Jonathan concludes, "give me the twenty acres of rock, the Bible, the cow, and Tabitha, and a little peaceable bundling." *The Contrast* was very popular and inspired many imitations. It illustrated the saving humor with which Americans could look at their present predicament of political independence and cultural immaturity. William Dunlap, the most successful early theatrical producer and a playwright as well, presented Shakespeare to American audiences more often than the work of any other playwright. He helped overcome the danger that in the longing for cultural independence Americans would neglect their great English inheritance.

The Arts

The rage for improvement and cultural independence produced a first generation of great American painters. In 1770, John Trumbull in his master's oration at Yale prophesied that Americans would overcome the British in the arts as well as by arms because they loved liberty and educated the whole people. He called for "some new Apelles" to paint the American scene, and his summons was answered by an astonishing group of painters. Benjamin West, a Pennsylvania Quaker, was acclaimed in London in 1771 for his *Death of General Wolfe,* and he accepted the post of Historical Painter to the King of England, but he did not forget his native land or its aspirations. In 1772, he explained to Englishmen that his painting, *Penn's Treaty with the Indians,* signified the conquest of a people without sword or dagger—a pointed rebuke to the British government's method of dealing with Americans. West established a school in London in which most of the leading American painters for two generations found encouragement.

John Singleton Copley of Boston was perhaps the greatest of the American "old masters." He painted New England patriots and Loyalists with impartial skill in his Beacon Hill studio until the oncoming war led him to follow West abroad. Sir Joshua Reynolds greeted him as unequaled among English painters. Critics still quarrel over the question whether Copley's work, like that of many other expatriate American artists, gained more in European refinement than it lost in native vigor as a result of his departure. Charles Willson Peale was content to commit his career to America because, as an ardent democrat, he noted that Americans had a growing taste for the arts "and are becoming more and more fond of encouraging their progress." After the Revolution, Peale painted its heroes and taught his chidren to paint. When George Washington granted him sittings, four painting Peales went to work on what the son Rembrandt Peale called "that dismal countenance." Rembrandt afterwards found a more congenial subject in the philosopher-democrat, Thomas Jefferson.

Gilbert Stuart became the most popular of all the portrait painters but his most famous work fell in a later period. Meanwhile, John Trumbull of Connecticut, a relative of the writer of the same name, claimed the title of "Painter of the Revolution." He served in Washington's Army long enough to witness and paint events from Bunker Hill to Trenton. In England, Trumbull was jailed in reprisal for the arrest of Major André, but West and Copley obtained his release. He made many portraits from life for his famous *Declaration of Independence.* For many years he toiled at heroic canvases celebrating battles and political events of the Revolution and he succeeded in fixing in American minds his rather romantic images of those events.

Emergent English romanticism dominated the Revolutionary generation of American painters, but in architecture English models gave way to a classicism believed to be more suited to the requirements of a libertarian republic. Thomas Jefferson, an amateur architect of great talent, was most responsible for the new trend in American building, especially public building. Thomas Paine challenged all imitation as unworthy of America, writing, "I have no notion of yielding the palm of the United States to any Grecians or Romans that were ever born." But

Jefferson followed the Italian and classical Palladio in believing that rules of good design were based on the laws of nature, and was convinced that temples erected by Romans to their gods were fit abodes for republican heroes. When he was minister to France after the American Revolution Jefferson gazed at the Maison Carrée in Nîmes "like a lover at his mistress," and he adapted this Roman temple to the needs of Virginia. The state capitol at Richmond was the result, and presently Roman and Greek temple forms complete with porticoes dotted the cities and the countryside in America.

Science

Jefferson was particularly interested in architecture because of its usefulness in a growing country, and he was glad to avail himself of the best classical and modern European models. He was also eager to draw on the science of other countries, and his own services, while minister in France, in sending home to the savants of the young republic information about the latest discoveries and inventions have caused him to be described as America's "scientific scout." This was in the spirit of the American Philosophical Society, founded in Philadelphia years before by Franklin, of which he was a member. The American Academy of Arts and Sciences in Boston, to which he also belonged, began its long and honorable history in 1780. Franklin's scientific pre-eminence in America was unchallenged until his death (1790); and next to him in scientific esteem was probably David Rittenhouse, the Philadelphia mathematician and astronomer.

Jefferson won his scientific fame chiefly as a naturalist, and his *Notes on Virginia,* first published in Paris in 1785 in a private edition, was destined to become the most famous American scientific work of the period. Described at the time as "a most excellent natural history not merely of Virginia but of North America and possibly equal or superior to that of any country yet published," it was notable not only for its scientific spirit but also for its patriotic fervor. While critical of certain institutions of his own state, including slavery and an insufficiently representative government, Jefferson sought to demonstrate that neither animal nor human life had degenerated in the New World, as certain French naturalists had rudely asserted, and he waxed eloquent in defense of the character of the Indians. Besides giving a large amount of accurate information, this informal and unpretentious scientific work defended the honor of human nature, challenged the doctrine of human inequality, and glorified the American philosophy of freedom. In its combination of universality and Americanism it was in the spirit of the Declaration of Independence.

Whether the civilization of the United States was more derivative than native at this stage is an idle question. Cultural independence had certainly not been achieved along with political, and without a doubt the American experiment had drawn profitably upon the whole heritage of Western civilization. But the citizens of this new country were doing their best to subject every item of that heritage to critical examination, aiming to reject what was outworn and to adapt to their purposes what was usable. At no other time in human history, probably, did a people ever set out so consciously to establish a civilization which should be, not rootless, but superior to its roots.

CHAPTER 12

The Confederation, 1781-1789

THE YEARS IMMEDIATELY FOLLOWING THE REVOLUTION and preceding the inauguration of President Washington were designated as the "critical period" of American history by the popular historian John Fiske. Writing a century later, Fiske held that the failure of the government the radicals had created in the Confederation brought on economic and political chaos and threatened the Republic with dissolution. The crisis, he believed, was surmounted only because conservatives succeeded in strengthening the central government by means of the Constitution of 1787, which went into effect two years later.

This interpretation gained wide acceptance and still persists to some degree, but in our century more careful historians have toned it down. In the light of present knowledge it would be foolish to say that the economic depression after the war was caused by the Articles of Confederation and cured by the Constitution; and it now seems that the dangers of domestic anarchy were exaggerated, though the perils of the international situation were not. The Articles of Confederation reflected the fears of a strong central government and reliance on the states that generally characterized the radicals, while the adoption of the Constitution of 1787 marked a conservative reaction. But we can now perceive the continuity of development and appreciate the extraordinary way in which these struggles were resolved in a new and better synthesis. Government under the Confederation was clearly inadequate in the domestic and even more in the international field, yet by its real services as well as its manifest failures it prepared the way for the better government and more perfect Union that followed.

GOVERNMENT UNDER THE ARTICLES

The American Republic, born on July 4, 1776, did not acquire a written constitution until March 1, 1781, when the Articles of Confederation were proclaimed. This was only six or seven months before the surrender of Lord Cornwallis at Yorktown brought the Revolution to a virtual end as a military conflict. All of the states except Connecticut and Rhode Island, which continued under their old charters after deleting references to the British Crown, had adopted constitutions by that time. Yet the famous resolutions of Richard Henry Lee, on June 7, 1776, called not only for a declaration of independence but also for the preparation of a plan of confederation. A committee for this purpose was promptly set up, under the chairmanship of John Dickinson of Pennsylvania, but independence was declared before his draft of "Articles of Confederation and Perpetual Union" was reported, and no action was taken on it that summer. To sever the tie with the mother country by resolution was far easier than to create a government that would be acceptable to thirteen different states then in the process of assuming full authority within their own borders. Young Edward Rutledge of South Carolina probably voiced the opinion that was dominant among all groups of patriots when he wrote: "I am resolved to vest the Congress with no more power than is absolutely necessary, and, to use a familiar expression, to keep the staff in our own hands." That is just what the states did—as long as possible.

Not until November 15, 1777, were the Articles formally adopted by Congress and submitted to the states. The struggle among the delegates had centered on the questions of the basis of voting, contributions to expenses, and common control of western lands. It was chiefly the last of these that delayed ratification. Most of the states ratified rather promptly, however, and long before the most reluctant of them, Maryland, gave her formal consent, Congress was guiding itself by the provisions of the Articles.

The general character of the Union is revealed at the very beginning of the document. This was to be a "confederacy," called "The United States of America," and consisting of states whose "sovereignty, freedom, and independence" were retained. The Confederation was described as "a firm league of friendship" for common defense and security, and in practice it was certainly much more like a league of nations than a union of the people. It worked best in times when there was fullest recognition of common danger.

To us it seems that the first central government was badly out of balance: framed in a time of reaction against executive power, it consisted of only a legislative body. Yet, in the light of historic developments elsewhere and particularly in England, it is clear that a legislature clothed with sufficient authority could have eventually created an adequate administrative and judicial system. The major fault was not so much that of imperfect form as of insufficient power. Congress was not authorized to set up a federal judiciary, beyond admiralty courts, and the administration of justice throughout the land was necessarily left to state and local courts. But Congress, in the effort to perform the limited functions that were committed to it, did create agencies and departments such as now fall within the executive branch of the government, and the services of these deserve more credit than they have generally received.

The chief sphere in which power was granted Congress was that of foreign relations. Only Congress could make war and peace, send and receive ambassadors, make treaties and alliances, and exercise maritime jurisdiction. In 1781, Congress created a Department of Foreign Affairs and elected Robert R. Livingston of New York as its first Secretary. He was succeeded after an interim by John Jay (1784), who performed the duties of this important office until Thomas Jefferson took them over in 1790 in President Washington's government. Early in 1781, Congress also set up a War Department under a single head—General Benjamin Lincoln in the first place. General Henry Knox assumed the office in 1785, held it throughout the rest of the Confederation's life, and was appointed Secretary of War by Washington.

The Department of Finances, established in the same year as the two others, was the most important of all during the administration of it by Robert Morris (1781-1784); he was even described as "pecuniary dictator." His views dominated Congress but that body had only limited authority to transmit to him. It lacked the power to tax, which the states had kept for themselves after denying it to the British government; and an amendment to the Articles which would have permitted a tax of 5 per cent on imports (called the Impost of 1781) was defeated in 1782 by Rhode Island. Congress could make requisitions on states for money, as it could for soldiers, but had no means of enforcement. It also lacked any authority over commerce. It could borrow money, emit bills of credit (paper money), and regulate coinage, weights, and measures. The adoption of the dollar and the decimal system of coinage, which was one of the constructive actions of the Confederation, came late in its life and was owing to Thomas Jefferson rather than to Robert Morris. It was on the recommendation of the "Financier," however, that Congress overcame its constitutional scruples and chartered the Bank of North America (1781). Morris expected this private institution to perform valuable services to the government, as it did, but it was too small and limited to serve Hamilton's purposes when he became Washington's Secretary of the Treasury. Morris, who was a very controversial figure, retired in the autumn of 1784, and financial matters were afterwards administered by a Board of Treasury.

Even in its own procedure Congress was hampered and at times gravely embarrassed by constitutional requirements. The equality of the states was assured by the provision that each state, large or small, would have one vote. Each state must send at least two and might send as many as seven delegates, and none of the important powers of Congress could be exercised without the favorable votes of at least nine states. But it frequently happened that fewer than nine states had two delegates present. For just this reason the ratification of the peace treaty with Great Britain was so long delayed that the formal notice reached England several weeks after the time limit had expired. Fortunately, the British made no point of the American failure to comply with the conditions. Unanimous action by all the delegations in Congress and agreement by all the states were necessary for the adoption of any amendment to the Articles. As the fate of the Impost of 1781 showed, the Articles were practically unamendable. This was a fatal weakness, for no unchangeable instrument of government can endure.

The Articles imposed co-operation among the states only to the extent usually required of sovereign governments entering into treaty relations. Each state gave full faith and credit to the public records, acts, and judicial proceedings of all the others; they were required to extradite criminals; and the citizens of one state were entitled to all the privileges and immunities granted in the several states. The Articles contained no bill of rights to prevent the central government from infringing on the rights of individuals, because the Confederation was created by and acted upon the state governments, not the individual citizens. The whole document was in effect a bill of *state* rights, and in practice Congress was like the central committee of a league, attempting to win the voluntary co-operation of the constituent nations. This has been aptly described as "government by supplication."

Creation of the National Domain

In one respect the Confederation turned out to be more than a league of sovereign states. It began to resemble a nation when it acquired title to a national domain. This was created from western lands to which certain states had claims resting on original charters. Maryland had no claims, and she refused to ratify the Articles of Confederation unless other states should give up their exclusive claims and turn them over to the central government. This was a reasonable attitude, because otherwise a few of the states would become so rich and powerful as to overawe the others—a situation with which modern planners of world government are quite familiar. The astonishing thing is that the states with claims did what the others asked, and their willingness to sacrifice particular interests to the common good attested their national patriotism.

Early in 1780, New York led the way in surrendering claims, saying that her action was designed "to accelerate the federal alliance." Actually, her claims were not strong. Virginia was the crucial state, for by charter she had the oldest and strongest claim to western lands, and she was much the largest by any reckoning. On September 6, 1780, Congress strongly recommended to the states that they make "a liberal surrender of their territorial claims," and at the same time it urged Maryland to ratify the Articles. Two Virginians, Joseph Jones and James Madison, then made proposals which were embodied by Congress in an important resolution on October 10: namely, that the ceded lands should be disposed of for the "common benefit" of the United States and be "settled and formed into distinct republican states, which shall become members of the federal union, and have the same rights of sovereignty, freedom and independence, as the other states." This was to be the basic principle of American expansion across the continent, and the formal recognition of it was a momentous act.

Meanwhile, another condition of cession was in the minds of leading Virginians, before they would yield an empire. Various speculative companies had acquired title to western lands from the gullible Indians, and there was fear that Congress, where these companies were very influential, might yield to their schemes. Jefferson in particular urged that the western lands be kept open on the most liberal terms for bona-fide settlers, especially small farmers; and Virginia in her own constitution had forbidden private purchases from the Indians.

By a resolution of January 2, 1781, the General Assembly of the Old Dominion, "for the sake of the public good," ceded to the general government all the territory northwest of the Ohio. The validity of this cession was contingent on the ratification of the Articles of Confederation by all the states (that is, by Maryland), and it was based on the expectation that similar cessions would be made by all the other states with claims to vacant territory. The resolution provided that in this area all deeds or grants from the Indians made for the benefit of private persons should be declared null and void. This ruled out the speculative companies. The Virginians also required that certain lands north of the Ohio be reserved for bounties to soldiers. While this offer was "not precisely conformable to the recommendations of Congress," the Marylanders decided to ratify the Articles.

When the Articles were proclaimed on March 1, 1781, the country finally had a constitution, but Congress was slow to accept the magnificent offer of the Virginians. This was chiefly because the land companies brought so much pressure that Congress would not consent to ignore their titles. It was not until 1783 that a committee of Congress worked out a compromise. Though an explicit annulment of the claims of the land companies was avoided in this proposal, the General Assembly of Virginia accepted it after making further provision for bounty lands to soldiers. What the Virginians reserved was a district between the Scioto and Little Miami rivers (shown on maps generally as the Virginia Military Reservation), and some 150,000 acres opposite Louisville for George Rogers Clark, "Conqueror of the Northwest" and his men. The deed of cession was presented to Congress by the Virginia delegation, headed by Jefferson who was now back in legislative harness. After considerable backing and filling Congress accepted it. It was signed on March 1, 1784, and the public domain may be said to date from then.

Other states followed the pattern that had now been set. The cession by Connecticut is of special interest, for she retained the lands below Lake Erie known as the Western Reserve. The southernmost states were slower in acting, but during the life of the Confederation it gained control of the region northwest of the Ohio. It was now more than the sum of thirteen sovereign states, for it held territory in its own name and began to administer this in the interest of all the American people.

CHARTERS FOR THE WEST

Next to winning independence, the government of the Confederation achieved its greatest success in formulating policies for the settlement and political development of the West. The relative failure of Congress in dealing with the Indians beyond the mountains was another count in the indictment of it by advocates of a stronger central government, but it set patterns for the future in its provisions for land sales and territorial government.

Ordinance of 1784

The Congressional leader who had the greatest faith in western frontiersmen and pioneers and the clearest vision of the future of the West was Jefferson, who started the Ordinance of 1784 on its legislative course. As chairman of a committee to prepare a plan of temporary government for the national domain he made a report immediately after Congress accepted the Virginia cession. Congress embodied in law its basic principle: that new states should be formed from the national domain and be admitted to the Union on an equal basis with the original members. Though imperial in size, the American Republic was not to be like the old British Empire in form or spirit. It was to be an expanding Union of self-governing commonwealths joined as a group of peers.

Unlike the more famous Ordinance of 1787 which superseded it, the Act of 1784 provided for the future government of all the territory that should be ceded by the states—that is, the region south as well as north of the Ohio. All of this was to be "forever" a part of the Confederation, and if Jefferson had had his way slavery would have been forbidden in the whole of it after 1800. Congress struck out the clause prohibiting the enlargement of the area of slavery, along with one forbidding hereditary titles. Also dropped were the polysyllabic names which Jefferson originally suggested for certain of the prospective states, though his Michigania and Illinoia afterward reappeared in the less classical rendering of Michigan and Illinois. The members of the committee were thinking of at least fourteen future states, even though there were only thirteen in the existing Union, and this is one measure of their audacity, for their own eastern states would be outnumbered. Provision was made for three stages of government in the West, and for self-government at every stage. First, the settlers in any one of these areas could adopt the constitution and laws of any one of the old states; this temporary government would continue until there were 20,000 free inhabitants, when they might frame a permanent government; and when there were as many inhabitants as in the least numerous of the original states of the Union they should be admitted as full partners. The idea of successive stages of government in the new regions persisted, but later acts did not allow self-government so soon.

This act of 1784 never went into effect, since it was contingent on the cession of all claims in the West by the old states, and its democratic provisions were never tested. Another member of the committee, David Howell of Rhode Island, well expressed the faith these men had in the "Western World." He said: "As a source of future population and strength, it is a guaranty of our independence. As its inhabitants will be mostly cultivators of the soil, republicanism looks to them as its guardians." But the Western World also opened an amazing financial prospect to the government. "It is equal to our debt," Howell said. Jefferson favored the most liberal of land policies—even to the giving of land away; but the treasury of the Confederation clamored for money and everybody recognized that Congress must gain some revenue from sales.

Land Ordinance of 1785

The Land Ordinance of 1785 required the division of all these public lands into townships 6 miles square, each consisting of thirty-six sections of 640 acres. One fortunate provision was that a section in each township should be set aside for education. The minimum lot was a section and the minimum price was $1.00 per acre. In requiring preliminary survey and providing for orderly sales of large blocks of land, the law was closer to the New England practice than to the more individualistic and less orderly Southern custom. Under the latter a settler could purchase a warrant, pick out his own land, and have it surveyed afterwards. The Southern practice was better adapted to frontier conditions and the law of 1785 was not encouraging to small, independent farmers. A section of 640 acres was more than a single family needed and the price of $640 was beyond the reach of the average settler. It is no wonder that the trend in later years was to

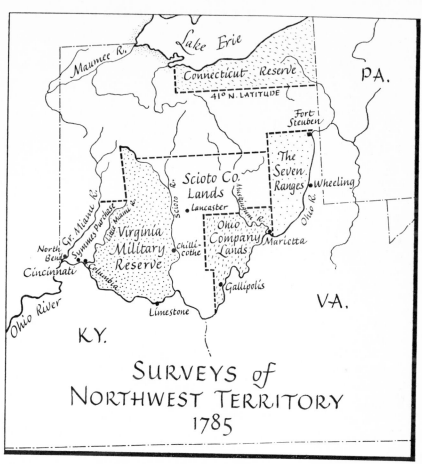

SURVEYS of NORTHWEST TERRITORY 1785

Lake Erie

Maumee R.

Connecticut Reserve

41° N. LATITUDE

P.A.

Fort Steuben

The Seven Ranges

Wheeling

Scioto Co. Lands

Lancaster

Virginia Military Reserve

Gr. Miami R.

Symmes Purchase

Little Miami R.

North Bend

Cincinnati

Columbia

Chilli-cothe

Ohio Company Lands

Marietta

Gallipolis

Scioto R.

Muskingum R.

Ohio R.

V.A.

Limestone

Ohio River

K.Y.

SYSTEM of PUBLIC LANDS SURVEY ~ 1796

Township

6 Miles

6	5	4	3	2	1
7	8	9	10	11	12
18	17	16	15	14	13
19	20	21	22	23	24
30	29	28	27	26	25
31.	32	33	34	35	36

6 Miles

Whole Section

640 Acres ~ 1 Mile Square

1 Mile

Half-section
320 acres

Quarter-section
160 acres

Half-quarter section
80 acres

Quarter-Quarter section
40 acres

reduce the size of the minimum purchase, nor is it surprising that under this law many became squatters on unsurveyed lands. Sales were by auctions, which were held regularly in the East. This provision favored large operators, who could buy whole townships and then parcel them out at a profit in small lots.

The treaties of Ft. Stanwix, Ft. McIntosh, and Ft. Finney gained important concessions from the Indians in the years 1784-1786, and the work of surveying was initiated under Thomas Hutchins, Geographer of the United States, in what became known as the Seven Ranges (beginning at the Pennsylvania line where it cut the Ohio River). But the surveying was necessarily slow and the Indian menace had not lifted. The first land auctions in 1787 brought the Treasury only about $175,000 in depreciated currency. Meanwhile, squatters were crossing the Ohio, asserting their right to take up vacant lands and establish their own governments. Troops vainly sought to displace them, and even George Washington described them as "banditti."

A group of speculators saw in this confused situation in the Northwest a great financial opportunity. Veterans of the Revolution had been paid off in Continental certificates of indebtedness which the government would accept for land but were otherwise almost worthless. General Rufus Putnam and other New England officers formed the Ohio Company, sold stock to veterans for their certificates, and proposed to Congress that it sell the company a giant tract at a few cents per acre, payable in certificates. Then the company could reap rich dividends by selling small plots. This was not according to the Land Ordinance of 1785. A shrewd lobbyist, the Reverend Manasseh Cutler, made the proposal to Congress. He found Congress little interested until William Duer, Secretary of the Board of Treasury which handled land sales, organized a group, including Congressmen who could not legally buy public land, into the Scioto Company; for this Cutler agreed that the Ohio Company would make purchases. Thereupon, with the authorization of Congress, the Board of Treasury sold more than 1.5 million acres to the Ohio Company at some 8 cents per acre, and gave it option on an even larger tract, which was destined for the Scioto Company. These lands lay between the Seven Ranges and the Virginia Military Reserve and bordered on the Ohio River.

Northwest Ordinance of 1787

Out of this sordid deal there emerged, very like a phoenix, the great Northwest Ordinance of 1787. Cutler told Congressmen that the company could not attract many settlers into the wilderness unless they were assured of the security of property in this lawless region. Congressmen knew that not only speculative interests but great national issues hinged upon western policy. From Vermont, which was a *de facto* republic threatening to rejoin the British Empire, to Tennessee (then a part of North Carolina), where John Sevier and others had set up the "State of Franklin," the West was seething with discontent and filled with the spirit of independence. On the other hand, conservative Easterners were certain that the wild frontiersmen could not be trusted to rule themselves and that, if they were granted equal statehood, radical Western farmers would soon control the central government and discriminate against Eastern interests. Congress had debated the issue for years; now in the summer of 1787 it quickly passed the Northwest Ordinance.

This was the most important law enacted by the government of the Confederation. Like the Ordinance of 1784, it provided for territories to become states by passing through three stages, but full self-government could be attained in only the last of these. The new system was colonial up to a point and then it became republican. In the first stage Congress would exercise authority through its own appointees—a territorial governor, a secretary, and three judges. When the adult male population reached 5000, the territory would enter the second stage; then the settlers would elect their own legislature to share control with a council of five appointed by the governor and Congress. This legislature could send a delegate to Congress who could speak but would have no vote. When the population reached 60,000 the territory could enter the final stage by framing a constitution and applying to Congress for admission to the Union on an equal footing with her older sisters.

Full statehood thus became a goal to be attained, but it was a sure one. Meanwhile, the individual settlers were granted protection against arbitrary power by a bill of rights. Among other things they were guaranteed freedom of religion, habeas corpus, jury trials, and security of contracts. Historically, the abolition of slavery was one of the most important features of the law but, unlike Jefferson's Ordinance of 1784, this law extended to only the region northwest of the Ohio. It also differed from the earlier act in that it provided for a smaller number of states in this region—not less than three nor more than five. In the course of time Ohio, Indiana, Illinois, Michigan, and Wisconsin were carved out of the Northwest Territory. The political provisions of the Ordinance were re-enacted by the federal Congress after the Constitution superseded the Articles of Confederation and this famous act provided precedents for later territorial legislation in other regions. Indeed, this American law offered a technique for the peaceful evolution of colonial areas into self-governing republics anywhere and set a model for the future liquidation of world empires.

Westerners were not entirely satisfied with it at the time. They detected Eastern fear and conservatism in several of its provisions: the

entire lack of self-government during the first stage, property qualifications for voters (50 acres) and legislators (200 acres), and the incon-
veniently large size of the prospective states. But these objections
dissolved as population grew and promises were kept. Settlers moved into
the Northwest Territory in swelling numbers. Despite its speculative
character, the Ohio Company proved to be paternalistic in practice, and
Marietta, which was established by it on the river in 1788, was a transplanted New England village with all that this implied in architecture,
education, and religion. Conditions were less happy in other places,
but Ohio eventually became a territory unto itself and, early in the
next century, a state. As one trans-Appalachian territory after another
was set up and state after state was admitted in good faith, the West
and particularly the Northwest became the most nationalistic of regions.
The original states had created the federal government, but that federal
government created the western states; it was the source and protector
of their rights and privileges. These settlers were not primarily New
Englanders or Virginians or Ohioans; they were first of all Americans.

THE ECONOMIC PROBLEM

While the Northwest Ordinance was a great achievement, it had little
immediate effect in enhancing the prestige of the feeble government of
the Confederation. By the date of its passage the general economic
situation, which had been at its worst about 1786, was improving, but this
was harder to see then than now. The difficulties of the previous years
were unforgettable. The economic problem had touched all levels of
private and public affairs. Debt and bankruptcy haunted farmers, planters,
merchants, state governments, and the Congress of the Confederation.
This state of affairs can be attributed to the fact that the artificial economy of wartime was followed by stagnation in time of peace, and that
inflation gave way to deflation. More specifically, the new international
situation was unfavorable to American commerce, and in a time of
heavy debts and taxes there was an appalling shortage of currency which
served to restrict if not to paralyze all forms of economic activity. The
conflicting interests of debtors and creditors underlay the political
struggles of the time. The attainment of general prosperity was contingent on the opening of markets and the creation of a sound and
sufficient currency. The government of the Confederation has been
blamed too much for a situation which could hardly have been escaped
by any government, but unhappily its powers were unequal to either
of these remedial tasks. Also, they were beyond the power of any single
state.

During the war there had been an abnormal military market, along
with risky but profitable foreign commerce. Prices rose because of the

large emissions of paper money and certificates of indebtedness by Congress and the state governments, and because of the activities of speculators and profiteers. But war prosperity quickly collapsed after the peace treaty of 1783. The prewar channels of commerce with the West Indies were closed, the French withdrew special privileges they had granted during the war, and the British imposed on American commerce such restrictions as they chose, being confident that they would get whatever trade they wanted. Independence carried with it a considerable degree of commercial isolation at first, and a major task of diplomacy was to provide ways of escape from this.

American merchants aggressively searched out new markets. In 1784 and 1785, for example, they opened trade with China. But these processes were slow, and not until the end of the period of Confederation did New England traders begin to pick up furs in the Pacific Northwest, take them to China, and barter them for Oriental products. Salem traders were making fabulous profits from this sort of business within a generation, but in the years just after the Revolution the region that suffered most from the depression was commercial New England. The most violent conflicts between creditors and debtors occurred there, for the merchants were hard pressed and the farmers were distressingly short of money. The southern planters and farmers suffered less, partly because the foreign demand for their staples reasserted itself, partly because they were better treated by their state governments.

The most difficult domestic problems of this time of depression were those of debts, taxes, and the currency—which were inseparable. Despite the virtual repudiation of the paper money by which the Revolution had been so largely financed, both the state governments and the Confederation emerged from the war in debt. The foreign debt of the Confederation need not concern us here, for the interest on part of it was paid well enough to maintain credit in the Dutch money market, and it was not now or ever a real political issue. The domestic debt of the Confederation was estimated by Alexander Hamilton as amounting in 1790 to about $42 million, including interest. Roughly speaking, it consisted of loan-office certificates, given in return for actual loans, and a variety of certificates of indebtedness for supplies and services. This paper had greatly depreciated but it circulated as a sort of currency. The loan-office certificates had generally come into the hands of northern merchants and financiers, while the certificates of indebtedness were more widely scattered. Since Congress had no power to tax it could not well take in and pay off this paper in a period of depression, or even pay the promised interest.

At the end of the period the state debts came to about half as much as the domestic debt of the Confederation. The states had the power to tax and they employed it in the postwar years. This was chiefly to pay interest charges, which consumed a very large part of state incomes. But, to cite a conspicuous example of successful state financing, Virginia paid off a large portion of the principal of her debt—especially the part of it which consisted of military certificates issued to soldiers. These certificates were exchanged for western lands (of which Virginia still had a plentiful supply) and were accepted in payment of taxes, then destroyed.

The great problem of individuals everywhere was to find something with which to pay taxes and private debts. Paper money had been repudiated at the close of the war, and in the course of trade specie had been drained abroad. The supply of money was disproportionately small in view of the resources of the country, and it was inadequate to the needs of the people. Farmers were at a special disadvantage, for such wealth as they had was in things not money. It is no wonder, therefore, that a clamor arose from farmers and debtors generally for new issues of paper money, for "tender acts" requiring creditors to accept land and produce in payment of debts, and for "stay laws" on collections. Men could be thrown into jail for debt, and they were in many places. On the other hand, farmers and debtors could gain control of state legislatures in a self-governing society.

By 1786, when the politico-economic struggle reached its crisis, seven states had adopted some form of paper money, though the conditions and fortunes of the emissions varied considerably. In South Carolina, where merchants backed an inflationary move and the large planters acceded to it, the paper money did not depreciate. It was also a recognized success in New York for a time, but it depreciated badly in North Carolina, where creditors bitterly opposed it, and that state was the most extreme case—next to Rhode Island.

Long noted for individualism, "Little Rhody" now provided conservatives with a flagrant example of the perils of popular rule. The farmer-debtor group came into full legislative control and translated its extreme demands into law. The paper money which was issued could be borrowed by debtors on easy terms and in theory creditors were forced to accept it. As a result some of the latter fled the state before their debtors while others refused to accept payment. This led to the famous case of Trevett vs. Weeden (1786), which the Supreme Court of the state dismissed on grounds of lack of jurisdiction while expressing the opinion that the act forcing creditors to accept paper money was unconstitutional. The judges were dismissed by the legislature, but in the end the law was repealed. By going to such extremes the farmer-radicals had played into the hands of the merchant-conservatives.

Shays's Rebellion

The most bitter of all these struggles between debtors and creditors occurred in Massachusetts, ending in the famous Shays's Rebellion. This was an instance of resort to violence by debt-ridden farmers who had failed to impose their wishes on the legislature. Massachusetts had tried to reduce her debt too fast and had not allowed enough for depreciation under the existing circumstances; the tax laws were weighted against the farmers; taxes were much higher than elsewhere in New England; and courts were harsh against debtors. This was all in the interest of the creditors, who were not only opposed to any form of relief but favored a deflationary policy which worsened the plight of debtors. Discontent was rife in the western part of the state where farmers comprised a more important segment of the population than along the coast, and when the legislature adjourned in July 1786 without taking any relief actions, meetings of protest were held in Worcester and Hatfield. These advocated an issue of paper money while condemning the political authorities. Violent action followed. Mobs prevented the meetings of courts in Northampton, Worcester, Great Barrington, and elsewhere. Captain Daniel Shays, a veteran of the Revolution, appeared as a leader of the insurgents in late September, when his followers confronted a body of militia in Springfield. The court sat, nonetheless, and the insurgents disbanded until their hopes of peaceful reform vanished; then the movement became an armed rebellion. Governor James Bowdoin, a merchant, declared the insurgents outlaws, and General Benjamin Lincoln was appointed by the legislature to suppress them. Shays's band was finally routed at Petersham; he fled to Vermont, and, although pardoned, he did not return to Massachusetts. This ignorant man believed that he was fighting the Revolution all over again and did not doubt that his method as well as his cause was just. The government of Massachusetts wisely refrained from reprisals and a few laws were passed that limited court actions against debtors.

The reverberations of Shays's Rebellion were very important. It frightened conservatives and moderates everywhere in the Union. George Washington wrote: "There are combustibles in every state which a spark might set fire to. I feel infinitely more than I can express for the disorders which have arisen. Good God! Who besides a Tory could have foreseen, or a Briton have predicted them?" This fear turned some conservatives to dreaming of an American monarchy as the only safe solution. At just this time, Jefferson, now in Europe and disliking kings more than ever since he had seen them in action, asserted that there was far more disorder in monarchial France than republican America. But he was too far away to have immediate influence on American opinion, and he was under no illusions about the Confederation. All conservatives agreed that Congress was helpless to solve the economic problem, and that restraint should be placed on the states in money matters. A central government which should have power to place the country's currency and public credit on a solid footing seemed to conservatives a minimum necessity if the country's economy was to be saved from ruin and its political institutions saved from rebels.

Still it is true that by 1787 some of the cause for conservatives' fears had disappeared. The defeat of Shays discredited violence as a means of redress. The vast majority of Americans, including radicals, accepted the peaceful processes of petition and election as making rebellion unnecessary and wrong. By 1787, deflation had run its course and prosperity was on the way. The movement for a stronger central government was supported chiefly by merchants and creditors, but certain of the outstanding leaders of the movement, notably James Madison, cannot be identified with creditor interests. Such leaders could see in the international situation a reason to strengthen the central government which, if less emotionally compelling than fear of internal revolt and control of states by radicals, was even more urgent.

FOREIGN AFFAIRS UNDER THE CONFEDERATION

Commercial Helplessness

The economic problem was itself inseparable from the foreign problem. The American economy was predominantly extractive. Products of the sea, the forests, and the fields had to be sold abroad for consumption or processing, and manufactured articles had to be imported if American prosperity was to be achieved. But trade had to be carried on in a world of powerful and predatory economic empires with which the government of the Confederation was inadequate to cope. Americans no longer enjoyed the privileges and protection that went with membership in the British mercantilist empire, and Britain herself now waged economic war against the young republic. William Pitt, a convert to the free-trade principles of Adam Smith, proposed to Parliament in 1783 that trade relations with the United States be reorganized on a basis of complete equality, but mercantilists and Tories would not so easily forgive the ungrateful Americans. Their views were summed up by Lord Sheffield in his influential pamphlet, *Observations on the Commerce of the United States* (1784). Sheffield argued that it was unnecessary to make any concessions to American trade, because this would be forced back into British channels anyway. At the moment he was right, and his views prevailed.

Refusing to enter into any commercial agreement whatever with the

United States, the British government proceeded to regulate American trade unilaterally by acts of Parliament and Orders in Council precisely as if the states were still colonies. Indeed, many of the regulations were more severe than before. American wheat, for example, was now excluded from the British market by prohibitive duties—the "Corn Laws," which were not repealed until 1846. Most injurious was the exclusion of American products from the British West Indies, which had formerly absorbed great quantities of American provisions. Britain was now determined to give her loyal colonies, particularly Canada, the benefit of markets the disloyal colonies had formerly enjoyed. The few articles which Americans could sell to British colonies had to be carried in British ships. This provision fully accorded with current mercantilist practice, but it was to the disadvantage of Americans in the carrying trade, especially New Englanders. American vessels were allowed to carry American cargoes to the British Isles, but they had to pay higher fees than British ships.

John Adams, after serving with Franklin and Jefferson on a commission to negotiate commercial treaties in Europe which had very slight success, was sent to England in 1785 as the first minister of the United States to that country, while Jefferson succeeded Franklin as minister to France. In England, Adams was practically ignored and sometimes snubbed. As told in his family, the story was that King George, at a public reception, turned his back on him and Jefferson, who was visiting him at the time. American merchants spoke threateningly of retaliations against British commerce and action was taken by some of the states, but Lord Sheffield had correctly foreseen that the Confederation could not impose a uniform policy on the thirteen sovereign commonwealths. Each could establish its own tariff laws, and, far from uniting for defense against British policy, they proceeded to use their power over interstate and foreign commerce to wage economic war against each other and to compete against each other for crumbs from the British table. When Adams asked British officials to negotiate a commercial treaty, the nearest thing to an answer that he got was a jibe that it would require not one but thirteen treaties.

In the Old World, British merchants alone offered long-term credits to Americans. By resuming in this respect the practices of colonial times they further exploited American weakness: American merchants could not resist the temptation to go ever more deeply into debt in order to obtain the British goods the American consumers needed. Hard money drained out of the United States into British hands even more rapidly after the Revolution than before, and rosy dreams of fruitful economic independence turned to fear of commercial bankruptcy. Some far-sighted Englishmen saw that a prosperous and solvent America would be a far better customer, but Tory mercantilism and vindictiveness were the bases of British policy.

Far-sighted Americans, on the other hand, saw that only a central government with exclusive authority over interstate and foreign trade could make equitable commercial arrangements with Great Britain and the other maritime powers. The United States already had a commercial treaty with France (1778) and the politeness with which Jefferson was received in that country contrasted sharply with the rudeness of British officials to him and Adams. Despite the weakness of his bargaining position, he gained some concessions from the French by patient negotiation. But, like every other leader concerned with the conduct of foreign affairs, he was convinced of the absolute necessity of strengthening national authority and power in this sphere.

More than commerce was involved. The inability of the Confederation to control the states' conduct toward foreign powers threatened to destroy the political as well as the economic independence of the United States. The three great imperial governments—Great Britain, Spain, and France—had no intention of allowing the parvenu republic to become genuinely independent and powerful within the generous boundaries of the peace treaty.

British Troops on American Soil

On April 8, 1784, the day before George III solemnly proclaimed ratification of the Treaty of 1783 and enjoined his subjects to obey it, his Secretary of State for Home Affairs secretly ordered the military governor in Quebec to ignore it and maintain British troops on American soil south of the Great Lakes. The British sought to retain control over the fur trade for the benefit of Canadian traders and their British backers, and to maintain alliances with the Indian tribes of the region who would serve as buffers against the expansion of American settlement beyond the mountains. The British had made promises to the Indians and feared that failure to keep these would provoke attacks on Canada. Also, they wanted to be in position to fall heir to the territory of the Old Northwest in case the young republic should collapse. The excuse made by them for retaining the posts in violation of the treaty was that the American states had committed prior violations by refusing to live up to the promises regarding debts and Loyalists. The American Secretary of Foreign Affairs, John Jay, was so disgusted with the states that he indiscreetly let it be known that he regarded the excuse of the British as valid. This made the latter all the more complacent and immovable. Congress was in no position to do anything about the gravest problem that an independent government can face—the presence of a foreign power on its own soil.

Spain and the Mississippi River

In the Southwest, the Spanish government compromised American independence even more seriously. Spain had signed no treaty with the United States and did not recognize its ownership of trans-Appalachia. Because of deep-seated fear of American freedom and expansion as threats to their own empire, Spanish officials determined to hem in the dangerous republic east of the mountains. The British-American Treaty of 1783 had designated the 31st parallel as the southern boundary of the United States, but Spain refused to be bound by this because the boundary of West Florida (now returned to Spain) had been more than one hundred miles further north when Britain had owned it (1763-1783). Spain also claimed territory as far north as the Tennessee River on grounds of military operations during the war. Beyond the Tennessee, Spain bought the loyalty of Indian tribes and bribed American settlers who were anxious to obtain the right to ship their produce to the depots of New Orleans. Thus Spain made American ownership of the whole territory south of the Ohio River a dead letter, and the promising settlements of Kentucky and Tennessee were in danger of becoming Spanish colonies.

The great geographic determinant of Western history was the Mississippi River. In 1780, John Jay wrote: "The Americans, almost to a man, believed that God Almighty had made that river a highway for the people of the upper country to go to sea by."

In 1784, Spain closed the Mississippi to American shipping. At the same time, certain favored Americans were given special permission to carry cargoes to New Orleans as a demonstration of the advantages of loyalty to Spain. Settlers were more inclined, however, to open the river by conquering New Orleans than by knuckling under to the Spanish dons. British agents talked to them about a British protectorate. George Washington traveled through the West and concluded that the settlers stood "as it were upon a pivot. The touch of a feather would turn them any way." But the majority hated both Spain and Britain and asked only that the American government should protect them from both and, most important, secure for them the right to navigate the great river.

During the war, Spain had temporarily relaxed her mercantilist restrictions against American trade, and this trade was a source of hard money, which was sorely needed. Don Diego de Gardoqui arrived in 1785 as Spanish minister empowered to negotiate a treaty, but he was forbidden by his government to concede navigation of the Mississippi. Congress at the same time forbade John Jay to negotiate a treaty which did *not* include the navigation right. The United States could obtain no trade concessions from Spain without virtually surrendering the Southwest to her. Caught in this dilemma, Jay gave in to the demands of Eastern merchants.

He and they induced Congress to change his instructions in 1786 and permit him to trade off navigation rights in return for commercial concessions.

News of this raised a fearful clamor in the West. Westerners threatened to join England or Spain or, better still, to organize an expedition down the river to exterminate the Spaniards. Southern states with western interests opposed the treaty, and without them a vote of nine states for ratification by Congress was impossible. Therefore Jay was forced to allow the negotiations to collapse. This experience led directly to the provision in the Federal Constitution of 1787 that a two-thirds vote by the Senate is necessary for approval of a treaty. The Jay-Gardoqui negotiations left behind them a heritage of western suspicion of the East, and at the time they nakedly exposed the impotence of the Confederation in the face of the Spanish threat.

Attitude of the French

The French menace was less immediate and less open. The Americans had abundant reason to be grateful to France for past services. The kingdom was still the ally of the republic and, in the opinion of Jefferson who was minister at the Court of Versailles (1785-1789), was still its surest friend. That was not much to say but it was something. At this time the French had no designs on American territory, but they were also allied with Spain and mindful of her interests. They valued the United States as a makeweight against the British, and the great foreign minister Vergennes had intervened in the Revolution for just that reason, but he had no desire for the young country to pursue a genuinely independent course and become too strong to manage. He counted on its being a satellite of France.

The official French attitude in the 1780's was reflected in a consular convention which Vergennes and Franklin negotiated in 1784, in fulfillment of a provision of the treaty of amity and commerce of 1778. This granted to French consuls in the United States privileges and powers which amounted to extraterritorial jurisdiction—that is, the authority of officials to administer the laws of their own country in another country. This may be reciprocal in form but when one country is far stronger than the other it is not reciprocal in fact. These provisions were incompatible with American sovereignty and constituted a threat against political independence. Congress, following the advice of John Jay, did not ratify this convention. Jefferson negotiated a new convention with Montmorin, the successor of Vergennes, and, without endangering the official friendship with France, managed to get rid of all the features of extraterritoriality but one: French consuls in the United States were given jurisdiction in civil cases arising there between French citizens, while the Ameri-

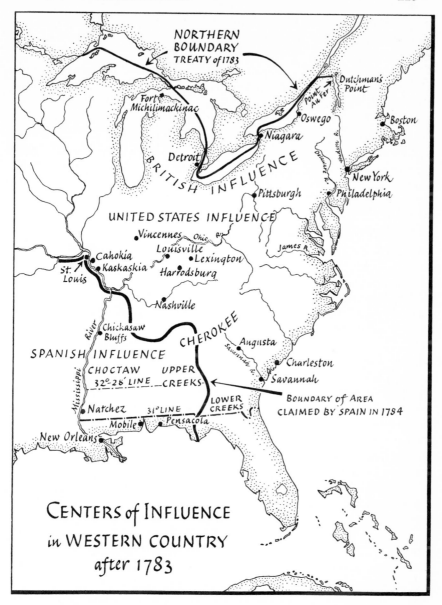

NORTHERN
BOUNDARY
TREATY of 1783

Dutchman's Point

Point Au Fer

Fort Michilimackinac

Oswego

Boston

Niagara

BRITISH INFLUENCE

Detroit

New York

Pittsburgh

Philadelphia

UNITED STATES INFLUENCE

Vincennes   Ohio R.

Louisville

James R.

Cahokia   Lexington

Kaskaskia   Harrodsburg

St. Louis

Nashville

CHEROKEE

Chickasaw Bluffs

Augusta

SPANISH INFLUENCE

CHOCTAW   UPPER

32° 28' LINE   CREEKS

Charleston

Savannah

Natchez   31° LINE   LOWER
CREEKS

Mobile   Pensacola

New Orleans

BOUNDARY of AREA
CLAIMED BY SPAIN IN 1784

CENTERS of INFLUENCE
in WESTERN COUNTRY
after 1783

can consuls were given this authority in connection with Americans in
France. Also he got the convention limited to twelve years. Jay recommended the ratification of this convention as a practical necessity. Actually it was the first international agreement approved by the United States
Senate (1789), but in this concession of a degree of infringement on
sovereignty it reflected American weakness under the Confederation.

In the 1780's the European powers did not expect or want the American experiment in revolution, liberty, and self-government to be successful. The state of American foreign relations offered the strongest of all arguments in favor of a new constitution. But the foreign and domestic problems were inseparable. A prosperous economy required a sound currency, the vitalization of public credit, and central control over interstate and foreign commerce; and all of these were prerequisite to the gaining of full independence from powers of the Old World which were not friendly to liberty.

CHAPTER 13

The Constitution of 1787

THE MEN WHO CREATED THE CONSTITUTION AND brought about its adoption had to overcome vast difficulties and their success still seems surprising. This constitutional movement as a whole has been described as a conservative revolution, in contrast to the radical revolution of 1776, but the most notable fact about it and the most wonderful is that the needs of the hour were met by the appeal of wise men to reason, rather than by the recourse of violent men to force. The leaders who met in the Federal Convention sought and found a middle way between anarchic localism and centralized tyranny; and as the Declaration of Independence voices a devotion to liberty which is characteristically American, the Constitution typifies American political realism and ability to compromise. There is no necessary conflict between these two great charters; and the Constitution, like the Declaration, was a supreme expression of the American mind.

THE FEDERAL CONVENTION

The members of the Congress, as James Madison said, had kept the Confederation afloat by working constantly at the pump, not by stopping the holes in the vessel. They were aware of the leaks, but all their efforts to render the ship seaworthy "had been frustrated by the selfishness or perverseness of some part or other of their constituency." Rhode Island, a "perverse sister," had blocked the Impost of 1781; and New York defeated the one of 1783 after a three-years' delay. The commercial state of New York was profiting greatly from the tariff duties she had imposed in her sovereign right and was disposed to grant no income from that source to Congress. Thus the effort to gain for the Confederation an independent income was a failure. An amendment granting Congress power to regulate foreign and interstate trade was debated in that body in 1784-1785, and this was defeated despite the provision that the duties would actually go to the states in which they were collected.

In the summer of 1786, a Congressional committee headed by James Monroe proposed amendments to the Articles which would have given Congress reasonable assurance of financial support and authority to regulate commerce, along with certain fresh powers to maintain full representation of the states and thus be able to carry on business. These amendments might have alleviated the most grievous ills of the immediate situation, but the legislative body never got around to passing them, and, judging from past experience, the states would not have accepted them if it had. The chances of any sort of constitutional change at the initiative of Congress had reached the vanishing point. Therefore, those who wanted change, whether great or small, centered their hopes in the winter of 1786-1787 on a movement which originated outside of the existing central government.

Preliminaries

The Convention in Philadelphia in the summer of 1787 was the consequence of two earlier interstate meetings of limited scope, the very inadequacy of which caused discerning men to conclude that a continental convention with broad purposes was necessary. The first of these two meetings was a very small one. In the summer of 1784, James Madison, who had completed a three-year tour of duty in Congress and was now an active member of the Virginia House of Delegates, made a motion in that body which led to the appointment of commissioners, including himself, to confer with representatives of Maryland about the navigation of the Potomac. This was a matter close to the heart of Washington, who lived on the banks of that river, and the deliberations took place in March 1785 at his hospitable home—which he described as a "well resorted tavern." Since Governor Patrick Henry forgot to inform Madison of the meeting he was not there, but an agreement was reached and he handled this interstate compact in the Virginia Assembly.

The Mount Vernon Conference, as this was called, dealt successfully with certain matters of commerce relating to two states, but Madison clearly saw that interstate and foreign trade could be effectively regulated only by the central government. The Virginia Assembly agreed (January 21, 1786) to a resolution which he drafted and John Tyler introduced, inviting all the states to send representatives to a commercial conference. The Annapolis Convention of September 1786 resulted.

Most of the states named deputies, but only a dozen men attended and they represented only five states. Madison, the moving spirit, gained powerful support from Alexander Hamilton, who came down from New York and drafted the address which was the only tangible result of the three-days' session. This went beyond commercial questions. It called upon all the states to appoint special commissioners to devise provisions which would render the Constitution "adequate to the exigencies of the Union." These proposals were to be reported to Congress and if approved by that body they were then to be referred to the states and confirmed by all of them. This little group of men made the specific suggestion that the meeting should be in Philadelphia on the second Monday in the following May.

Half a dozen states appointed delegates without waiting for Congressional action. Virginia was the first, and her action was made all the more impressive by the selection of George Washington to head her distinguished delegation. Madison induced him to accept. New Jersey, Pennsylvania, North Carolina, Delaware, and Georgia followed; and on February 21, 1787, Congress passed a resolution making the call for the Convention official. Congress admitted that there were "defects" in the Confederation and recognized that a convention was probably the best means of "establishing in these states a firm national government." The language itself was significant, and the changes were afterwards rung on the word "national." The Convention was to revise the Articles so as to render them "adequate to the exigencies of government and the preservation of the Union," and it was to report to Congress and the various legislatures.

The passage of this resolution encouraged other states to act. Shays's Rebellion had just occurred in Massachusetts, and this accelerated the movement for a stronger government. One New England state had no share whatsoever in these developments, however: Rhode Island stuck to her independent course and was never represented in the Convention. All the other states sent delegates, though those from New Hampshire did not arrive until the sessions were half over, because her government had trouble finding the money for their expenses.

The Federal Convention met in the Pennsylvania State House, where the Declaration of Independence had been adopted. On May 25, when at length a majority of the states were represented, the meeting was organized by the unanimous election of George Washington as president. The rules of procedure were that all voting should be by states, as in Congress, and that a majority of the states present would be sufficient to decide any question. But for the first provision the meeting would have broken up, and without the second very little would have been accomplished. With only slight interruption, the daily sessions continued until September 17, when the engrossed Constitution was signed in the names of all the states present by all of the delegates present except three.

This close approximation of unanimity is something to marvel at. It could hardly have been attained if the proceedings had not been strictly secret, and if these men had not been wholly free to change as well as to speak their minds. This secrecy was deplored by some leaders who were not there, Jefferson for instance, but it now seems exceedingly fortunate that the delegates did not have to talk and vote in the glare of publicity. Some fifty-five men attended the meetings at one time or another, but the average number present was only about thirty. This group was more like a large committee than a modern legislative body.

An "Assembly of Demigods"

Two of the leading statesmen of the day whose names are inseparable from the Declaration of Independence—Thomas Jefferson and John Adams—could not share in the making of the Constitution since they were on missions abroad. Writing from Paris to his friend Adams in London, Jefferson described this Convention as an "assembly of demigods." George Washington, now at the peak of popularity, came as near being a demigod in the eyes of his countrymen as any American who ever lived, and the prestige which he contributed to this gathering was an indispensable factor in its success. Second only to him in American esteem, and second to no one in world-wide reputation, was Benjamin Franklin, now eighty-one years old but still wise and witty. Nobody else who was there matched these two in fame then or afterwards, but James Madison and Alexander Hamilton stand very high on any list of American immortals. Madison, who was now thirty-six, was personally unimpressive but by common consent he was the most effective member of this body. On the other hand, Hamilton, who was even younger, played no important part. Outvoted by his two colleagues from New York, he attended relatively few sessions and his advice was little heeded.

Much more important was James Wilson of Pennsylvania, a near-sighted Scot whose national vision was far-reaching. Gouverneur Morris from the same state, a gallant with a shrunken arm and wooden leg, was one of the most brilliant of all the delegates though distrusted by some, and he left his mark on the language of the Constitution. Other men who made distinct contributions, when the time came for compromise, were Roger Sherman and Oliver Ellsworth of Connecticut; and John Rutledge of South Carolina was one of the more useful members. Governor Edmund Randolph of Virginia and George Mason, author of the Virginia Declaration of Rights, belong on any list of distinguished and influential delegates, even though they declined to sign the Constitution in the end, along with Elbridge Gerry of Massachusetts. Some of the delegations were mediocre; but almost all of these representatives had held important offices in their own communities and most of them had served at some time in Congress. They were men of large experience in state and Continental affairs and above all things they were practical.

In his notable book, *An Economic Interpretation of the Constitution of the United States* (first published in 1913), Charles A. Beard laid great emphasis on the identification of these men with the propertied class, especially the creditor class, and on the lack of representation of the small farmers and artisans. It is unquestionably true that the delegates belonged to the upper economic group from which the political leaders of the time were almost invariably drawn. The same can be said of most of the signers of the Declaration of Independence. It is also true that they were opposed to the sort of policies that had been carried through the legislature of Rhode Island by the debtor-farmers and had been championed by Daniel Shays and his followers in Massachusetts. The delegates had no sympathy with what they supposed to be an attempt to abolish private and public debts by legislative action or, worse still, by physical revolt. It would be a great mistake, nevertheless, to assume that everybody who was against Shays and the states' paper money was thinking solely or primarily of the particular interests of the creditor class. If we make a sharp distinction, as Beard did, between real property (such as land) and personalty (in some sort of paper), the southern planters were chiefly concerned about the former, and, despite some holdings of state and Continental paper, they were more often debtors than creditors. Special concern for the commercial and creditor groups was best exemplified in this period by Hamilton, who was of little influence in the Convention though of vast importance later. The dominant spirit of that body can be best ascertained by reading the mind of Madison. In financial matters he was characteristically conservative, he was strongly opposed to any form of repudiation, and to a notable degree he spoke for the general interest which comprehended all classes.

Madison held no securities which stood to appreciate in value by the establishment of a strong central government, and he had a conspicuous record as a defender of the rights of all men as individual human beings. It was he who carried through the Virginia Assembly, in Jefferson's absence abroad, the latter's notable revisal of the state's laws and, most particularly, the famous bill for establishing religious freedom. He deserved a lion's share of credit for the "philosophical legislation" of Virginia which won the admiration of enlightened liberals on both sides of the Atlantic. At the same time he was a political and economic realist. No leader of his day appreciated more fully than he that political conflicts more often arise from economic causes than any other; and he described this clash of interests so well that his words have been endlessly quoted. He recognized rich and poor, creditors and debtors, a landed interest, a manufacturing interest, a mercantile interest, a moneyed interest, along with many others; and he saw in the regulation of these the major task of government. But, unlike Hamilton, he did not believe in the dominance of the few over the many; and, unlike Karl Marx, he did not believe in the dominance of the many over the few. He believed that these various conflicting interests would balance each other off and cancel each other out sufficiently to avoid injustice, and his hope lay in the diversity of a large country. At this stage of his career he was specially fearful of what was afterward called the "tyranny of the majority," and he saw a dangerous possibility of this in state actions against private property. But he was not thinking of one kind of property in preference to another, and his record showed that he was concerned to protect religious as well as economic minorities. He contributed signally to American political philosophy by preaching the blessings of diversity; and if his thought is hard to grasp when stated abstractly it has been illustrated a thousand times in the history of his country. His chief conviction was that tyranny has been rare where interests have been many and no one of them has been able to gain predominance.

One of Madison's colleagues in the Convention said that he was always the best informed delegate on any point that came up in debate. This was no accident. Ever the scholar in politics, he had prepared himself fully and specifically for this occasion. His special preparations, which extended over a period of at least two years, were greatly facilitated by the books his friend Jefferson sent him from Europe. These enabled him to make a particular study of ancient and modern confederacies, and it was in the light of historical as well as personal experience that he viewed the existing American Constitution and perceived its "mortal ills." The simplest statement of the purposes he brought to Philadelphia is that he wanted this Confederacy to be transformed into a nation.

One can argue endlessly about what constitutes a nation, but the extreme alternatives which these men faced can be stated simply. On the one hand was a group of virtually independent states and on the other a consolidated republic in which the states would virtually disappear. Madison was looking for middle ground which would "support a due supremacy of the national authority, and leave in force the local authorities so far as they can be subordinately useful." It was characteristic of him to seek a working balance and to oppose most strongly the evils which were greatest at a particular time. He talked a good deal about the rights of the states in later years, but his chief concern now was to reduce centrifugal forces and to strengthen the central authority of the republic.

Extreme advocates of national authority were relatively unimportant in the Convention and the most extreme group of all was without a voice. There were in the country old army officers, members of the Society of the Cincinnati, who would have liked to establish a military dictatorship and make George Washington the King. But for Washington's own absolute refusal, such a movement might have gained great headway while the Confederation was faltering. In 1787, however, representatives of this point of view were conspicuously absent from the Convention, just as the farmer-debtors were.

FRAMING THE CONSTITUTION

The Virginia Plan

A few days after the Convention was organized, Edmund Randolph presented to it on behalf of the entire delegation from his state a set of fifteen resolutions comprising what is known as the Virginia Plan. After introducing the resolutions on May 29, Randolph withdrew the first of them the next day. This had implied that a mere correction of the Articles of Confederation would be sufficient. The three resolutions that he offered in place of the first on May 30 stated forcefully that a mere "federal" Union would not be sufficient, and that a "national" government, consisting of a *supreme* legislature, executive, and judiciary, should be created.

The Virginia Plan provided the basis of discussion in the Convention for more than two weeks, and not until June 15 was it challenged as a whole. It called for a central government with three branches. A legislature in two houses was recommended, along with a national executive and national judiciary. This was to be a new government in structure. But the three branches lacked the degree of mutual independence that was finally granted them, since the legislature would have elected the executive and the judges. The best clue to the nationalism of the Virginia Plan is to be found in its provisions for representation. Here, also, is the best explanation of the lengths to which Madison was willing to go in granting authority to the legislature. He was willing to trust it if it could be based on the sovereignty of the whole people. The crucial resolution was the one calling for representation in the legislature in proportion to quotas of contributions or to free population. This struck directly at the equality of the states in voting, which was the fundamental principle of the Confederation and had made it a league rather than a nation.

The injustice of the existing situation was obvious to the Virginians, whose state had no more voice in Congress than Delaware though it was believed to have sixteen times as many people. More than the interests of particular states was involved; this was a question of the basis of representative government. Should the basis be the states as governments (meaning in practice the legislatures) or the states as people? The Virginia Plan called for the election of the members of one house of the central legislature by the people and for the election of the members of the other by the first house from nominees of the state legislatures. The lower, popularly-elected house was to be the most important part of the central structure. Furthermore, the final resolution called for the submission of the new Constitution to conventions which were "expressly chosen by the people." The whole new structure was to be grounded on popular approval. This recognition of popular sovereignty is the more significant because of the antidemocratic reaction of the times.

The Virginia Plan appealed to states with a relatively large population or with such a large area that they might expect to be populous in the future; and when the Committee of the Whole approved the three-fifths rule for slaves the principle of proportionate representation in both houses of Congress became generally acceptable to the Southern states. But the fears of the small Northern states were rising. Quite clearly they were going to have a much smaller share in the new government than they had had in the Confederation, and they became increasingly reluctant to surrender the principle of state equality. Some of their delegates were now arguing that, if proportionate representation should obtain, the only fair procedure would be to throw all the states into "hotchpotch" and redivide them so as to make them equivalent in size. Representatives of the large states, such as Virginia and Pennsylvania, described this proposal as wholly impracticable, but they could not properly object to the request of certain small states for delay in order that they might present a plan of their own.

The New Jersey Plan

The plan that William Paterson of New Jersey offered on June 15 called merely for a strengthening of the Confederation without changing its character as a league of states centering on Congress. Additional powers were given that body to raise revenue, control commerce, and make requisitions on the states. There was to be an executive, consisting of more than one person and elected by Congress, and a judiciary without inferior courts and with only appellate jurisdiction. The strongest of the resolutions provided that acts of Congress and treaties should be the "supreme law" of the states and that the various state courts should be bound by them. This sweeping assertion of national authority afterwards got into the Constitution, but in the New Jersey Plan it was coupled with a government which was structurally weak and could never have been truly representative. The fatal flaw of the Plan lay in its basic assumption that the states were governments first of all, rather than people, and that they were equal in authority in the Union.

In the course of the discussion of the New Jersey Plan, Alexander Hamilton expressed his unfavorable opinion of it in no uncertain terms, and at the same time manifested his dissatisfaction with the Virginia Plan. His alternative proposals were not offered to the Convention; he merely read them and gave them to Madison to file. It was fortunate for his public popularity that his speech and proposals were not published until long after his death and that only a few of his contemporaries knew how doubtful he was of the success of the American Republic. The

British government was the best in the world, he believed, and the only one that united "public strength with individual security." He wanted a new American government, with decisive powers and complete sovereignty, but he was not one to stress the sovereignty of the people. He spoke of the "amazing violence and turbulence of the democratic spirit," and, while approving the election of members of the House of Representatives by popular vote, he wanted the Senate, as well as the Executive, to be chosen by electors one or two removes from the populace and to hold office for life, thus serving as a barrier against pernicious innovations after the manner of the House of Lords. Not only did he favor a President for life; he favored giving this officer a full veto over all laws passed by Congress and the right to appoint all the governors of states, who should have a similar authority over the actions of state legislators. This would have been consolidation with a vengeance, and if it was not monarchical in name it was almost that in spirit.

Hamilton's antidemocratic sentiments were undoubtedly approved by some members of the Convention, but not even he thought it feasible to set up as consolidated a system as he favored in theory. Nor were many delegations now satisfied with the sort of federation the New Jersey Plan would have maintained. Consequently, when the matter was put to a vote in the Committee of the Whole on June 19, the amended Virginia Plan was preferred to the one Paterson had submitted. Strong opposition to proportionate representation in both houses of Congress continued, however. The feeling in late June and early July was so intense that some delegates believed the Convention to be on the verge of dissolution, and Benjamin Franklin proposed that the sessions be opened with prayer for Divine assistance.

The Great Compromise

A committee containing a representative of each state recommended what has come to be known as the Great Compromise of the Constitution, and after the working out of certain details it was formally adopted on July 16. The crucial feature of this was the concession to the small states of an equal vote in the Senate. The provision for representation in the lower House was essentially the same as had already been agreed to: namely, representation was to be based on the respective numbers of inhabitants, slaves being counted as three-fifths. The provision that direct taxes should be apportioned on the same basis may be regarded as a concession by the Northern states, since it assured the Southerners that slaves would not be taxed as such. Part of the proposal was that money bills should originate in the House of Representatives and not be amendable by the Senate, though they might be rejected. Madison correctly judged this concession meaningless, and in the end the

Senate was left as free to amend money bills as any others. It was generally believed, nonetheless, that the House would be the more important legislative branch. The number of representatives from each state was specified in the first instance, and there was a good deal of guesswork in the absence of precise information about the population; but provision was made for an enumeration within three years of the first meeting of Congress and within every ten years thereafter.

On the other hand, the concession of state equality in the Senate made it impossible for that body to be genuinely representative of the American people. The convention at a later time made this situation irremediable: in the Article of the Constitution dealing with Amendments it include the specific declaration that no state may be deprived of its equal suffrage in the Senate without its own consent. Thus the Great Compromise based the membership of the legislative branch of the government on geography as well as population and imparted to Congress a federal as well as a national character. Some of the leading delegates, like Madison, and some of the largest states, like Virginia and Pennsylvania, opposed this settlement, but they came to recognize it as the necessary price of Union. After the Great Compromise, a report got into a newspaper that a proposal had been made to give the name "Unanimity Hall" to the room where the Convention was meeting. From this time on, the small states were more eager than the large ones to strengthen the central government, realizing that they would have a larger share in it than was warranted by their population or their wealth.

The Federalism of the Constitution

One of the most important of the questions which were still unsettled when the Committee on Detail was elected was that between an enumeration of the powers of the central government and a general grant of power. On this point the states had been evenly divided and the alignment was not determined by their size. As the problem was finally worked out, the central government was to be one of specified powers and functions but the scope and exercise of these were broadened by certain general expressions, chiefly the "general welfare clause" and the "necessary and proper clause." Also, a whole group of powers formerly exercised by states and falling mostly in the fiscal and commercial fields were to be explicitly denied the states. There remained, however, a very large residue of powers that were neither granted the central government nor denied the states, and by necessary implication these remained with the latter or the people. This was not explicitly stated in the Constitution drafted in Philadelphia, but the Tenth Amendment (1791) soon made that point entirely clear.

The Fathers had arrived at a dual system. This involved not merely the division of the field of government in a large country through force of practical necessity, but also the recognition in principle of both the general idea of the Union and the local idea of the individual state. The Union and the states were coexistent, and neither was at the mercy of the other. Expounding the Constitution a few weeks after the Convention, Madison said that it was neither national nor federal but a "composition of both." It was on a fresh pattern which was neither that of a league nor a consolidated republic. Conceivably it might veer in either direction and the draftsmen regarded excessive localism as the more immediate danger, but they sought to strike a balance and show the middle way. A fresh term was needed to describe their point of view, and the one most commonly employed in the next few years was "federalist." Like many other terms, this one was eventually abused by politicians, but through the generations it has been used to designate the basic American doctrine as embodied in the Constitution, and federalism is perhaps the most important American contribution to political science.

The Presidency

In the course of time the Presidency came to be regarded as a major contribution to the instrumentalities of government. There was little dispute in the Convention about the desirability of making the chief executive an important officer, but the question of his election proved difficult and was not settled until the last weeks. So long as the original proposal that he be elected by the legislature was agreed to, the general feeling was that he should have a rather long term and be ineligible for re-election. That is, he should be under no temptation to cater to Congress after he was elected. As the Convention went on, important delegates like Madison and James Wilson came to prefer his election by the people, directly or indirectly. The electoral system, which Wilson proposed, was designed to render the President independent of the legislative department from the very beginning and to vest his election in a group of qualified men who were selected for this express purpose.

The electors were to be chosen in any way that the legislatures of the various states should direct, and it was presumed that they would follow their own judgment in voting. They came to follow party judgments rather than personal opinions after parties arose, and in the course of time they were chosen everywhere by popular vote. According to the original system, each elector was to vote for two men, one at least of whom must be an inhabitant of another state. The man receiving the largest vote, if a majority, was to be President and the next man Vice-President. In case no one had a majority, the House of Representatives was to choose from the five highest on the list, voting by states. Time proved this system to be impracticable and it was changed by amendment. The term of the President was now set at four years and no limit was imposed upon his re-election. The number of electors from any state was to equal the whole number of Senators and Representatives from the state. The original system permitted adjustment to later democratic developments, and it could be rightfully said in later years that Presidents went into office with a mandate from the people, but the electoral system perpetuated the inequities of the Great Compromise. In the choice of a President the small states were to have a disproportionate voice, as they were to have in Congress.

Provision for Ratification

In form, the provision for the adoption of the Constitution was revolutionary. The delegates had set out to amend the Articles of Confederation, and the specified procedure was for amendments to be agreed to in Congress and afterwards confirmed by the legislatures of all the states. But, following the proposal in the Virginia Plan, the Convention decided that this new instrument should be ratified by conventions, not legislatures, and that it should go into effect when ratified by nine states among the states so ratifying. One reason for this disregard of the express requirements of the Articles was that unanimous ratification was doubtful or likely to be long delayed, and that conventions were more likely to ratify than legislatures, since the latter had a vested interest in state authority and would be reluctant to surrender any part of it. Also, there was an important philosophical reason. It was believed by many at this time, following the example of Massachusetts, that a convention chosen by vote of the electorate for a specific purpose was the fullest possible expression of the people's will; and, as Madison expressed it, a major difference between a nation and a league was that the former rested on the people, not on the state governments.

The American people were divided by state lines, however, and the precise language of the Preamble—"We the People of the United States" —was somewhat fortuitous. It would have been more accurate to say: "We the people of New Hampshire, Massachusetts," and so on. But nobody knew at the time what nine states would ratify first, and it would have been improper to list one that declined to ratify. The general expression in the Constitution voiced a hope rather than a reality: it was the desire of the Fathers that the new instrument should be based on the will of the sovereign people as a whole. Not all of the people voted then, to be sure, but the Constitution left requirements for the suffrage precisely where they were already—that is, in the hands of the states. It is worthy of note that no property qualifications were imposed on the holders of federal office under the proposed new government.

RATIFICATION

Some months after the Federal Convention adjourned, Madison described the Constitution as "the best that could be obtained from the jarring interests of states, and the miscellaneous opinions of politicians"; and Benjamin Franklin at the time sagely remarked that another convention could not be expected to produce a better one. This was the almost unanimous opinion of the delegates who had struggled with these problems for so many weeks. But Congress and the states had not had the benefit of these secret deliberations and the new charter of government now had to withstand public scrutiny. At the outset George Washington had issued a grave exhortation: "Let us raise a standard to which the wise and honest can repair. The event is in the hands of God." The Fathers of the Constitution did not content themselves with reliance on Divine Providence, however. They conducted a vigorous campaign for ratification and this was a major reason why the work of their hands was accepted.

The Convention sent the Constitution to Congress, then sitting in New York, with the recommendation that it be submitted to conventions in the various states, as specified in the document. On September 28, Congress, by unanimous vote of the states present, resolved to follow the prescribed procedure. In view of the sweeping changes in the government that were proposed, and the revolutionary nature of the provisions for ratification, this docility may seem surprising. But most of these men recognized the seriousness of the public situation, and sentiment favorable to the proposed plan of government increased when a dozen members of the Convention who were also regularly elected delegates to Congress came from Philadelphia to New York and joined the latter body. Conspicuous among these was Madison, who strongly defended the Convention against the charge that it had exceeded its instructions. A contradiction might be perceived in the instructions themselves, he said, since it was not possible to set up a *"national* and *adequate"* government merely by altering the Articles of Confederation. The essence of his argument was that the end justified the means, and the judgment of posterity has been that it did, especially since the means themselves were reasonable and peaceful. As Thomas Jefferson said a little later, the United States had set the world the admirable example of "changing a consitution by assembling the wise men of the State, instead of assembling armies."

Madison attributed the forbearance of the public to the "irresistible conviction" that it would be absurd to subject the fate of twelve states to "the perverseness or corruption of the thirteenth." The necessity of waiving the requirement of unanimity was generally conceded; and even those members of Congress who were turning against the Constitution, like Richard Henry Lee of Virginia, thought that the only proper procedure was to refer it to the states. The state legislatures, except for that of Rhode Island, accepted the recommendation and called specially-elected ratifying conventions, without insisting on their own right under the Articles to do the ratifying or the rejecting. This was a constitutional revolution and some have even described it as a *coup d'état*.

The ratification campaign represented a triumph of organization and skillful political management. The supporters of the Constitution, now called Federalists, were united while its various foes were divided; and the former, having seized the initiative, proceeded to keep it. During the winter of 1787-1788 and the succeeding spring and summer, eleven of the states accepted the Constitution. North Carolina, where the Anti-Federalists gained control, deferred decision, and Rhode Island did not act at all in this period. The remaining eleven commonwealths may be divided into three groups in the order of ratification:

(1) Delaware, Pennsylvania, New Jersey, Georgia, and Connecticut. These five states ratified in December and January. Their action was prompt, either because of the absence of effective opposition or the desire to forestall it. The vote in the conventions of Delaware and New Jersey was unanimous, and apparently it was in Georgia. It was two-to-one in Pennsylvania and more than three-to-one in Connecticut. The procedure in Pennsylvania was regarded by a vocal minority as hasty and high-handed and the vote may not have been a true index of the opinion of the electorate; but with this possible exception the Federalist sentiment in these five states was overwhelming. Furthermore, these early actions imparted to the movement for the Constitution a momentum it never lost.

(2) Massachusetts, Maryland, South Carolina, and New Hampshire (February 6—June 21, 1788). In Maryland and South Carolina, where action was very deliberate, the vote left no doubt of the overpowering strength of Federalist opinion. Massachusetts and New Hampshire were in very doubtful case, however, and the acceptance of the Constitution by the former by a close vote was accompanied by the strong recommendation of specific amendments. In many quarters, opponents of the Constitution were urging that another federal convention be called to consider amendments. The result of this would have been to throw the country back into the chaos of doubt from which it was emerging, and the specification by individual states of particular amendments as an absolute condition of ratification would have resulted in vast uncertainty and confusion. The example of Massachusetts in attaching recommendations rather than conditions to her act of ratification was followed by several other states. Ratification by New Hampshire was decisive, since she

was the ninth state and the establishment of the new government was thus assured. This government could hardly have hoped to endure, however, without further accessions.

(3) Virginia and New York (June 26 and July 26, 1788). Because of their size and geographical position these were key states, and the most severe battles occurred within them. Ratification was by a close vote in each case, at the end of a long campaign. The famous series of essays called *The Federalist* arose out of the conflict in New York and was employed very effectively there and in Virginia.

The heroes of the ratification fight in Virginia and New York were Madison and Hamilton, and in each instance the opposition was led and symbolized by the most popular political figure in the state—Patrick Henry in Virginia and Governor George Clinton in New York. With Henry, whose power lay in his voice and not his pen and who appeared in this conflict primarily as a localist, was ranged George Mason, who strongly criticized the new Constitution for its omission of guarantees of individual freedom. He had declined to sign it chiefly for this reason, and he also thought it went too far in the direction of consolidation. The position of Richard Henry Lee was strikingly like that of Mason. Before the end of 1787, Lee published his *Letters of the Federal Farmer*, which became a sort of textbook of the opposition. In New York, in September of the same year, Clinton, under the pseudonym "Cato," began a series of newspaper articles against the Constitution. His grounds of opposition, like those of Patrick Henry, appear to have been chiefly local; he did not want his strategically-placed state to be absorbed into a stronger Union.

The Federalist *Papers*

Realizing the difficulties of the situation in New York, Hamilton conceived the idea of a series of articles in which the Constitution should be thoroughly expounded. He himself did not think that document went far enough in granting power to the central government, but he was determined that it should be adopted and he brought to his self-imposed task unexcelled powers of exposition and persuasion. About a month after Clinton's first article appeared, Hamilton published his first as "Publius." He had gained the promise of assistance from John Jay, who was specially competent in the field of foreign relations, but that gentleman fell ill after doing four numbers and was able to do only one more. Under these circumstances Hamilton turned to Madison, who was in New York as a delegate to Congress and remained there through the winter. The result was one of the most fruitful collaborations in American history. *The Federalist* consisted of 85 numbers altogether, the last appearing in a newspaper in May 1788. All were signed "Publius" and it now appears that Hamilton wrote 59 of them, Jay 5, and Madison 29. The series was published almost immediately in book form, and competent contemporary judgment of it is reflected in the statement of Jefferson that it was "the best commentary on the principles of government which was ever written." More particularly, it was a commentary on the proposed government for the United States, written for the very practical purpose of gaining support for it.

Though they followed the orderly plan which Hamilton had formulated, the authors worked independently and the views of the two main ones were not identical. They were in complete agreement about the value of union, the gross inadequacy of the Confederation, and the necessity of adopting the Constitution. But the differences between them that had appeared in the Convention were reflected here in a difference in emphasis. Hamilton sought to show the necessity of a government "at least equally energetic with the one proposed," and quite obviously he would have preferred one that was considerably more energetic. To Madison fell the appropriate and congenial task of describing the actual problems that the Convention had faced, of showing the "conformity of the proposed Constitution to the true principles of republican government," and of defining the system of checks and balances which had been designed to prevent tyranny. In describing the operations of the new government, he dealt primarily with the House of Representatives, while Hamilton dealt with the Senate, the Executive, and the Judiciary.

Hamilton exercised considerably more restraint than he had in the Convention, but in these pages as elsewhere he appears as a major prophet of national power. Madison was closer to the spirit of the Convention itself, and he convincingly answered the criticisms of the proposed government as a "consolidation." He was setting the stage for his coming duel with Patrick Henry. The best-remembered characterization of the Constitution by that rural orator is that it "squinted" toward monarchy, and there was this special reason why Madsion should emphasize its republican form and character. Like other American political experiments, it rested on "the capacity of mankind for self-government," he said. His definition of republican government was destined to become a classic, and he gave as clear a statement as has ever been made of the extent to which the government of the United States was to be national on the one hand and federal on the other.

Virginia and New York

The Federalist served as a textbook for one side in the debate in Richmond—the greatest debate of them all. Madison had succeeded in wooing Edmund Randolph back to the side of the Constitution, partly by appealing to his distrust of Patrick Henry—a distrust which was shared by

Madison himself and Thomas Jefferson. The latter was outside this particular fight and Washington was not there. Edmund Pendleton and young John Marshall battled for the Constitution, while George Mason and James Monroe were against it. But the main antagonists were Henry and Madison: eloquence was matched and finally borne down by patient argument and explanation. The final vote was 89 to 79. It was the hardest fight and the greatest victory of Madison's long and useful life.

In Virginia as elsewhere the opponents of the Constitution could not agree on their objections. One that is specially worthy of note, however, was to the control of commerce by the Union. The fears that were now being expressed harked back to the old negotiations of John Jay about the navigation of the Mississippi. The danger that this might be surrendered in the interest of the Northern commercial states was specially alarming to representatives of the Kentucky counties, and despite Madison's own clear record on the issue these fears could not be wholly dissipated. A majority of the delegates were convinced that the proper procedure was to ratify first and amend afterwards. The Virginia convention recommended to the consideration of the first Congress a bill of rights in twenty parts, and a score of amendments to the body of the Constitution. The first of the latter, like the First Amendment proposed by Massachusetts, called for an explicit statement that the powers not specifically delegated to Congress should be retained by the states. Basic guarantees of individual liberty and this degree of protection of the rights of the states were expected of the new government, though not made an express condition of ratification. There was another expectation in the minds of the Virginians—that George Washington would be the first President—and this reconciled many opponents of the Constitution to the decision in its favor.

It has been estimated that when the New York convention first assembled, from two-thirds to three-fourths of its members were opposed to ratification, though sentiment in New York City was strongly favorable. Under the leadership of Hamilton the Federalists fought a delaying action, and the conventions in New Hampshire and Virginia acted favorably in the meantime. Hamilton was skillful in maneuver and powerful in debate, and eventually a favorable vote of 30 to 27 was attained. The convention affirmed what amounted to a bill of rights, put on record its own interpretation of certain phrases in the Constitution, and proposed a set of amendments. It assumed that there would be another federal convention, and the next legislature of the state actually called on the first Congress under the Constitution to summon one. No doubt the Federalists had concluded that any sort of ratification was better than none.

A few days after New York finally acted, North Carolina adopted a Declaration of Rights and proposed twenty-six amendments to the

Constitution, but neglected to ratify that document. One of her delegates in the Congress of the Confederation wrote to another of his country-men sarcastically: "It appears that North Carolina has at length thrown herself out of the Union, but happily she is not alone; the large, upright and respectable State of Rhode Island is her associate."

To the Congress of the Confederation it now appeared that the Constitution had been ratified, but this body delayed proclaiming that event because the delegates could not agree just where the new govern-ment should get started. They finally concluded to follow the path of least resistance and leave it in its present seat, which happened to be New York. Not until September 13 did the old Congress resolve that the new one should meet on the first Wednesday in March 1789, following the choice of electors in January and their assembling to vote for the Presi-dent in February.

The Bill of Rights

The most serious and general objection to the new Constitution was its lack of a bill of rights. Early in the first session of the first Congress, Madison introduced one, and as passed by both houses this consisted of twelve amendments. Two of these, dealing with the membership of Congress and the pay of Congressmen, were never ratified by the states but the ten others were. Proclaimed in 1791, they have ever since been regarded as virtually a part of the original Constitution. They begin with the guarantee that Congress shall make no law respecting an establish-ment of religion, or prohibiting the free exercise thereof; and they end, in the Tenth Amendment, with the express declaration that undelegated powers, not prohibited to the states, are reserved to the states or to the people. All ten are restrictions on the federal government, not the indi-vidual state governments. They were regarded as the honest fulfillment of a tacit pledge and they served to make the Constitution the guardian of liberty as well as the instrument of power.

This action was in direct response to public opinion, but there was no popular referendum on the Constitution at any time—just as there was none on the Declaration of Independence. Judging from the popular vote for delegates to the various conventions, the sentiment of the voters in several of the states that ratified the document in 1787-1788 was adverse or doubtful in the first instance. It should be borne in mind, also, that in practically all cases the suffrage was considerably restricted. Thus the movement for the Constitution, like that for independence from the mother country, was the work of a minority. Considering the times, this was not at all surprising, and both movements must be judged at last by their purposes and fruits.

In the ratification fight the lines of cleavage were not always clear but they tended to coincide with those of economic interest. The groups which had been specially imperiled under the Confederation, or were specially conscious of their peril—merchants and creditors generally— tended to favor the Constitution, which provided safeguards for their property against state actions. The two states which had been most conspicuous in connection with paper money and the relief of debtors, North Carolina and Rhode Island, did not ratify until after the new government had been set up; and opposition was most manifest among small farmers and debtors. By and large, the coastal and commercial districts favored the Constitution, while the back country tended to oppose it. But there was good reason to hope that all groups would prosper in a more perfect Union.

The Success of the Constitution

Within a remarkably short time after the Constitution became effective, opposition to it almost wholly ceased, and as soon as national political parties appeared they vied with each other in avowing their devotion to what was already becoming a sacred document. It has been said that the Americans enthroned it in place of a king; and from the presidency of George Washington until the present day the common assumption among them has been that their country has enjoyed the best of all forms of government. How can we explain the extraordinary success and popularity of the charter which issued from a closed room in Philadelphia and over the merits of which men had so fiercely battled?

The immediate success of the first administration under the Constitution was owing to various personal, political, and economic factors which appeared in happy combination. But full credit must be given the Fathers for their great skill in correcting the structural ills of the Confederation, which they understood so well from personal experience. The Union now had a government which could really function.

Unlike the Articles of Confederation, the Constitution did not contain the expression "perpetual Union," and dissolution was to be threatened a number of times before the supreme threat of the 1860's. We may now wonder why the Fathers did not speak more categorically on this point, but it was a sign of their practical wisdom that they did not deal in absolutes or peer too far into the distant future. By necessity as well as choice they set up a dual rather than a consolidated system: while declaring the supremacy of the laws of the United States they divided sovereignty between the Union and the individual commonwealths, leaving an unexplored borderland; and they left a host of unanswered questions to the arbitrament of time. Extending central authority as far as they safely could by specific grant, they made undefined general grants which could form the basis for expanding power, if there should be later need for it and if circumstances should permit its growth.

It is because of this capacity for growth and adjustment to changing circumstances that the Constitution has endured from the age of the stagecoach and post rider to that of the airplane and atomic power. By means of general expressions, such as the "elastic" and "general welfare" clauses, the Fathers made it possible for the enumerated powers of Congress to be expanded. They did not anticipate the interpretation that Abraham Lincoln would give to his war powers, but they made the President the commander-in-chief of the armed forces. They could hardly have foreseen the full development of the doctrine of judicial review under Chief Justice Marshall and his successors, but they made the Constitution and the laws and treaties of the United States the supreme law of the land, and extended the judicial power to all cases arising under these.

While the *powers* of the new government proved to be flexible, the Fathers imparted a certain rigidity to the governmental *structure* which has characterized it ever since. They made provision for precise terms of office and tried to draw a sharp line of demarcation between the branches of the United States government. Thus they made it difficult to assign responsibility for public acts and made conflict between the branches almost inevitable. The conflict between Congress and the President runs through the whole of American political history, and it has caused many thoughtful Americans to long for a more unified and responsible government like that of England. But in their age of absolute monarchs in Europe and highhanded local legislatures in America, the framers of the Constitution sought to make tyranny difficult if not impossible. To them, as to Montesquieu, there were three distinct types of power—legislative, executive, and judicial—and the junction of these spelled tyranny. Efficiency may be hard to attain under the American system of divided authority and responsibility, but in our own age, when totalitarianism threatens all mankind, we can be grateful that we have been so well guarded against consolidated despotism.

The Constitution was least effective when it departed furthest from past experience and relied most on theory. If the separation of powers and system of checks and balances are not a case in point, the electoral system surely is. This novel device was a practical failure; and despite its modification by the Twelfth Amendment and the later practice of choosing electors by popular vote within each state, it remains as a sort of vermiform appendix in the constitutional system.

Other unfortunate features of the Constitution may be attributed to the necessity for compromise. The concession of equality of the states in the Senate, wholly without regard to population, is one of them; and this inequity is perpetuated also in the electoral system. The three-fifths ratio for slaves, without which the southern states would probably not have agreed to the Constitution, was destined to cause much future trouble. Mention may also be made of the denial to Congress of the right to prohibit the foreign slave trade for twenty years, which was balanced at the time by the concession to the northern states that navigation laws could be passed by a majority rather than a two-thirds vote.

It has sometimes been argued that amendment of the Constitution was made too difficult, and it is a fact that after the adoption of the Twelfth Amendment in 1804, there was no other until 1865. This led to the saying that a war is required to amend the Constitution. But the process was far easier than it had been under the Articles of Confederation. No state can be deprived of its equality in the Senate without its own consent, however, and a combination of sparsely settled states can block changes in the government even though an overwhelming majority of the whole people may regard these as imperative. This is a fault of the dual system which was otherwise particularly adapted to the American situation. A division of authority between states and nation is essential to the American system, and the provision for the admission of new states permitted the indefinite expansion of the Union.

The Constitution cannot be properly described as what Gladstone called it, "the greatest work that was ever struck off at a given time by the brain and purpose of man." Nor can one justly claim that since 1789 the people of United States have lived under the best of all possible governments. But within the framework which the experienced statesmen of 1787 set up it has been possible for a great nation to develop and for a diverse people to enjoy a fuller measure of freedom, prosperity, and happiness than has generally been offered mortal men in older countries. The Fathers had an uncommon measure of wisdom and they builded even better than they thought. The enduring Republic is their living monument.

SELECT BIBLIOGRAPHY

General Statement

READING IN MORE DETAILED WORKS CAN ENORMOUSLY ENRICH AND ENLIVEN the story which is inevitably compressed in a book like this; and original sources can provide a vividness of impression that secondary narratives rarely convey. Part of the continuing appeal of historical study arises from the fact that there is always something more which anybody can learn about the past and that the closer one gets to the actual people and events the more vivid and real they become. To some extent every student can become an explorer in his own right, and in the investigation of some appealing topic can taste the joy of discovery.

The purpose of the present bibliography is to acquaint the student and reader with the most useful aids—stress being laid on those that are most accessible—and, without making any pretence of exhaustiveness, to mention selected books which can be read to advantage and sources which can be explored with relative ease. Comments are frequently attached—sometimes as a sort of warning but more often as an invitation to particular items in the historical feast.

First, there is a relatively brief list of works bearing on the whole or most of this volume; then, both general and specific suggestions are given chapter by chapter. These can be richly supplemented from the bibliographical items and suggestions in many of the listed books.

Basic Reference Works

The most important single bibliographical aid is the *Harvard Guide to American History* (1954), edited by Oscar Handlin. Besides excellent chapters on the materials and tools of American history and convenient lists of books in various categories, it contains suggestions for reading on the various periods and topics which go far beyond any that can be given here.

Every historical shelf should have the *Encyclopedia of American History* (1953), edited by R. B. Morris, a handy volume which is invaluable for facts and dates. The arrangement is both chronological and topical.

Among the larger reference works with which students should familiarize themselves is the *Dictionary of American Biography* (20 vols., 1928-36), edited by Allen Johnson and Dumas Malone; supplementary volumes edited by H. E. Starr (1944), and R. L. Schuyler (1958). This co-operative work provides rich personal materials for the whole of American history. A good way to turn mere names into real persons is to look them up in this collection of articles. Those desiring to read further will find suggestions in the bibliographies. (A selected list of biographies is given in the *Harvard Guide*, pp. 190-206).

Excellent examples of large collections of the writings of great Americans are Washington's *Writings*, edited by J. C. Fitzpatrick (39 vols., 1931-44); and

Lincoln's *Collected Works*, edited by R. P. Basler (9 vols., 1953). Among extensive collections now in process the pace-setter is Jefferson's *Papers*, edited by Julian P. Boyd, 16 vols. of which had appeared by 1964. A number of handy one-volume collections are mentioned hereafter.

The *Dictionary of American History* (5 vols., 1940), edited by J. T. Adams, is abridged in *Concise Dictionary of American History* (1962), edited by Wayne Andrews. The *Encyclopedia of the Social Sciences* (15 vols., 1930-34), edited by E. R. A. Seligman, is a work of much wider scope.

Fascinating statistical materials can be found in the publications of the Bureau of the Census, *A Century of Population Growth* . . . *1790-1900* (1909), and *Historical Statistics of the U.S., Colonial Times to 1957: A Statistical Abstract Supplement* (1960). The *Biographical Directory of the American Congress, 1774-1949* (1950), besides giving the lists of members of the successive Congresses (and also of executive officers), contains brief biographical sketches.

Good maps are of the first importance. Two older collections have not yet been excelled for general historical use: W. R. Shepherd, *Historical Atlas* (1911), which deals with Europe as well as America; and *Harper's Atlas of American History* (1920), consisting of maps from the old *American Nation* series. Later school atlases of wide use include: C. E. and E. H. Lord, *Historical Atlas of the United States* (1944); and J. T. Adams, *Atlas of American History* (1943). The fullest and most authoritative work is C. O. Paullin, *Atlas of the Historical Geography of the United States* (1932), edited by J. K. Wright. While too big and cumbersome for frequent use, this is valuable for boundary disputes and other matters of concern to advanced students and specialists.

Much work has been done in making old and recent pictures available. The first extensive modern compilation was *The Pageant of America* (15 vols., 1926-29), edited by R. H. Gabriel. The *Harvard Guide*, pp. 65-66, has a list of later general collections. Some works of special value dealing with particular periods or subjects will be referred to hereafter at appropriate points. Naturally, pictorial records became more accurate as well as more extensive with the development of photography, but the older paintings and prints often convey a delightful sense of their own day.

Convenient Collections of Documents and Readings

The best general collection of documents in convenient form and a strong contender for any historian's bookshelf is *Documents of American History* (7 edn., 1963), edited by H. S. Commager. Besides official documents, this contains party platforms, important speeches, etc. It can be supplemented by L. B. Evans, *Cases on American Constitutional Law*, revised edition by C. G. Fenwick (1948), or by *Cases in Constitutional Law*, by Robert E. and Robert F. Cushman (2 edn., 1963), both of which are fuller in a more limited field. Treaties and diplomatic documents can be best consulted in R. J. Bartlett, ed., *The Record of American Diplomacy* (1950), a book which should stand on the shelf with Commager.

A rich collection of readings bearing especially on social and intellectual matters is *American Issues*, Vol. I, "The Social Record" (rev. edn., 1955), edited by Willard Thorp, Merle Curti, and Carlos Baker. Another good collection, which is more economic and political in emphasis, is *The Shaping of the American Tradition* (1947), edited by L. M. Hacker, whose relatively long introductions are illuminating and provocative. The older and less accessible work, G. S. Callender, ed., *Selections from the Economic History of the United States, 1765-1868* (1909), contains, besides readings, brief but unusually penetrating introductions which comprise a summary of economic history.

The Making of American History (rev. edn., 1954), edited by Donald Sheehan, is an anthology which contains 35 long extracts from historical writers dealing with major topics. Some of these will be specifically referred to hereafter. *Understanding the American Past* (1954), edited by E. N. Saveth, is a similar work.

Problems in American Civilization: Readings Selected by the Department of American Studies, Amherst College (1947-   ) comprise a useful series of paper-bound booklets. Each deals with a particular topic and contains selections from authors with varying views. Somewhat more than a dozen have been issued to date and they offer one of the best methods of studying controversial questions. Individual booklets will be mentioned hereafter.

Larger General Histories

Every student and serious reader should become acquainted with major long histories and series, and should dip into them to some extent. The present list is confined to works or sets covering the whole or most of American history.

Edward Channing, *History of the United States* (6 vols., 1905-25) extends through 1865. To some extent it reflects the author's Northeastern environment and at time his caprices, but generally it is judicious and temperate.

The Chronicles of America (50 vols., 1918-21), edited by Allen Johnson, comprise an unusually readable series of small volumes which inevitably vary in quality.

A History of American Life (13 vols., 1927-48), edited by A. M. Schlesinger and D. R. Fox, is the standard series for social history. The bibliographies are excellent.

The old series, *The American Nation: A History* (26 vols., 1904-08; additional vol., 1918), edited by A. B. Hart, has a distinguished position in American historiography and certain volumes are still of great value. *The New American Nation Series*, edited by H. S. Commager and R. B. Morris, to comprise about 40 vols., is in process. The volumes are of a handy size and contain full and up-to-date bibliographies.

A History of the South, edited by W. H. Stephenson and E. M. Coulter (1947-   ), projected in 10 vols., of which 8 fall in the period to 1877, is an admirable series, now almost done. The bibliographies are detailed and comprehensive.

Topical Histories

GEOGRAPHY AND ABORIGINES

There is need for a readable work on American historical geography in convenient size. The two following books are useful for reference: J. R. Smith and

M. O. Phillips, *North America* (rev. edn., 1940), a lengthy regional treatment of the United States, Canada, and Central America; R. H. Brown, *Historical Geography of the United States* (1948), a sound work, following the order of settlement. In the field of oceanography, Rachel Carson, *The Sea around Us* (1951), is fascinating. An excellent account of the Indians, written for the layman, is R. M. Underhill, *Red Man's America* (1953).

SETTLEMENT AND IMMIGRATION

Most general works pay considerable attention to the process of settlement and there are many specialized studies of particular areas. A comprehensive but compact book is R. A. Billington, *Westward Expansion; A History of the American Frontier* (1949), dealing also with transportation and land policies. *The Frontier in America* (1921), a collection of essays by F. J. Turner, is a classic.

The larger problems of immigration are illuminated by three books by M. L. Hansen: *The Atlantic Migration, 1607-1860* (1940), and *The Immigrant in American History* (1941), both edited by A. M. Schlesinger, and *The Mingling of the Canadian and American Peoples* (1940), completed by J. B. Brebner. A good general treatment is Carl Wittke, *We Who Built America: The Saga of the Immigrant* (1939). Works on the Negro and particular ethnic groups are cited hereafter.

ECONOMIC AND FINANCIAL HISTORY

Among general economic histories in one volume are H. U. Faulkner, *American Economic History* (8 edn., 1959); E. C. Kirkland, *A History of American Economic Life* (3 edn., 1951); F. A. Shannon, *America's Economic Growth* (rev. edn., 1951); and Robert R. Russel, *A History of the American Economic System* (1964). The older and more restricted works, D. R. Dewey, *Financial History of the United States* (12 edn., 1934), and F. W. Taussig, *Tariff History of the United States* (7 edn., 1923) are still useful handbooks.

AGRICULTURAL HISTORY

The standard works for the period covered by this volume are P. W. Bidwell and J. I. Falconer, *History of Agriculture in the Northern United States, 1620-1860* (1925), and L. C. Gray, *History of Agriculture in the Southern United States to 1860* (2 vols., 1933). While too detailed for general reading, these books are invaluable to those wishing to explore any part of this vital subject.

INTELLECTUAL HISTORY

Merle Curti, in *The Growth of American Thought* (2 edn., 1951), covers the whole period systematically and has unusually valuable bibliographies for his chapters. V. L. Parrington, *Main Currents in American Thought* (3 vols., 1927-30), is highly stimulating and a delight to read, even when one disputes the author's judgment. R. H. Gabriel, *The Course of American Democratic Thought* (2 edn., 1956), deals admirably with the period after 1815. Harvey

Wish, *Society and Thought in Early America* (1950), covers social as well as intellectual history to 1865.

LITERARY HISTORY

Abundant materials are available in R. E. Spiller and others, *Literary History of the United States* (3 vols., 1948), the third volume of which is an elaborate bibliography; and A. H. Quinn, ed., *The Literature of the American People* (1951).

LABOR

F. R. Dulles, *Labor in America* (1949), is a convenient general treatment.

CONSTITUTIONAL HISTORY AND PARTIES

For general use the best works on their subject are C. B. Swisher, *American Constitutional Development* (1943); and A. H. Kelly and W. A. Harbison, *The American Constitution: Its Origins and Development* (1948). A. C. McLaughlin, *A Constitutional History of the United States* (1935) becomes less valuable after the early national period. W. E. Binkley, *American Political Parties: Their Natural History* (3 edn., 1958), is a good survey.

DIPLOMACY

General treatments are: J. W. Pratt, *A History of United States Foreign Policy* (1955), a well-proportioned and judicious recent work; the old reliable, S. F. Bemis, *A Diplomatic History of the United States* (rev. edn., 1950); T. A. Bailey, *A Diplomatic History of the American People* (7 edn., 1964); Alexander De Conde, *A History of American Foreign Policy* (1963). There is much information and interpretation in S. F. Bemis, ed., *The American Secretaries of State and Their Diplomacy* (10 vols., 1927-29).

RELIGION, SCIENCE, AND EDUCATION

General treatments are disappointing, but the following works are useful: W. W. Sweet, *The Story of Religion in America* (rev. edn., 1939); D. J. Struik, *Yankee Science in the Making* (1948); E. P. Cubberly, *Public Education in the United States* (rev. edn., 1934) E. E. Slosson, *The American Spirit in Education* (1921, *Chronicles of America*). M. E. Curti, *Social Ideas of American Educators* (1935), is excellent. Richard Hofstadter and Wilson Smith, eds., *American Higher Education: A Documentary History* (1961), is basic. J. W. Smith and A. L. Jamison, eds., *Religion in American Life*, vols. I, II, IV (1961), is a significant contribution.

ARCHITECTURE AND ART

The main lines of development are shown in T. F. Hamlin, *The American Spirit in Architecture* (1926); T. F. Tallmadge, *The Story of Architecture in America* (rev. edn., 1936); W. C. Andrews, *Americans, Ambition and Architecture*

(1955); Samuel Isham, *The History of American Painting*, supplemented by Royal Cortissoz (1927).

MILITARY AND NAVAL

The fruitfulness of scholarship in this field is best shown in specialized studies. General works do not yet fully reflect it, but the following are useful: W. A. Ganoe, *A History of the United States Army* (1942); O. L. Spaulding, *The United States Army in War and Peace* (1937); D. W. Knox, *A History of the United States Navy* (rev. edn., 1948); H. H. and Margaret Sprout, *The Rise of American Naval Power, 1776-1918* (1939). The old army textbook, M. F. Steele, *American Campaigns* (2 vols., last edn., 1922), with its maps, is still helpful.

Part I: Colonial Foundations, to 1763

General

A good one-volume history of the entire period is C. P. Nettels, *The Roots of American Civilization* (1938). The most comprehensive general treatment is C. M. Andrews, *The Colonial Period of American History* (4 vols., 1934-38); Vols. I-III are devoted to the settlements, and Vol. IV to the British system. Political institutions are treated exhaustively in H. L. Osgood, *The American Colonies in the Seventeenth Century* (3 vols., 1904-07), and *The American Colonies in the Eighteenth Century* (4 vols., 1924-25), which is not the equal of its predecessor; the style of both works is dull. Social developments are described in early volumes of *A History of American Life*. Literary and intellectual developments are treated in works cited under Topical Histories.

Special

See suggestions under individual chapters. It should be noted that, as the treatment in the text is considerably more compressed in Part I of this work than in the Parts which follow, the bibliography is correspondingly curtailed. Anyone wishing to explore the extensive literature of the colonial period will find abundant suggestions in the *Harvard Guide*, Chs. 6-9.

1. EUROPEAN BACKGROUNDS

General

Since the entire history of western Europe from the late Middle Ages provides backgrounds for American history, students will naturally turn to general works which themselves offer further suggestions for reading. Among these the following are specially helpful: J. W. Thompson, *Economic and Social History of Europe in the Later Middle Ages, 1300-1530* (1931); W. C. Abbott, *The Expansion of Europe* (1938); E. P. Cheyney, *The Dawn of a New Era* (1936); C. H. H. Hayes, *Political and Cultural History of Modern Europe* (1939);

Preserved Smith, *The Age of the Reformation* (1920). The course of thought is dealt with more specifically in J. H. Randall, *The Making of the Modern Mind* (1926); Crane Brinton, *Ideas and Men, The Story of Western Thought* (1950); Preserved Smith, *A History of Modern Culture*, Vols. I, II (1930, 1934); W. C. Dampier-Whetham, *History of Science* (1932).

Special

Pre-Columbian discoveries are described in H. R. Holand, *Westward from Vinland: An Account of Norse Discoveries and Explorations in America* (1940). R. H. Tawney, *Religion and the Rise of Capitalism* (1926), and Max Weber, *The Protestant Ethic and the Spirit of Capitalism* (1930), are stimulating treatments of a pertinent controversial subject. See also E. D. Adams, *The Power of Ideals in American History* (1913).

2. CONTINENTAL POWERS AND THE NEW WORLD

General

Works in European history cited for the previous chapter, especially Abbott, *Expansion of Europe;* Channing, *History of the United States*, Vol. I; J. B. Brebner, *Explorers of North America* (1933); Priestley, *Coming of the White Man (History of American Life)*, Chs. 1-3; H. E. Bolton and T. M. Marshall, *The Colonization of North America, 1492-1783* (1920).

Special

Supplementary reading on this huge topic can be profitably centered on a particular Power or outstanding leader.

PORTUGAL: J. P. Oliveira Martins, *Golden Age of Prince Henry the Navigator* (1914). SPAIN: E. G. Bourne, *Spain in America, 1450-1580*, (1905, *American Nation*); C. H. Haring, *Spanish Empire in America* (1952); E. D. Salmon, *Imperial Spain* (1931); H. E. Bolton, *Spanish Borderlands* (1921, *Chronicles of America*), for the North American Southwest. FRANCE: Francis Parkman, *Pioneers of France in the New World* (1885); G. M. Wrong, *Rise and Fall of New France* (1928). DUTCH: E. L. Raesly, *Portrait of New Netherland* (1945).

Those preferring the biographical approach can find fascinating reading in S. E. Morison, *Admiral of the Ocean Sea* (1942), and the same author's briefer book, written for a wider audience, *Christopher Columbus, Mariner* (1955); Germán Arciniegas, *Amerigo and the New World: The Life and Times of Amerigo Vespucci* (1955, trans. from the Spanish); H. E. Bolton, *Coronado* (1949); C. M. Parr, *So Noble a Captain: The Life and Times of Magellan* (1953).

Recent abridgements of classic works are: *The Battle for North America* (1948), edited by John Tebbel from the Works of Francis Parkman; S. E. Morison, ed., *The Parkman Reader* (1955); Prescott's *The Conquest of Mexico, Designed for Modern Reading*, by Marshall McClintock (1948).

3. EARLY ENGLISH SETTLEMENTS:
VIRGINIA AND MARYLAND

General

W. F. Craven, *The Southern Colonies in the Seventeenth Century, 1607-1689* (1949), Chs. 1-6, an admirable account with full bibliography; T. J. Wertenbaker, *The First Americans* (1927, *History of American Life*), Ch. 2, for social history; C. M. Andrews, "Factors Influencing Colonization," in Sheehan, *Making of American History*, pp. 4-30 (from *Colonial Period of American History*).

Special

ENGLISH BACKGROUNDS

G. M. Trevelyan, *England under the Stuarts* (12 edn., 1927), a brilliant narrative history; Wallace Notestein, *The English People on the Eve of Colonization, 1603-1630* (1954, *New American Nation Series*), an illuminating study of English society; J. A. Williamson, *The Age of Drake* (1938); W. E. Lingelbach, *Merchant Adventurers of England* (1902); G. L. Beer, *Origins of the British Colonial System, 1578-1660* (1908), a detailed treatment.

VIRGINIA

T. J. Wertenbaker, in *Virginia under the Stuarts, 1607-1688* (1914), *The Planters of Colonial Virginia* (1922), and other works has freshly interpreted the history and society of the Old Dominion in the seventeenth century, emphasizing the yeoman farmers. The stimulating book of L. B. Wright, *The First Gentlemen of Virginia* (1940), describes the aristocrats, with greater emphasis on the eighteenth century. R. L. Morton, *Colonial Virginia* (2 vols., 1960), is the fullest general account.

MARYLAND

The best discussion of Maryland's early history is that of C. M. Andrews in *The Colonial Period of American History*, Vol. II, Chs. 8-9. Among special studies of value are C. C. Hall, *The Lords Baltimore and the Maryland Palatinate* (1902); B. C. Steiner, *Beginnings of Maryland, 1631-1639* (1903); N. D. Mereness, *Maryland as a Proprietary Province* (1901). In view of the particular significance of religious developments in Maryland to Catholics, special mention should be made of John G. Shea, *A History of the Catholic Church within the Limits of the United States* (4 vols., 1886-92).

SLAVES AND INDENTURED SERVANTS

The beginnings of slavery in the southern colonies are described in general works, such as U. B. Phillips, *American Negro Slavery* (1929), and J. H. Franklin, *From Slavery to Freedom: A History of American Negroes* (1947). A scholarly treatment of bound white labor is A. E. Smith, *Colonists in Bondage: White Servitude and Convict Labor in America, 1607-1776* (1947). R. B.

Morris, *Government and Labor in Early America* (1946) is valuable for both facts and interpretation.

4. THE NEW ENGLAND COLONIES

General

Good narratives are plentiful. C. M. Andrews gives a full story in *Colonial Period of American History*, Vol. I, Chs. 12-22; Vol. II, Chs. 1-4; and a brief one in *Fathers of New England* (1919, *Chronicles of America*). See also Channing, *History*, Vol. I, Chs. 10-14. J. T. Adams, *The Founding of New England* (1921) is good reading but the rather iconoclastic tone which heightened its popularity when the work was published has caused it to be frowned upon by many historians who take a more favorable view of the Puritans. T. J. Wertenbaker, *The Puritan Oligarchy* (1947) is stimulating and readable. For the Pilgrims, see G. F. Willison, *Saints and Strangers* (1945).

Special

William Bradford's classic, *Of Plymouth Plantation, 1620-1647*, has appeared in an edition by S. E. Morison (1953). Along with this may be read Bradford Smith, *Bradford of Plymouth* (1951). Other biographical works are S. E. Morison, *Builders of the Bay Colony* (1930); S. H. Brockunier, *The Irrepressible Democrat: Roger Williams* (1940); D. E. Winslow, *Master Roger Williams* (1957); W. K. Rugg, *Unafraid: A Life of Anne Hutchinson* (1930).

Puritanism is discussed in the general accounts. For able and sympathetic treatment of its theological aspects and intellectual emphasis, see Perry Miller, *Orthodoxy in Massachusetts* (1933), and *The New England Mind* (1939); the introduction to the documentary collection, *The Puritans*, edited by Miller and F. H. Johnson; S. E. Morison, *Founding of Harvard College* (1935); *Puritan Pronaos* (1936); and *Builders of the Bay Colony*. Parrington, in *Main Currents in American Thought*, Vol. I, is less sympathetic. The booklet, *Puritanism in Early America*, in the Amherst *Problems in American Civilization*, offers excellent materials for discussion.

For Witchcraft, see M. L. Starkey, *The Devil in Massachusetts* (1949); G. L. Kittredge, *Witchcraft in Old and New England* (1928). It would be difficult to find in a modern mystery or psychological novel a more engrossing story than that of the actual events in Salem.

5. ORGANIZATION AND DEVELOPMENT OF THE EMPIRE

General

Over-all accounts in Channing, *History*, Vol. II; Nettels, *Roots of American Civilization;* T. J. Wertenbaker, *The Founding of American Civilization: The Middle Colonies* (1938), written in the author's characteristically interesting style; W. F. Craven, *Southern Colonies in the Seventeenth Century*, Chs. 7-11.

Special

British policy, which becomes so important at this time, is ably described and discussed in Andrews, *Colonial Period*, Vol. IV; G. L. Beer, *The Old Colonial System, 1660-1754* (1912); L. A. Harper, *English Navigation Laws* (1939). For the most important non-British group of settlers, see A. B. Faust, *The German Element in the United States* (2 vols., 1909); for the Scotch-Irish and others, see Wittke, *We Who Built America*, and other general accounts of immigration. Other works of special interest are: W. I. Hill, *William Penn* (1937); R. M. Jones, *Quakers in the American Colonies* (1911); T. J. Wertenbaker, *Torchbearer of the Revolution* (1940), an account of Nathaniel Bacon, and W. E. Washburn, *The Governor and the Rebel: A History of Bacon's Rebellion in Virginia* (1957), arriving at different conclusions.

6. COLONIAL LIFE IN THE EIGHTEENTH CENTURY

General

On the process of settlement: R. A. Billington, *Westward Expansion*, Chs. 2-4; F. J. Turner, *Frontier in American History*, Chs. 1, 2; T. P. Abernethy, *Three Virginia Frontiers* (1949). Social, economic, and cultural developments and conditions are described in J. T. Adams, *Provincial Society* (1927, *History of American Life*); C. M. Andrews, *Colonial Folkways* (1919, *Chronicles of America*); T. J. Wertenbaker, *The Golden Age of Colonial Culture* (1942); L. B. Wright, *The Atlantic Frontier* (1947), and *The Cultural Life of the American Colonies, 1607-1763* (1957). Intellectual developments in Curti, *Growth of American Thought*, Part I; Max Savelle, *Seeds of Liberty: The Genesis of the American Mind* (1948); Parrington, *Main Currents in American Thought*, Vol. I. A stimulating fresh study is D. J. Boorstin, *The Americans: The Colonial Experience* (1958).

Special

The following brief list can be readily supplemented from the bibliographies of many of the general works above and from the *Harvard Guide*, pp. 285-289 (sections 103-104); it can cover only a few of the numerous topics of interest and must be merely suggestive: Carl Bridenbaugh, *Cities in the Wilderness: The First Century of Urban Life in America, 1625-1744* (1939), and *Cities in Revolt: Urban Life in America, 1743-1776* (1955); R. G. Albion, *Forests and Sea Power* (1926); V. D. Harrington, *The New York Merchant on the Eve of the Revolution* (1931); R. B. Morris, *Government and Labor in Early America* (1946); L. C. Wroth, *The Colonial Printer* (1938); E. E. Slosson, *The American Spirit in Education* (1921, *Chronicles of America*); O. W. Larkin, *Art and Life in America* (1949); Carl Van Doren, *Benjamin Franklin* (1938), especially Chs. 1-11—an excellent biography of the man who best embodied the diversity of colonial achievement and culture.

7. POLITICS AND WARS

General

Accounts in Channing, *History*, Vol. II; Nettels, *Roots of American Civilization;* E. B. Greene, *Provincial America* (1905, *American Nation*). L. W. Labaree, *Royal Government in America* (1930), well describes the form of government under which most of the colonists lived; it has a full bibliography. The struggle with the French is described briefly by G. M. Wrong in *The Conquest of New France* (1918, *Chronicles of America*), more fully in *The Rise and Fall of New France*. Francis Parkman has written classic works on this topic, reaching the climax in *Montcalm and Wolfe* (2 vols., 1884); in reduced form this comprises Part VI of *The Battle for North America*, ed. by John Tebbel. See also Billington, *Westward Expansion*, Ch. 6; Bolton, *Spanish Borderlands*.

Special

POLITICAL INSTITUTIONS: O. M. Dickerson, *American Colonial Government, 1696-1765* (1912); R. B. Morris, *Studies in the History of American Law* (1930). MERCANTILIST REGULATIONS: G. L. Beer, *British Colonial Policy, 1754-1765* (1937); O. M. Dickerson, *Navigation Acts and the American Revolution* (1951); L. A. Harper, *English Navigation Laws.* INTERNATIONAL STRUGGLE AND COLONIAL WARS: G. S. Graham, *Empire of the North Atlantic: The Maritime Struggle for North America* (1950); L. H. Gipson, *The British Empire before the Revolution* (9 vols., 1936-56), a monumental work, sympathetic with the imperial idea; D. S. Freeman, *George Washington*, Vol. II (1948), giving a detailed and authoritative account of the ill-fated western campaign; Max Savelle, *A Diplomatic History of the Canadian-American Boundary, 1749-1763* (1940), brilliantly summarizing the stakes in the war.

Part II: Beginnings of the Republic, 1763-1789

8. REORGANIZATION OF THE EMPIRE, 1763-1774

General

The story of events in this and the two following chapters is told much more fully in a number of unusually interesting books. These include: C. L. Becker, *The Eve of the Revolution* (1918, in *Chronicles of America*); J. C. Miller, *The Origins of the American Revolution* (1943), and *The Triumph of Freedom, 1775-1783* (1948); L. H. Gipson, *The Coming of the Revolution, 1763-1775* (1954), and J. R. Alden, *The American Revolution, 1775-1783* (1954); J. R. Alden, *The South in the Revolution, 1763-1789* (1957); W. E. H. Lecky, *The American Revolution, 1763-1783* (1898), a temperate English work which retains its value. E. B. Greene, *A Revolutionary Generation, 1763-1790* (1943, in *History of American Life*) provides the social background for the entire period.

Special

Few controversies in American history invite study and stimulate discussion more than that between the colonies and the mother country before the Revolution. Imperial problems at the beginning of the era are treated sympathetically by G. L. Beer in *British Colonial Policy, 1754-1765* (1907). C. M. Andrews views them in the large in *The Colonial Background of the American Revolution* (1924), a brief but illuminating book. The constitutional question within the empire is discussed by C. H. McIlwain in *The American Revolution: A Constitutional Interpretation* (1923), and R. L. Schuyler in *Parliament and the British Empire* (1929), these two eminent scholars arriving at different conclusions. For the ideological conflict see also R. G. Adams, *Political Ideas of the American Revolution, 1763-1783* (1922); Clinton Rossiter, *Seedtime of the Republic* (1953); Philip Davidson, *Propaganda and the American Revolution, 1763-1783* (1941); A. M. Schlesinger, *Prelude to Independence: The Newspaper War on Britain, 1764-1776* (1958). The emphasis is more economic in A. M. Schlesinger, *Colonial Merchants and the American Revolution* (1918); and T. P. Abernethy, *Western Lands and the American Revolution* (1937), a detailed work. The land question is dealt with by C. W. Alvord in *The Mississippi Valley in British Politics* (2 vols., 1917), and by R. A. Billington in his general account, *Westward Expansion.*

Sources and Documents Illustrating the American Revolution, 1764-1788 (1929), edited by S. E. Morison, is a useful collection with excellent comments. The booklet, *The Causes of the American Revolution,* in Amherst *Problems in American Civilization,* provides an admirable basis for discussion.

9. TOWARDS AMERICAN INDEPENDENCE, 1774-1776

General

For the political story see the works referred to in the previous chapter. Early military events are covered in Allen French, *The First Year of the American Revolution* (1934). For other military works see the next chapter. E. C. Burnett, *The Continental Congress* (1941), the standard work on its subject, describes the deliberations and actions of that body.

Special

Interpretative works of interest are: W. A. Brown, *Empire or Independence: A Study in Failure of Reconciliation, 1774-1783* (1941); G. H. Guttridge, *English Whiggism and the American Revolution* (1942); C. H. Van Tyne, *Causes of the War of Independence* (1922).

One of the best ways to gain a vivid view of the course of the revolt is to follow it in a particular locality. Attitudes and developments in Massachussetts are described by Esther Forbes, in *Paul Revere and the World He Lived In* (1942), and Harold Murdock, in *The Nineteenth of April 1775* (1923); and in New York by T. J. Wertenbaker, in *Father Knickerbocker Rebels* (1948). See also A. M. Baldwin, *The New England Clergy and the American Revolution* (1928). H. J. Eckenrode, *The Revolution in Virginia* (1916) is outmoded by recent biographies of leading Virginians but is best in its early chapters.

For the student of political ideas the literature on this era is abundant. Besides the works referred to in the previous chapter, the following are specially commended: A. C. McLaughlin, *The Foundations of American Constitutionalism* (1932); R. B. Perry, *Puritanism and Democracy* (1944), especially Chs. 6-7; Z. S. Fink, *Classical Republicans* (1932); B. F. Wright, *American Interpretations of Natural Law* (1931). Particular thinkers can be looked up in M. C. Tyler, *Literary History of the American Revolution* (2 vols., 1897), an old work which is still valuable. For the attitudes of those who opposed the revolt, see C. H. Van Tyne, *Loyalists in the American Revolution* (1929).

The Declaration of Independence has a literature of its own. A brilliant work on the subject is C. L. Becker, *The Declaration of Independence: A Study in the History of Ideas* (reprinted 1951). Edward Dumbauld, *The Declaration of Independence and What It Means Today* (1951) spells out the terms and charges so as to make them comprehensible to the modern layman. J. H. Hazelton, *The Declaration of Independence: Its History* (1906), is the fullest account of events and a standard work, though too rare a book and too detailed a study for general use. J. P. Boyd, *The Declaration of Independence: The Evolution of the Text* (1945), reproduces the documents in facsimile and discusses them expertly. *The Story of the Declaration of Independence* (1954), text by Dumas Malone, pictures by Hirst Milhollen and Milton Kaplan, is a richly illustrated book; it contains brief sketches of all the Signers.

Biographies of leading men become specially important in this period. Among these may be mentioned: J. C. Miller, *Sam Adams: Pioneer in Propaganda* (1936); Carl Becker, *Benjamin Franklin* (1946), a brilliant sketch originally published in *Dictionary of American Biography*; Carl Van Doren, *Benjamin Franklin*, esp. Chs. 17-18; R. D. Meade, *Patrick Henry: Patriot in the Making* (1957); Catherine Drinker Bowen, *John Adams and the American Revolution* (1950), with fictionalized conversations but fundamentally accurate; Page Smith, *John Adams* (2 vols., 1962); D. S. Freeman, *George Washington*, esp. Vol. III, Chs. 15-18; Dumas Malone, *Jefferson the Virginian* (1948, Vol. I of *Jefferson and His Time*), esp. Chs. 13-16. H. H. Clark, ed., *Thomas Paine: Representative Selections* (1944, *American Writers Series*), is an unusually good one-volume edn.; it contains "Common Sense" and offers an admirable introduction to the most effective popular writer of the day.

10. THE AMERICAN REVOLUTION

General

On the military side, W. M. Wallace, *Appeal to Arms* (1951) is an excellent general account. Christopher Ward, *War of the Revolution* (2 vols., 1952) is fuller. For international relations see, besides the general diplomatic histories, A. B. Darling, *Our Rising Empire, 1763-1803* (1940).

Special Military

Freeman, in *George Washington*, Vol. IV (1951), carries his detailed story through Valley Forge, and in Vol. V (1952) through Yorktown. Bernhard Knollenberg, *Washington and the Revolution* (1940), takes a less favorable view of Washington. See also T. G. Frothingham, *Washington, Commander in Chief* (1930). Particular campaigns, battles, and episodes can be studied in Ward and Freeman, and in specialized works like the following: Hoffman Nickerson, *The Turning Point of the Revolution, or Burgoyne in America* (1928); A. H. Bill, *Valley Forge* (1952); Carl Van Doren, *Secret History of the American Revolution* (1951), giving an account of the conspiracy of Benedict Arnold and others. Important aspects of the war are dealt with by Allen Bowman, *The Morale of the American Revolutionary Army* (1943); Herbert Richmond, *Statesmen and Sea Power* (1946). A good view of John Paul Jones can be gained from the article on him in *Dictionary of American Biography*.

Special International

Among studies of value are: S. F. Bemis, *The Diplomacy of the American Revolution* (1935); E. S. Corwin, *French Policy and the American Alliance* (1916); Bernard Faÿ, *The Revolutionary Spirit in France and America* (1927); D. M. Clark, *British Opinion and the American Revolution* (1930). The simplest way to live through the diplomatic problems of the time is to follow the career of Benjamin Franklin, in Van Doren, Chs. 20-23, or elsewhere.

11. THE INTERNAL REVOLUTION

General

Internal developments are treated in varying degree in general accounts of the Revolution, and the larger social background is given in Greene, *Revolutionary Generation*. J. F. Jameson, *The American Revolution as a Social Movement* (1940) is brief and suggestive.

Special

Political developments are emphasized in Allan Nevins, *The American States during and after the Revolution* (1924), which can be supplemented by M. B. Macmillan, *War Governors in the American Revolution* (1943); E. P. Douglass, *Rebels and Democrats: The Struggle for Equal Political Rights and Majority Rule During the American Revolution* (1955); and R. A. Rutland, *The Birth of the Bill of Rights, 1776-1791* (1955). R. A. East, *Business Enterprise in the American Revolutionary Era* (1938) is a stimulating study.

The movement for religious freedom is treated in various monographic works, like H. J. Eckenrode, *Separation of Church and State in Virginia* (1910), and in general works, such as E. B. Greene, *Religion and the State* (1941), and W. W. Sweet, *The Story of Religion in America* (1939). An important biography of a religious leader is P. K. Guilday, *Life and Times of John Carroll* (2 vols., 1922).

For cultural developments, the student will naturally turn first to histories of American thought, literature, architecture, art, etc. To those already listed may be added A. H. Quinn, *A History of the American Drama* (1943).

The important services of Jefferson and Madison to the cause of individual freedom in this period are described in Malone, *Jefferson the Virginian*, Chs. 17-20; Irving Brant, *James Madison* (1948), Vol. II, Ch. 22; Adrienne Koch, *Jefferson and Madison* (1950), Chs. 1-2; and in other biographies of these men. The situation respecting slavery is described briefly in general histories of American slavery, and more specifically in M. S. Locke, *Anti-Slavery Sentiment in America 1619-1808* (1901).

12. THE CONFEDERATION

General

John Fiske, *The Critical Period of American History* (1888), while now recognized as extreme and inaccurate, is still good reading. The Confederation has been most staunchly defended in recent years by Merrill Jensen in *The Articles of Confederation* (1948), and *The New Nation: A History of the United States during the Confederation, 1781-1789* (1950). The volume in the old *American Nation* series, A. C. McLaughlin, *Confederation and Constitution* (1904), still has value; and works very useful for this period are Burnett, *Continental Congress*, and Nettels, *Roots of American Civilization*.

Special

P. J. Treat, *The National Land System* (1910) is full of detailed information. The traditional story of Maryland's refusal to ratify the Articles and of Virginia's cession of western lands has been considerably modified by Abernethy, in *Western Lands and the American Revolution*, by Jensen and others. The documents in the case are in *Papers of Thomas Jefferson*, edited by J. P. Boyd, III, 625-636; IV, 386-391; VI, 571-580, with able and illuminating notes. The lengthy note on Jefferson's plan for the government of the western territory (VI, 581-600) is the best treatment of this topic in print.

For the events of Shays's Rebellion, see J. T. Adams, *New England in the Republic, 1776-1850* (1926); Jonathan Smith, *Some Features of Shays's Rebellion* (1903; reprinted in *William and Mary Quarterly*, 1948). For the political use of this affair, see R. A. East, "The Massachusetts Conservatives in the Critical Period," in *Era of the American Revolution* (1939), edited by R. B. Morris.

On economics and finance, see C. P. Nettels, *Emergence of a National Economy, 1775-1815* (1962); Dewey, *Financial History;* C. L. Ver Steeg, *Robert Morris, Revolutionary Financier* (1954); E. J. Ferguson, *The Power of the Purse: A History of American Public Finance, 1776-1790* (1961). On trade expansion, see S. E. Morison, *Maritime History of Massachusetts, 1783-1860* (1921), a brilliant book with which all who are sea-going in spirit should become acquainted. International problems are covered by the diplomatic histories already listed. See also: G. S. Graham, *Sea Power and British North America, 1783-1820* (1941); S. F. Bemis, "John Jay," in *American Secretaries of State and Their Diplomacy,* I (1927).

13. THE CONSTITUTION OF 1787

General

Narrative accounts are: Max Farrand, *Framing of the Constitution* (1913); Charles Warren, *The Making of the Constitution* (1928); Carl Van Doren, *The Great Rehearsal* (1948). See also R. L. Schuyler, *The Constitution of the United States* (1923); E. S. Corwin, *The Constitution and What It Means Today* (1954).

Special

On ratification, see O. G. Libby, *Geographical Distribution of the Vote on the Constitution* (1894). C. A. Beard criticizes this in *An Economic Interpretation of the Constitution* (1913), a book which in turn has been subjected to much criticism, as in R. E. Brown, *Charles Beard and the Constitution* (1956), but which every serious student of the Constitution must read.

Irving Brant, *James Madison,* Vol. III (1950), is of the first importance for both the Convention and the ratification fight. Other biographies of special value in this connection are: C. P. Smith, *James Wilson: Founding Father, 1742-1798* (1956); Nathan Schachner, *Alexander Hamilton* (1946); Broadus Mitchell, *Alexander Hamilton: Youth to Maturity, 1755-1788* (1957); D. J. Mays, *Edmund Pendleton,* Vol. II (1952); A. J. Beveridge, *Life of John Marshall,* Vol. I (1916); Clinton Rossiter, *Alexander Hamilton and the Constitution* (1964). J. T. Main, *The Anti-federalists: Critics of the Constitution, 1781-1788* (1961), is a good study.

Documents are indispensable in any study of the Constitution. The following are standard: Department of State, *Documentary History of the Constitution of the United States* (5 vols., 1894-1905); Max Farrand, ed., *Records of the Federal Convention* (3 vols., 1911); Jonathan Elliott, ed., *Debates in the Several State Conventions on the Adoption of the Federal Constitution* (5 vols., 1861). *The Federalist Papers* of Hamilton, Madison, and John Jay have been published in numerous editions.

APPENDICES

DECLARATION OF INDEPENDENCE

In Congress, July 4, 1776

A DECLARATION BY THE REPRESENTATIVES OF THE UNITED STATES OF AMERICA, IN CONGRESS ASSEMBLED

WHEN, IN THE COURSE OF HUMAN EVENTS, IT BECOMES NECESSARY FOR ONE people to dissolve the political bands which have connected them with another, and to assume, among the powers of the earth, the separate and equal station to which the laws of nature and of nature's God entitle them, a decent respect to the opinions of mankind requires that they should declare the causes which impel them to the separation.

We hold these truths to be self-evident:—That all men are created equal; that they are endowed by their Creator with certain unalienable rights; that among these are life, liberty, and the pursuit of happiness. That, to secure these rights, governments are instituted among men, deriving their just powers from the consent of the governed; that, whenever any form of government becomes destructive of these ends, it is the right of the people to alter or to abolish it, and to institute a new government, laying its foundation on such principles, and organizing its powers in such form, as to them shall seem most likely to effect their safety and happiness. Prudence, indeed, will dictate, that governments long established should not be changed for light and transient causes; and accordingly all experience hath shown that mankind are more disposed to suffer while evils are sufferable, than to right themselves by abolishing the forms to which they are accustomed. But when a long train of abuses and usurpations, pursuing invariably the same object, evinces a design to reduce them under absolute despotism, it is their right, it is their duty, to throw off such government, and to provide new guards for their future security. Such has been the patient sufferance of these colonies; and such is now the necessity which constrains them to alter their former systems of government. The history of the present King of Great Britain is a history of repeated injuries and usurpations, all having in direct object the establishment of an absolute tyranny over these states. To prove this, let facts be submitted to a candid world.

He has refused his assent to laws the most wholesome and necessary for the public good.

He has forbidden his governors to pass laws of immediate and pressing importance, unless suspended in their operation till his assent should be obtained; and when so suspended, he has utterly neglected to attend to them.

He has refused to pass other laws for the accommodation of large districts of people, unless those people would relinquish the right of representation in the legislature—a right inestimable to them, and formidable to tyrants only.

He has called together legislative bodies at places unusual, uncomfortable, and distant from the depository of their public records, for the sole purpose of fatiguing them into compliance with his measure.

He has dissolved representative houses repeatedly, for opposing, with manly firmness, his invasions on the rights of the people.

He has refused, for a long time after such dissolutions, to cause others to be elected, whereby the legislative powers, incapable of annihilation, have returned to the people at large for their exercise; the State remaining, in the mean time, exposed to all the dangers of invasions from without, and convulsions within.

He has endeavored to prevent the population of these States; for that purpose obstructing the laws for the naturalization of foreigners; refusing to pass others to encourage their migration hither, and raising the conditions of new appropriations of lands.

He has obstructed the administration of justice, by refusing his assent to laws for establishing judiciary powers.

He has made judges dependent on his will alone for the tenure of their offices, and the amount and payment of their salaries.

He has erected a multitude of new offices, and sent hither swarms of officers to harass our people and eat out their substance.

He has kept among us in times of peace, standing armies, without the consent of our legislatures.

He has affected to render the military independent of, and superior to, the civil power.

He has combined with others to subject us to a jurisdiction foreign to our constitutions, and unacknowledged by our laws; giving his assent to their acts of pretended legislation:

For quartering large bodies of armed troops among us;

For protecting them, by a mock trial, from punishment for any murders which they should commit on the inhabitants of these States;

For cutting off our trade with all parts of the world;

For imposing taxes on us without our consent;

For depriving us, in many cases, of the benefits of trial by jury;

For transporting us beyond seas, to be tried for pretended offences;

For abolishing the free system of English laws in a neighboring province, establishing therein an arbitrary government, and enlarging its boundaries, so as to render it at once an example and fit instrument for introducing the same absolute rule into these colonies;

For taking away our charters, abolishing our most valuable laws, and altering, fundamentally, the forms of our governments;

For suspending our own legislatures, and declaring themselves invested with power to legislate for us in all cases whatsoever.

He has abdicated government here, by declaring us out of his protection, and waging war against us.

He has plundered our seas, ravaged our coasts, burned our towns, and destroyed the lives of our people.

He is at this time transporting large armies of foreign mercenaries to complete the works of death, desolation and tyranny, already begun with circumstances of cruelty and perfidy scarcely paralleled in the most barbarous ages, and totally unworthy the head of a civilized nation.

He has constrained our fellow-citizens, taken captive on the high seas, to bear arms against their country, to become the executioners of their friends and brethren, or to fall themselves by their hands.

He has excited domestic insurrection among us, and has endeavored to bring on the inhabitants of our frontiers the merciless Indian savages, whose known rule of warfare is an undistinguished destruction of all ages, sexes, and conditions.

In every stage of these oppressions we have petitioned for redress in the most humble terms; our repeated petitions have been answered only by repeated injury. A prince whose character is thus marked by every act which may define a tyrant, is unfit to be the ruler of a free people.

Nor have we been wanting in our attentions to our British brethren. We have warned them, from time to time, of attempts by their legislature to extend an unwarrantable jurisdiction over us. We have reminded them of the circumstances of our emigration and settlement here. We have appealed to their native justice and magnanimity; and we have conjured them, by the ties of our common kindred, to disavow these usurpations, which would inevitably interrupt our connections and correspondence. They, too, have been deaf to the voice of justice and consanguinity. We must, therefore, acquiesce in the necessity which denounces our separation, and hold them, as we hold the rest of mankind, enemies in war, in peace friends.

We, therefore, the Representatives of the United States of America, in General Congress assembled, appealing to the Supreme Judge of the world for the rectitude of our intentions, do, in the name and by the authority of the good people of these colonies, solemnly publish and declare, That these united Colonies are, and of right ought to be, free and independent states; that they are absolved from all allegiance to the British crown, and that all political connection between them and the state of Great Britain is, and ought to be, totally dissolved; and that, as free and independent states, they have full power to levy war, conclude peace, contract alliances, establish commerce, and do all other acts and things which independent states may of right do. And, for the support of this declaration, with a firm reliance on the protection of Divine Providence, we mutually pledge to each other our lives, our fortunes, and our sacred honor.

The foregoing Declaration was, by order of Congress, engrossed, and signed by the following members:

JOHN HANCOCK

NEW HAMPSHIRE
JOSIAH BARTLETT
WILLIAM WHIPPLE
MATTHEW THORNTON

MASSACHUSETTS BAY
SAMUEL ADAMS
JOHN ADAMS
ROBERT TREAT PAINE
ELBRIDGE GERRY

RHODE ISLAND
STEPHEN HOPKINS
WILLIAM ELLERY

CONNECTICUT
ROGER SHERMAN
SAMUEL HUNTINGTON
WILLIAM WILLIAMS
OLIVER WOLCOTT

NEW YORK
WILLIAM FLOYD
PHILIP LIVINGSTON
FRANCIS LEWIS
LEWIS MORRIS

NEW JERSEY
RICHARD STOCKTON
JOHN WITHERSPOON
FRANCIS HOPKINSON
JOHN HART
ABRAHAM CLARK

PENNSYLVANIA
ROBERT MORRIS
BENJAMIN RUSH
BENJAMIN FRANKLIN
JOHN MORTON
GEORGE CLYMER
JAMES SMITH
GEORGE TAYLOR
JAMES WILSON
GEORGE ROSS

DELAWARE
CAESAR RODNEY
GEORGE READ
THOMAS M'KEAN

MARYLAND
SAMUEL CHASE
WILLIAM PACA
THOMAS STONE

CHARLES CARROLL, of
   Carrollton

VIRGINIA
GEORGE WYTHE
RICHARD HENRY LEE
THOMAS JEFFERSON
BENJAMIN HARRISON
THOMAS NELSON, JR.
FRANCIS LIGHTFOOT LEE
CARTER BRAXTON

NORTH CAROLINA
WILLIAM HOOPER
JOSEPH HEWES
JOHN PENN

SOUTH CAROLINA
EDWARD RUTLEDGE
THOMAS HEYWARD, JR.
THOMAS LYNCH, JR.
ARTHUR MIDDLETON

GEORGIA
BUTTON GWINNETT
LYMAN HALL
GEORGE WALTON

THE
CONSTITUTION
OF THE
UNITED STATES OF AMERICA

WE, THE PEOPLE OF THE UNITED STATES, IN ORDER TO FORM A MORE PERFECT union, establish justice, insure domestic tranquillity, provide for the common defence, promote the general welfare, and secure the blessings of liberty to ourselves and our posterity, do ordain and establish this constitution for the United States of America.

ARTICLE I
SECTION 1

ALL LEGISLATIVE POWERS HEREIN GRANTED SHALL BE VESTED IN A CONGRESS OF the United States, which shall consist of a Senate and a House of Representatives.

SECTION 2

The House of Representatives shall be composed of Members chosen every second Year by the People of the several States, and the Electors in each State shall have the Qualifications requisite for Electors of the most numerous Branch of the State Legislature.

No Person shall be a Representative who shall not have attained to the Age of twenty-five Years, and been seven Years a Citizen of the United States, and who shall not, when elected, be an Inhabitant of that State in which he shall be chosen.

[Representatives and direct Taxes shall be apportioned among the several States which may be included within this Union, according to their respective Numbers, which shall be determined by adding to the whole Number of free Persons, including those bound to Service for a Term of Years, and excluding Indians not taxed, three fifths of all other Persons.]* The actual Enumeration shall be made within three Years after the first Meeting of the Congress of the United States, and within every subsequent Term of ten Years, in such Manner as they shall by Law direct. The Number of Representatives shall not exceed one for every thirty Thousand, but each State shall have at Least one

* Repealed by Section 2 of Amendment XIV.

Representative; and until such enumeration shall be made, the State of New Hampshire shall be entitled to chuse three, Massachusetts eight, Rhode-Island and Providence Plantations one, Connecticut five, New-York six, New Jersey four, Pennsylvania eight, Delaware one, Maryland six, Virginia ten, North Carolina five, South Carolina five, and Georgia three.

When vacancies happen in the Representation from any State, the Executive Authority thereof shall issue Writs of Election to fill such Vacancies.

The House of Representatives shall chuse their Speaker and other Officers; and shall have the sole Power of Impeachment.

Section 3

The Senate of the United States shall be composed of two Senators from each State, [chosen by the Legislature thereof,]* for six Years; and each Senator shall have one Vote.

Immediately after they shall be assembled in Consequence of the first Election, they shall be divided as equally as may be into three Classes. The Seats of the Senators of the first Class shall be vacated at the Expiration of the second Year, of the second Class at the Expiration of the fourth Year, and of the third Class at the Expiration of the sixth Year, so that one-third may be chosen every second Year; [and if Vacancies happen by Resignation, or otherwise, during the Recess of the Legislature of any State, the Executive thereof may make temporary Appointments until the next Meeting of the Legislature, which shall then fill such Vacancies.]†

No person shall be a Senator who shall not have attained to the Age of thirty Years, and been nine Years a Citizen of the United States, and who shall not, when elected, be an Inhabitant of that State for which he shall be chosen.

The Vice President of the United States shall be President of the Senate, but shall have no Vote, unless they be equally divided.

The Senate shall chuse their other Officers, and also a President pro tempore, in the Absence of the Vice President, or when he shall exercise the Office of President of the United States.

The Senate shall have the sole Power to try all Impeachments. When sitting for that Purpose, they shall be an Oath or Affirmation. When the President of the United States is tried, the Chief Justice shall preside: And no Person shall be convicted without the Concurrence of two thirds of the Members present.

Judgment in Cases of Impeachment shall not extend further than to removal from Office, and disqualification to hold and enjoy any Office of honor, Trust or Profit under the United States: but the Party convicted shall nevertheless be liable and subject to Indictment, Trial, Judgment and Punishment, according to Law.

Section 4

The Times, Places and Manner of holding Elections for Senators and Representatives, shall be prescribed in each State by the Legislature thereof; but the Congress may at any time by Law make or alter such Regulations, except as to the Places of chusing Senators.

* Replaced by Section 1 of Amendment XVII.
† Changed by Clause 2 of Amendment XVII.

The Congress shall assemble at least once in every Year, and such Meeting* shall [be on the first Monday in December] unless they shall by Law appoint a different Day.

Section 5

Each House shall be the Judge of the Elections, Returns and Qualifications of its own Members, and a Majority of each shall constitute a Quorum to do Business; but a smaller Number may adjourn from day to day, and may be authorized to compel the Attendance of absent Members, in such Manner, and under such Penalties as each House may provide.

Each House may determine the Rules of its Proceedings, punish its Members for disorderly Behavior, and, with the Concurrence of two thirds, expel a Member.

Each House shall keep a Journal of its Proceedings, and from time to time publish the same, excepting such Parts as may in their Judgment require Secrecy; and the Yeas and Nays of the Members of either House on any question shall, at the Desire of one fifth of those present, be entered on the Journal.

Neither House, during the Session of Congress, shall, without the Consent of the other, adjourn for more than three days, nor to any other Place than that in which the two Houses shall be sitting.

Section 6

The Senators and Representatives shall receive a Compensation for their Services, to be ascertained by Law, and paid out of the Treasury of the United States. They shall in all Cases, except Treason, Felony and Breach of the Peace, be privileged from Arrest during their Attendance at the Session of their respective Houses, and in going to and returning from the same; and for any Speech or Debate in either House, they shall not be questioned in any other Place.

No Senator or Representative shall, during the Time for which he was elected, be appointed to any civil Office under the Authority of the United States, which shall have been created, or the Emoluments whereof shall have been encreased during such time; and no Person holding any Office under the United States, shall be a Member of either House during his Continuance in Office.

Section 7

All Bills for raising Revenue shall originate in the House of Representatives; but the Senate may propose or concur with Amendments as on other Bills.

Every Bill which shall have passed the House of Representatives and the Senate, shall, before it become a Law, be presented to the President of the United States; If he approve he shall sign it, but if not he shall return it, with his Objections to that House in which it shall have originated, who shall enter the Objections at large on their Journal, and proceed to reconsider it. If after such Reconsideration two thirds of that House shall agree to pass the Bill, it shall be sent, together with the Objections, to the other House, by which it shall likewise be reconsidered, and if approved by two thirds of that House, it

* Changed by Section 2 of Amendment XX.

shall become a Law. But in all such Cases the Votes of both Houses shall be determined by Yeas and Nays, and the Names of the Persons voting for and against the Bill shall be entered on the Journal of each House respectively. If any Bill shall not be returned by the President within ten Days (Sundays excepted) after it shall have been presented to him, the Same shall be a Law, in like Manner as if he had signed it, unless the Congress by their Adjournment prevent its Return, in which Case it shall not be a Law.

Every Order, Resolution, or Vote to which the Concurrence of the Senate and House of Representatives may be necessary (except on a question of Adjournment) shall be presented to the President of the United States; and before the Same shall take Effect, shall be approved by him, or being disapproved by him, shall be repassed by two thirds of the Senate and House of Representatives, according to the Rules and Limitations prescribed in the Case of a Bill.

SECTION 8*

The Congress shall have Power To lay and collect Taxes, Duties, Imposts and Excises, to pay the Debts and provide for the common Defence and general Welfare of the United States; but all Duties, Imposts and Excises shall be uniform throughout the United States;

To borrow Money on the credit of the United States;

To regulate Commerce with foreign Nations, and among the several States, and with the Indian Tribes;

To establish an uniform Rule of Naturalization, and uniform Laws on the subject of Bankruptcies throughout the United States;

To coin Money, regulate the Value thereof, and of foreign Coin, and fix the Standard of Weights and Measures;

To provide for the Punishment of counterfeiting the Securities and current Coin of the United States;

To establish Post Offices and post Roads;

To promote the Progress of Science and useful Arts, by securing for limited Times to Authors and Inventors the exclusive Right to their respective Writings and Discoveries;

To constitute Tribunals inferior to the supreme Court;

To define and punish Piracies and Felonies committed on the high Seas, and Offences against the Law of Nations;

To declare War, grant Letters of Marque and Reprisal, and make Rules concerning Captures on Land and Water;

To raise and support Armies, but no Appropriation of Money to that Use shall be for a longer Term than two Years;

To provide and maintain a Navy;

To make Rules for the Government and Regulation of the land and naval Forces;

To provide for calling forth the Militia to execute the Laws of the Union, suppress Insurrections and repel Invasions;

To provide for organizing, arming, and disciplining the Militia, and for governing such Part of them as may be employed in the Service of the United States, reserving to the States respectively, the Appointment of the Officers,

* Paragraphs 1-17 of Section 8 contain the "enumerated powers" of Congress.

and the Authority of training the Militia according to the discipline prescribed by Congress;

To exercise exclusive Legislation in all Cases whatsoever, over such District (not exceeding ten Miles square) as may, by Cession of particular States, and the Acceptance of Congress, become the Seat of the Government of the United States, and to exercise like Authority over all Places purchased by the Consent of the Legislature of the State in which the Same shall be, for the Erection of Forts, Magazines, Arsenals, dock-Yards, and other needful Buildings;—And

To make all Laws which shall be necessary and proper° for carrying into Execution the foregoing Powers, and all other Powers vested by this Constitution in the Government of the United States, or in any Department or Officer thereof.

SECTION 9†

The Migration or Importation of such Persons as any of the States now existing shall think proper to admit, shall not be prohibited by the Congress prior to the Year one thousand eight hundred and eight, but a Tax or duty may be imposed on such Importation, not exceeding ten dollars for each Person.

The Privilege of the Writ of Habeas Corpus shall not be suspended, unless when in Cases of Rebellion or Invasion the public Safety may require it.

No Bill of Attainder or ex post facto Law shall be passed.

No Capitation, or other direct, tax shall be laid, unless in Proportion to the Census or Enumeration herein before directed to be taken.

No Tax or Duty shall be laid on Articles exported from any State.

No Preference shall be given by any Regulation of Commerce or Revenue to the Ports of one State over those of another: nor shall Vessels bound to, or from, one State, be obliged to enter, clear, or pay Duties in another.

No Money shall be drawn from the Treasury, but in Consequence of Appropriations made by Law; and a regular Statement and Account of the Receipts and Expenditures of all public Money shall be published from time to time.

No Title of Nobility shall be granted by the United States: And no Person holding any Office of Profit or Trust under them, shall, without the Consent of the Congress, accept of any present, Emolument, Office, or Title, of any kind whatever, from any King, Prince, or foreign State.

SECTION 10‡

No State shall enter into any Treaty, Alliance, or Confederation; grant Letters of Marque and Reprisal; coin Money; emit Bills of Credit; make any Thing but gold and silver Coin a Tender in Payment of Debts; pass any Bill of Attainder, ex post facto Law, or Law impairing the Obligation of Contracts,§ or grant any Title of Nobility.

No State shall, without the Consent of the Congress, lay any Imposts or Duties on Imports or Exports, except what may be absolutely necessary for

° The "coefficient clause" (or "Elastic Clause" or "Necessary and Proper" clause) of the Constitution.
† This section imposes certain limitations on the powers of Congress.
‡ This section imposes certain limitations on the States.
§ The "Obligation of Contract" clause.

executing it's inspection Laws: and the net Produce of all Duties and Imposts, laid by any State on Imports or Exports, shall be for the Use of the Treasury of the United States; and all such Laws shall be subject to the Revision and Control of the Congress.

No State shall, without the Consent of Congress, lay any Duty of Tonnage, keep Troops, or Ships of War in time of Peace, enter into any Agreement or Compact with another State, or with a foreign Power, or engage in War, unless actually invaded, or in such imminent Danger as will not admit of delay.

ARTICLE II

Section 1

The executive Power shall be vested in a President of the United States of America. He shall hold his Office during the Term of four Years, and, together with the Vice President, chosen for the same Term, be elected, as follows:

Each State shall appoint, in such Manner as the Legislature thereof may direct, a Number of Electors, equal to the whole Number of Senators and Representatives to which the State may be entitled in the Congress: but no Senator or Representative, or Person holding an Office of Trust or Profit under the United States, shall be appointed an Elector.

[The electors shall meet in their respective States, and vote by ballot for two Persons, of whom one at least shall not be an Inhabitant of the same State with themselves. And they shall make a List of all the Persons voted for, and of the Number of Votes for each; which List they shall sign and certify, and transmit sealed to the Seat of the Government of the United States, directed to the President of the Senate. The President of the Senate shall, in the Presence of the Senate and House of Representatives, open all the Certificates, and the Votes shall then be counted. The Person having the greatest Number of Votes shall be the President, if such Number be a Majority of the whole Number of Electors appointed; and if there be more than one who have such Majority, and have an equal Number of Votes, then the House of Representatives shall immediately chuse by Ballot one of them for President; and if no Person have a Majority, then from the five highest on the List the said House shall in like Manner chuse the President. But in chusing the President, the Votes shall be taken by States, the Representation from each State having one Vote; A quorum for this Purpose shall consist of a Member or Members from two thirds of the States, and a Majority of all the States shall be necessary to a Choice. In every Case, after the Choice of the President, the Person having the greatest Number of Votes of the Electors shall be the Vice President. But if there should remain two or more who have equal Votes, the Senate shall chuse from them by Ballot the Vice President.]°

The Congress may determine the Time of chusing the Electors, and the Day on which they shall give their Votes; which Day shall be the same throughout the United States.

No Person except a natural born Citizen, or a Citizen of the United States, at the time of the Adoption of this Constitution, shall be eligible to the Office of

° Superseded by Amendment XII.

President; neither shall any Person be eligible to that Office who shall not have attained to the Age of thirty five Years, and been fourteen Years a Resident within the United States.

In Case of the Removal of the President from Office, or of his Death, Resignation or Inability to discharge the Powers and Duties of the said Office, the same shall devolve on the Vice President, and the Congress may by Law provide for the Case of Removal, Death, Resignation or Inability, both of the President and Vice President, declaring what Officer shall then act as President, and such Officer shall act accordingly, until the Disability be removed, or a President shall be elected.

The President shall, at stated Times, receive for his Services, a Compensation, which shall neither be encreased nor diminished during the Period for which he shall have been elected, and he shall not receive within that Period any other Emolument from the United States, or any of them.

Before he enter on the Execution of his Office, he shall take the following Oath or Affirmation:—"I do solemnly swear (or affirm) that I will faithfully execute the Office of President of the United States, and will to the best of my Ability, preserve, protect and defend the Constitution of the United States."

SECTION 2

The President shall be Commander in Chief of the Army and Navy of the United States, and of the Militia of the several States, when called into the actual Service of the United States; he may require the Opinion, in writing, of the principal Officer in each of the executive Departments, upon any Subject relating to the Duties of their respective Offices, and he shall have Power to grant Reprieves and Pardons for Offences against the United States, except in Cases of Impeachment.

He shall have Power,* by and with the Advice and Consent of the Senate, to make Treaties, provided two thirds of the Senators present concur; and he shall nominate, and by and with the Advice and Consent of the Senate, shall appoint Ambassadors, other public Ministers and Consuls, Judges of the supreme Court, and all other Officers of the United States, whose Appointments are not herein otherwise provided for, and which shall be established by Law: but the Congress may by Law vest the Appointment of such inferior Officers, as they think proper, in the President alone, in the Courts of Law, or in the Heads of Departments.

The President shall have Power to fill up all Vacancies that may happen during the Recess of the Senate, by granting Commissions which shall expire at the End of their next Session.

SECTION 3

He shall from time to time give to the Congress Information of the State of the Union, and recommend to their Consideration such Measures as he shall judge necessary and expedient; he may, on extraordinary Occasions, convene both Houses, or either of them, and, in Case of Disagreement between them, with Respect to the Time of Adjournment, he may adjourn them to such Time as he shall think proper; he shall receive Ambassadors and other public Min-

* The "Treaty Making Power" is contained in this sentence.

isters; he shall take Care that the Laws be faithfully executed, and shall Commission all the Officers of the United States.

SECTION 4

The President, Vice President and all civil Officers of the United States, shall be removed from Office on Impeachment for, and Conviction of, Treason, Bribery, or other high Crimes and Misdemeanors.

ARTICLE III

SECTION 1

The judicial Power of the United States, shall be vested in one supreme Court, and in such inferior Courts as the Congress may from time to time ordain and establish. The Judges, both of the supreme and inferior Courts, shall hold their Offices during good Behaviour, and shall, at stated Times, receive for their Services, a Compensation, which shall not be diminished during their Continuance in Office.

SECTION 2

The judicial Power shall extend to all Cases, in Law and Equity, arising under this Constitution, the Laws of the United States, and Treaties made, or which shall be made, under their Authority;—to all Cases affecting Ambassadors, other public Ministers and Consuls;—to all Cases of admiralty and maritime Jurisdiction;—to Controversies to which the United States shall be a Party;—to Controversies between two or more States;—between a State and Citizens of another State;—between Citizens of different States,—between Citizens of the same State claiming Lands under Grants of different States, and between a State, or the Citizens thereof, and foreign States, Citizens or Subjects.

In all Cases affecting Ambassadors, other public Ministers and Consuls, and those in which a State shall be Party, the supreme Court shall have original Jurisdiction. In all the other Cases before mentioned, the supreme Court shall have appellate Jurisdiction, both as to Law and Fact, with such Exceptions, and under such Regulations as the Congress shall make.

The Trial of all Crimes, except in Cases of Impeachment, shall be by Jury; and such Trial shall be held in the State where the said Crimes shall have been committed; but when not committed within any State, the Trial shall be at such Place or Places as the Congress may by Law have directed.

SECTION 3

Treason against the United States, shall consist only in levying War against them, or in adhering to their Enemies, giving them Aid and Comfort. No Person shall be convicted of Treason unless on the Testimony of two Witnesses to the same overt Act, or on Confession in open Court.

The Congress shall have Power to declare the Punishment of Treason, but no Attainder of Treason shall work Corruption of Blood, or Forfeiture except during the Life of the Person attainted.

ARTICLE IV

SECTION 1

Full Faith and Credit shall be given in each State to the public Acts, Records, and judicial Proceedings of every other State. And the Congress may by general Laws prescribe the Manner in which such Acts, Records and Proceedings shall be proved, and the Effect thereof.

SECTION 2

The Citizens of each State shall be entitled to all Privileges and Immunities of Citizens in the several States.

A person charged in any State with Treason, Felony, or other Crime, who shall flee from Justice, and be found in another State, shall on Demand of the executive Authority of the State from which he fled, be delivered up, to be removed to the State having Jurisdiction of the Crime.

No Person held to Service or Labour in one State, under the Laws thereof, escaping into another, shall, in Consequence of any Law or Regulation therein, be discharged from such Service or Labour, but shall be delivered up on Claim of the Party to whom such Service or Labour may be due.

SECTION 3

New States may be admitted by the Congress into this Union; but no new State shall be formed or erected within the Jurisdiction of any other State; nor any State be formed by the Junction of two or more States, or Parts of States, without the Consent of the Legislatures of the States concerned as well as of the Congress.

The Congress shall have Power to dispose of and make all needful Rules and Regulations respecting the Territory or other Property belonging to the United States; and nothing in this Constitution shall be so construed as to Prejudice any Claims of the United States, or of any particular State.

SECTION 4

The United States shall guarantee to every State in this Union a Republican Form of Government, and shall protect each of them against Invasion; and on Application of the Legislature, or of the Executive (when the Legislature cannot be convened) against domestic Violence.

ARTICLE V

The Congress, whenever two thirds of both Houses shall deem it necessary, shall propose Amendments to this Constitution,* or, on the Application of the Legislatures of two thirds of the several States, shall call a Convention for proposing Amendments, which, in either Case, shall be valid to all Intents and Purposes, as Part of this Constitution, when ratified by the Legislatures of three fourths of the several States, or by Conventions in three fourths thereof, as the one or the other Mode of Ratification may be proposed by the Congress; Provided that no Amendment which may be made prior to the Year One thousand eight hundred and eight shall in any Manner affect the first and fourth

* The Amending power.

Clauses in the Ninth Section of the first Article; and that no State, without its Consent, shall be deprived of its equal Suffrage in the Senate.

ARTICLE VI

All Debts contracted and Engagements entered into, before the Adoption of this Constitution, shall be as valid against the United States under this Constitution, as under the Confederation.

This Constitution, and the Laws of the United States which shall be made in Pursuance thereof; and all Treaties made, or which shall be made, under the Authority of the United States, shall be the supreme Law of the Land; and the Judges in every State shall be bound thereby, any Thing in the Constitution or Laws of any State to the Contrary notwithstanding.

The Senators and Representatives before mentioned, and the Members of the several State Legislatures, and all executive and judicial Officers, both of the United States and of the several States, shall be bound by Oath or Affirmation, to support this Constitution; but no religious Test shall ever be required as a Qualification to any Office or public Trust under the United States.

ARTICLE VII

The Ratification of the Conventions of nine States, shall be sufficient for the Establishment of this Constitution between the States so ratifying the Same.

DONE in Convention by the Unanimous Consent of the States present the Seventeenth Day of September in the Year of our Lord one thousand seven hundred and Eighty seven and of the Independence of the United States of America the Twelfth. IN WITNESS whereof We have hereunto subscribed our Names.

G° WASHINGTON
Presid* and deputy from Virginia

NEW HAMPSHIRE	JOHN LANGDON NICHOLAS GILMAN
MASSACHUSETTS	NATHANIEL GORHAM RUFUS KING
CONNECTICUT	WM. SAML. JOHNSON ROGER SHERMAN
NEW YORK	ALEXANDER HAMILTON
NEW JERSEY	WIL: LIVINGSTON DAVID BREARLEY WM. PATERSON JONA: DAYTON
PENNSYLVANIA	B FRANKLIN THOMAS MIFFLIN ROBT. MORRIS GEO. CLYMER THOS. FITZSIMONS JARED INGERSOLL JAMES WILSON GOUV MORRIS

DELAWARE	GEO: READ GUNNING BEDFORD jun JOHN DICKINSON RICHARD BASSETT JACO: BROOM
MARYLAND	JAMES MCHENRY DAN OF ST. THOS. JENIFER DANL. CARROLL
VIRGINIA	JOHN BLAIR — JAMES MADISON JR.
NORTH CAROLINA	WM. BLOUNT RICHD. DOBBS SPAIGHT HU WILLIAMSON
SOUTH CAROLINA	J. RUTLEDGE CHARLES COTESWORTH PINCKNEY CHARLES PINCKNEY PIERCE BUTLER
GEORGIA	WILLIAM FEW ABR BALDWIN

Attest WILLIAM JACKSON *Secretary*

AMENDMENTS

ARTICLE I

Congress shall make no law respecting an establishment of religion, or prohibiting the free exercise thereof; or abridging the freedom of speech, or of the press; or the right of the people peaceably to assemble, and to petition the Government for a redress of grievances.

ARTICLE II

A well regulated Militia, being necessary to the security of a free State, the right of the people to keep and bear Arms, shall not be infringed.

ARTICLE III

No Soldier shall, in time of peace, be quartered in any house, without the consent of the Owner, nor in time of war, but in a manner to be prescribed by law.

ARTICLE IV

The right of the people to be secure in their persons, houses, papers, and effects, against unreasonable searches and seizures, shall not be violated, and no Warrants shall issue, but upon probable cause, supported by Oath or affirmation, and particularly describing the place to be searched, and the persons or things to be seized.

ARTICLE V

No person shall be held to answer for a capital, or otherwise infamous crime, unless on a presentment or indictment of a Grand Jury, except in cases arising in the land or naval forces, or in the Militia, when in actual service in time of War or public danger; nor shall any person be subject for the same offence to be twice put in jeopardy of life or limb; nor shall be compelled in any Criminal Case to be a witness against himself, nor be deprived of life, liberty, or property, without due process of law; nor shall private property be taken for public use, without just compensation.

ARTICLE VI

In all criminal prosecutions, the accused shall enjoy the right to a speedy and public trial, by an impartial jury of the State and district wherein the crime shall have been committed, which district shall have been previously ascertained by law, and to be informed of the nature and cause of the accusation; to be confronted with the witnesses against him; to have compulsory process for obtaining Witnesses in his favor, and to have the Assistance of Counsel for his defence.

ARTICLE VII

In suits at common law, where the value in controversy shall exceed twenty dollars, the right of trial by jury shall be preserved, and no fact tried by a jury shall be otherwise re-examined in any Court of the United States, than according to the rules of the common law.

ARTICLE VIII

Excessive bail shall not be required, nor excessive fines imposed, nor cruel and unusual punishments inflicted.

ARTICLE IX

The enumeration in the Constitution, of certain rights, shall not be construed to deny or disparage others retained by the people.

ARTICLE X

The powers not delegated to the United States by the Constitution, nor prohibited by it to the States, are reserved to the States respectively, or to the people.

[THE FIRST TEN ARTICLES PROPOSED 25 SEPTEMBER 1789; DECLARED IN FORCE 15 DECEMBER 1791]*

ARTICLE XI

[DECLARED RATIFIED 8 JANUARY 1798]

The Judicial power of the United States shall not be construed to extend to any suit in law or equity, commenced or prosecuted against one of the United States by Citizens of another State, or by Citizens or Subjects of any Foreign State.

ARTICLE XII

[DECLARED RATIFIED 25 SEPTEMBER 1804]

The Electors shall meet in their respective states, and vote by ballot for President and Vice-President, one of whom, at least, shall not be an inhabitant of the same state with themselves; they shall name in their ballots the person voted for as President, and in distinct ballots the person voted for as Vice-President, and they shall make distinct lists of all persons voted for as President, and of all persons voted for as Vice-President, and of the number of votes for each, which lists they shall sign and certify, and transmit sealed to the seat of the Government of the United States, directed to the President of the Senate;— The President of the Senate shall, in the presence of the Senate and House of Representatives, open all the certificates and the votes shall then be counted;— The person having the greatest number of votes for President, shall be the President, if such number be a majority of the whole number of Electors appointed; and if no person have such majority, then from the persons having the highest numbers not exceeding three on the list of those voted for as President, the House of Representatives shall choose immediately, by ballot, the President. But in choosing the President, the votes shall be taken by states, the representation from each state having one vote; a quorum for this purpose shall consist of

---

* These amendments bind only the National Government, but these rights are not infrequently binding against State authority because of the Court's interpretation of the "due process clause" of Amendment XIV.

a member or members from two-thirds of the states, and a majority of all the states shall be necessary to a choice. And if the House of Representatives shall not choose a President whenever the right of choice shall devolve upon them, before the fourth day of March next following, then the Vice-President shall act as President, as in the case of the death or other constitutional disability of the President. The person having the greatest number of votes as Vice-President, shall be the Vice-President, if such number be a majority of the whole number of Electors appointed, and if no person have a majority, then from the two highest numbers on the list, the Senate shall choose the Vice-President; a quorum for the purpose shall consist of two-thirds of the whole number of Senators, and a majority of the whole number shall be necessary to a choice. But no person constitutionally ineligible to the office of President shall be eligible to that of Vice-President of the United States.

ARTICLE XIII

[DECLARED RATIFIED 18 DECEMBER 1865]

SECTION 1

Neither slavery nor involuntary servitude, except as a punishment for crime whereof the party shall have been duly convicted, shall exist within the United States, or any place subject to their jurisdiction.

SECTION 2

Congress shall have power to enforce this article by appropriate legislation.

ARTICLE XIV

[DECLARED RATIFIED 28 JULY 1868]*

SECTION 1

All persons born or naturalized in the United States, and subject to the jurisdiction thereof, are citizens of the United States and of the State wherein they reside. No State shall make or enforce any law which shall abridge the privileges or immunities of citizens of the United States; nor shall any State deprive any person of life, liberty, or property, without due process of law; nor deny to any person within its jurisdiction the equal protection of the law.

SECTION 2

Representatives shall be apportioned among the several States according to their respective numbers, counting the whole number of persons in each State, excluding Indians not taxed. But when the right to vote at any election for the choice of electors for President and Vice-President of the United States, Representatives in Congress, the Executive and Judicial officers of a State, or the members of the Legislature thereof, is denied to any of the male inhabitants of such State, being twenty-one years of age, and citizens of the United States, or in any way abridged, except for participation in rebellion, or other crime, the basis of representation therein shall be reduced in the proportion which the

* Prior to date of ratification of the twenty-eighth state, Ohio and New Jersey "withdrew" their earlier assents to the amendment. Congress passed a joint resolution on July 21, 1868 declaring the amendment a part of the Constitution and directing the Secretary of State to promulgate it as such. On July 13th South Carolina ratified and on July 21 Georgia added its ratification.

number of such male citizens shall bear to the whole number of male citizens twenty-one years of age in such State.

SECTION 3

No person shall be a Senator or Representative in Congress, or elector of President and Vice-President, or hold any office, civil, or military, under the United States, or under any State, who, having previously taken an oath, as a member of Congress, or as an officer of the United States, or as a member of any State legislature, or as an executive or judicial officer of any State, to support the Constitution of the United States, shall have engaged in insurrection or rebellion against the same, or given aid or comfort to the enemies thereof. But Congress may by a vote of two-thirds of each House, remove such disability.

SECTION 4

The validity of the public debt of the United States, authorized by law, including debts incurred for payment of pensions and bounties for services in suppressing insurrection or rebellion, shall not be questioned. But neither the United States nor any State shall assume or pay any debt or obligation incurred in aid of insurrection or rebellion against the United States, or any claim for the loss or emancipation of any slave; but all such debts, obligations and claims shall be held illegal and void.

SECTION 5

The Congress shall have power to enforce, by appropriate legislation, the provisions of this article.

ARTICLE XV

[DECLARED RATIFIED 30 MARCH 1870]

SECTION 1

The right of citizens of the United States to vote shall not be denied or abridged by the United States or by any State on account of race, color, or previous condition of servitude.

SECTION 2

The Congress shall have power to enforce this article by appropriate legislation.

ARTICLE XVI

[PROPOSED 12 JULY 1909; DECLARED RATIFIED 25 FEBRUARY 1913]

The Congress shall have power to lay and collect taxes on incomes, from whatever source derived, without apportionment among the several States, and without regard to any census or enumeration.

ARTICLE XVII

[DECLARED RATIFIED 31 MAY 1913]

The Senate of the United States shall be composed of two senators from each State, elected by the people thereof, for six years; and each Senator shall have one vote. The electors in each State shall have the qualifications requisite for electors of the most numerous branch of the State legislature.

When vacancies happen in the representation of any State in the Senate, the executive authority of such State shall issue writs of election to fill such vacancies: PROVIDED, That the legislature of any State may empower the executive thereof to make temporary appointments until the people fill the vacancies by election as the legislature may direct.

This amendment shall not be so construed as to affect the election or term of any senator chosen before it becomes valid as part of the Constitution.

ARTICLE XVIII*
[DECLARED RATIFIED 29 JANUARY 1919]

After one year from the ratification of this article, the manufacture, sale, or transportation of intoxicating liquors within, the importation thereof into, or the exportation thereof from the United States and all territory subject to the jurisdiction thereof for beverage purposes is hereby prohibited.

The Congress and the several States shall have concurrent power to enforce this article by appropriate legislation.

This article shall be inoperative unless it shall have been ratified as an amendment to the Constitution by the legislatures of the several States, as provided in the Constitution, within seven years from the date of the submission hereof to the States by the Congress.

ARTICLE XIX
[PROPOSED 4 JUNE 1919; DECLARED RATIFIED 26 AUGUST 1920]

The right of citizens of the United States to vote shall not be denied or abridged by the United States or by any States on account of sex.

The Congress shall have power, by appropriate legislation, to enforce the provisions of this article.

ARTICLE XX
[DECLARED RATIFIED 6 FEBRUARY 1933]
SECTION 1

The terms of the President and Vice-President shall end at noon on the twentieth day of January, and the terms of Senators and Representatives at noon on the third day of January, of the years in which such terms would have ended if this article had not been ratified; and the terms of their successors shall then begin.

SECTION 2

The Congress shall assemble at least once in every year, and such meeting shall begin at noon on the third day of January, unless they shall by law appoint a different day.

SECTION 3

If, at the time fixed for the beginning of the term of the President, the President-elect shall have died, the Vice-President-elect shall become President. If a President shall not have been choosen before the time fixed for the beginning of his term, or if the President-elect shall have failed to qualify, then the Vice-President-elect shall act as President until a President shall have qualified;

* Repealed by section 1 of Amendment XXI.

and the Congress may by law provide for the case wherein neither a President-elect nor a Vice-President-elect shall have qualified, declaring who shall then act as President, or the manner in which one who is to act shall be selected, and such person shall act accordingly until a President or Vice-President shall have qualified.

SECTION 4

The Congress may by law provide for the case of the death of any of the persons from whom the House of Representatives may choose a President whenever the right of choice shall have devolved upon them, and for the case of the death of any of the persons from whom the Senate may choose a Vice-President whenever the right of choice shall have devolved upon them.

SECTION 5

Sections 1 and 2 shall take effect on the 15th day of October following the ratification of this article.

SECTION 6

This article shall be inoperative unless it shall have been ratified as an amendment to the Constitution by the legislatures of three-fourths of the several States within seven years from the date of its submission.

ARTICLE XXI

[DECLARED RATIFIED 5 DECEMBER 1933]

SECTION 1

The eighteenth article of amendment to the Constitution of the United States is hereby repealed.

SECTION 2

The transportation or importation into any State, Territory or possession of the United States for delivery or use therein of intoxicating liquors, in violation of the laws thereof, is hereby prohibited.

SECTION 3

This article shall be inoperative unless it shall have been ratified as an amendment to the Constitution by convention in the several States, as provided in the Constitution, within seven years from the date of the submission hereof to the States by the Congress.

ARTICLE XXII

[DECLARED RATIFIED 1 MARCH 1951]

SECTION 1

No person shall be elected to the office of President more than twice, and no person who has held the office of President, or acted as President, for more than two years of a term to which some other person was elected President shall be elected to the office of the President more than once. But this article shall not apply to any person holding the office of President when this article was proposed by the Congress, and shall not prevent any person who may be holding the office of President, or acting as President, during the term within which this Article becomes operative from holding the office of President or acting as President during the remainder of such term.

SECTION 2

This Article shall be inoperative unless it shall have been ratified as an amendment to the Constitution by the legislatures of three-fourths of the several States within seven years from the date of its submission to the States by the Congress.

ARTICLE XXIII

[DECLARED RATIFIED 3 APRIL 1961]

SECTION 1

The District constituting the seat of Government of the United States shall appoint in such manner as the Congress may direct:

A number of electors of President and Vice President equal to the whole number of Senators and Representatives in Congress to which the District would be entitled if it were a State, but in no event more than the least populous State; they shall be in addition to those appointed by the States, but they shall be considered, for the purposes of the election of President and Vice President, to be electors appointed by a State; and they shall meet in the District and perform such duties as provided by the twelfth article of amendment.

SECTION 2

The Congress shall have power to enforce this article by appropriate legislation.

ARTICLE XXIV

[DECLARED RATIFIED 5 FEBRUARY 1964]

SECTION 1

The right of citizens of the United States to vote in any primary or other election for President or Vice President, for electors for President or Vice President, or for Senator or Representative in Congress, shall not be denied or abridged by the United States or any State by reason of failure to pay any poll tax or other tax.

SECTION 2

The Congress shall have power to enforce this article by appropriate legislation.

UNRATIFIED AMENDMENTS

Twenty-two Amendments have been ratified by the required three-fourths of the states, 5 others have been submitted to the States but have not been ratified.

In *Coleman vs Miller,* 307 U.S. 433, (1939) the U.S. Supreme Court ruled that the reasonableness of time for ratification was a political question to be determined by Congress.

THE TWO UNRATIFIED AMENDMENTS OF THE PROPOSED BILL OF RIGHTS (1789)

ARTICLE I

After the first enumeration required by the first article of the Constitution, there shall be one Representative for every thirty thousand, until the number shall amount to one hundred, after which the proportion shall be so regulated by Congress, that there shall be no less than one hundred Representatives, nor less than one Representative for every forty thousand persons, until the number of Representatives shall amount to two hundred; after which the proportion shall be so regulated by Congress, that there shall not be less than two hundred Representatives for every fifty thousand persons.

ARTICLE II

No law varying the compensation for the services of the Senators and Representatives shall take effect, until an election of Representatives shall have intervened.

THE UNRATIFIED AMENDMENT RELATING TO TITLES OF NOBILITY OF FOREIGN GOVERNMENTS
(proposed by 2nd Session of the 11th Congress)

Resolved by the Senate and House of Representatives of the United States of America in Congress assembled (two-thirds of both Houses concurring), That the following section be submitted to the legislatures of the several states, which, when ratified by the legislatures of three-fourths of the states, shall be valid and binding, as a part of the constitution of the United States.

If any citizen of the United States shall accept, claim, receive or retain any title of nobility or honour, or shall, without the consent of Congress, accept and retain any present, pension, office of emolument of any kind whatever, from any emperor, king, prince or foreign power, such person shall cease to be a citizen of the United States, and shall be incapable of holding any office of trust or profit under them, or either of them.

THE UNRATIFIED 13TH AMENDMENT (proposed by the 36th Congress, March 2, 1861)

This was signed by President Lincoln the day after the seizure of Fort Sumter. This is the only proposed amendment ever signed by the President. The President's signature is not considered necessary because of the constitutional provision that two-thirds of both Houses of Congress must concur before the amendment can be submitted to the States for ratification.

Resolved by the Senate and House of Representatives of the United States of America in Congress assembled, That the following article be proposed to the Legislatures of the several States as an amendment to the Constitution of the United States, which, when ratified by three-fourths of said Legislatures, shall be valid, to all intents and purposes, as part of the said Constitution, viz:

ARTICLE XIII

No amendment shall be made to the Constitution which will authorize or give to Congress the power to abolish or interfere, within any State, with the domestic institutions thereof, including that of persons held to labor or service by the laws of said State.

THE UNRATIFIED CHILD-LABOR AMENDMENT (proposed by the 1st Session of the 68th Congress in June 1924)

Resolved by the Senate and House of Representatives of the United States of America in Congress assembled (two-thirds of each House concurring therein), That the following article is proposed as an amendment to the Constitution of the United States, which, when ratified by the legislatures of three-fourths of the several States, shall be valid to all intents and purposes as a part of the Constitution:

ARTICLE ———

SECTION 1. The Congress shall have power to limit, regulate, and prohibit the labor of persons under 18 years of age.

SECTION 2. The power of the several States is unimpaired by this article except that the operation of State laws shall be suspended to the extent necessary to give effect to legislation enacted by the Congress.

INDEX